The Trouble with Foreign Investor Protection

The Trouble with Foreign Investor Protection

GUS VAN HARTEN

OXFORD
UNIVERSITY PRESS

OXFORD
UNIVERSITY PRESS

Great Clarendon Street, Oxford, OX2 6DP,
United Kingdom

Oxford University Press is a department of the University of Oxford.
It furthers the University's objective of excellence in research, scholarship,
and education by publishing worldwide. Oxford is a registered trade mark of
Oxford University Press in the UK and in certain other countries

First Edition published in 2020

Impression: 2

Published in the United States of America by Oxford University Press
198 Madison Avenue, New York, NY 10016, United States of America

British Library Cataloguing in Publication Data
Data available

Library of Congress Control Number: 2020934578

ISBN 978–0–19–886621–3

Printed and bound by
CPI Group (UK) Ltd, Croydon, CR0 4YY

Preface

In this book, I present a more fundamental critique of investment treaty arbitration (commonly known as investor–state dispute settlement—ISDS) than is typical in legal academic work on the subject. I do so because ISDS treaty reform is rightly under discussion by governments and, in that vein, it seems important to be clear about the crux of the problem and how the treaties appear to warrant more extensive reforms than most governments have pursued thus far.

At their core, ISDS treaties are flawed because they very firmly institute wealth-based inequality under international law. I will dissect that claim. The treaties are wealth based because they use cross-border ownership of assets (ie 'foreign investment') as the gateway to extraordinary legal benefits. They are unequal because the many people who lack enough wealth, or the right kind of wealth, are denied these benefits and disadvantaged by the cost of providing them to 'investors'. The wealth-based inequality is very firmly instituted under international law, since it emerges from treaties that establish the most powerful adjudicative mechanism in international law (and perhaps all law) to protect private actors—here, primarily multinationals and tycoons—in their relations with sovereigns. Thus, on close examination, ISDS treaties have the main effect of safeguarding a shockingly awesome set of rights and privileges for the ultra-wealthy, at the expense of countries and their populations.

This perspective on ISDS is elaborated in the book from different angles. It is shown how ISDS has exploded in a global context of extreme concentration of wealth and of widespread poverty. The history of early ISDS treaties is introduced to highlight their ties to decolonization and, at times, extreme violence and authoritarianism. Focusing on early ISDS lawsuits and rulings, it is shown how a small group of lawyers and arbitrators worked to create the legal foundations for massive growth of ISDS since around 2000. ISDS-based protections for investors are examined in detail to demonstrate how they provide exceptional advantages in law to the wealthy. Various examples are given of how these protections have been used to elevate the interests of foreign investors within state decision making and to shift sovereign minds in their favour. Finally, the ongoing efforts of many governments to reform ISDS are surveyed, with a call for countries to go further or, best of all, to withdraw from the treaties.

I am grateful to the editorial team of Oxford University Press and my local editor, Nicole Langlois, for their close review of the text. I am grateful to Mandi Byrd, Rosie Hatton, and Leah Horzempa for their dedicated research assistance and feedback. I acknowledge with thanks the financial support of the Social Sciences and Humanities Research Council of Canada and of Osgoode Hall Law School and York University for supporting the research behind the book, especially on ISDS and regulatory chill. When studying ISDS, I have at times thought with appreciation of the materially poor but spiritually rich families with whom I lived for a time in Guatemala in the 1990s, and of how ISDS relates to the interests of people like them. Finally, I am conscious that any book I write could well be my last, so above all and with strong feelings I dedicate this one with love to Susanne, Olivia, Mattias, and all my family.

Gus Van Harten

Contents

Table of Cases

INVESTMENT ARBITRATION CASES

OTHER DOMESTIC AND INTERNATIONAL CASES

Table of Treaties

BILATERAL INVESTMENT TREATIES

[Texts of all treaties referenced below are available online: UNCTAD International Investment Agreements Navigator.]

OTHER TREATIES

Table of Domestic Statutes and Other Instruments

EUROPEAN DIRECTIVE

List of Key Websites

Global Affairs Canada <https://www.international.gc.ca/trade-agreements-accords-commerciaux/topics-domaines/disp-diff/nafta.aspx?lang=eng> (awards and party submissions in NAFTA Chapter 11 investment arbitration claims).

International Centre for Settlement of Investment Disputes (ICSID) <https://icsid.worldbank.org/en/Pages/cases/SearchCases.aspx> (awards and annulment decisions in ICSID arbitrations).

Investment Claims <http://www.investmentclaims.com> (awards and other documents in investment treaty arbitrations).

Investment Treaty Arbitration (ITA Law) <http://www.italaw.com> (awards and other documents in investment treaty arbitrations).

NAFTA Claims <http://www.naftaclaims.com> accessed 24 March 2020 (awards and documents in NAFTA arbitrations).

Permanent Court of Arbitration (PCA) <https://pca-cpa.org/cases/> accessed 24 March 2020 (awards in UNCITRAL Rules investment arbitrations).

Secretaría de Economía (Mexico) <https://www.gob.mx/se/acciones-y-programas/comercio-exterior-solucion-de-controversias?state=published> (awards and party submissions in NAFTA claims against the United States).

UN Conference on Trade and Development (UNCTAD) International Investment Agreements Navigator: <https://investmentpolicy.unctad.org/international-investment-agreements> (texts of investment treaties).

US State Department: <https://2009-2017.state.gov/s/l/c3439.htm> (awards and party submissions in NAFTA claims against the United States).

List of Abbreviations

AIT	Agreement on Internal Trade
AUS	Australian dollars
BIT	bilateral investment treaty
CAD	Canadian dollars
CAFTA	Dominican Republic–Central America–United States Free Trade Agreement
CETA	Comprehensive Economic and Trade Agreement
CIA	Central Intelligence Agency
CPTPP	Comprehensive and Progressive Agreement for Trans-Pacific Partnership
ECHR	European Convention on Human Rights
ECJ	European Court of Justice
ECT	Energy Charter Treaty
EPA	Economic Partnership Agreement
EU	European Union
EUR	Euros
FAO	Food and Agriculture Organization
FDI	foreign direct investment
IBA	International Bar Association
ICC	International Chamber of Commerce
ICJ	International Court of Justice
ICOMOS	International Council on Monuments and Sites
ICS	Investment Court System
ICSID	International Centre for Settlement of Investment Disputes
IPCC	Intergovernmental Panel on Climate Change
ISDS	investor–state dispute settlement
ITA	investment treaty arbitration
MFN	most-favoured-nation
MMT	methylcyclopentadienyl manganese tricarbonyl
NAFTA	North American Free Trade Agreement
OECD	Organisation for Economic Co-operation and Development
PAHO	Pan American Health Organization
PCA	Permanent Court of Arbitration
SCC	Stockholm Chamber of Commerce
SEATCA	Southeast Asia Tobacco Control Alliance
SIAC	Singapore International Arbitration Centre
TTIP	Transatlantic Trade and Investment Partnership
UN	United Nations
UNCITRAL	United Nations Commission on International Trade Law

UNCTAD	United Nations Conference on Trade and Development
UNESCO	United Nations Educational, Scientific and Cultural Organization
USD	United States dollars
WHO	World Health Organization
WTO	World Trade Organization

1
Fortifying Inequality

In 1997, international arbitrators ordered war-torn Congo to pay USD 9 million to a foreign investor whose factory had been looted by soldiers. In 2003, they ordered the Czech Republic to pay USD 395 million to an American billionaire, Ralph Lauder, after he had a dispute with the country's broadcasting regulators. In 2007, they ordered Argentina to pay USD 278 million to German multinational Siemens, and USD 219 million to UK multinational BG Group for losses the companies had faced in the course of a national economic crisis. In 2012, it was Ecuador—ordered to pay over USD 2 billion to oil giant Occidental Petroleum—and, in 2019, arbitrators ordered Pakistan to pay a crippling USD 6 billion to two mining corporations whose approvals had been annulled by the country's supreme court. Each case was ground breaking at the time. Each was made possible by a novel set of 'investment' treaties, where countries give extraordinary powers and protections to owners of international wealth, mostly huge corporations and ultra-wealthy individuals,[1] without also giving them corresponding responsibilities.

If we live in a new gilded age,[2] foreign investor protections are one of its key symbols and guarantors. They exist in a category that is unique in international law, supported in the treaties by the most powerful international enforcement mechanism available anywhere to companies and individuals in their disputes with the sovereign. The enforcement mechanism, commonly called 'investor–state dispute settlement' (ISDS),[3] authorizes investors to bring claims for huge sums against a country if it uses its institutions to enact laws or policies, investigate alleged offences, withhold or revoke licences, enforce court decisions, make public statements, or take other steps which the investor does not want. Scrutiny of ISDS reveals how states have written international rules to favour the wealthy and how those rules have been activated by powerful economic actors, aided by

[1] I refer here to companies with over USD 1 billion in annual revenue and to individuals with over USD 100 million in net wealth. G Van Harten and P Malysheuski, 'Who Has Benefited Financially from Investment Treaty Arbitration? An Evaluation of the Size and Wealth of Claimants', Osgoode Hall Law School Legal Studies Research Paper No 14 (2016) 1.

[2] UBS and PricewaterhouseCoopers, *New Visionaries and the Chinese Century: Billionaires' Insights 2018* (UBS and PricewaterhouseCoopers 2018) 24.

[3] The European Commission put the name 'ISDS' into widespread usage—to describe the foreign investor protections and arbitrations by which they are enforced—around 2009, when the European Union (EU) first began negotiating ISDS provisions in its trade agreements. However, the Commission shifted away from this name in 2015 after it became unpopular. Other common names are 'investor–state arbitration' or 'investment treaty arbitration'. I use 'ISDS' in this book because it appears the most widely recognized.

ISDS lawyers and arbitrators. In ISDS, one finds examples of unfairness, conflicts of interest, and public money flowing to private actors on dubious grounds. Yet one also finds a simple way to change the law and help countries confront pressing concerns of human welfare and survival by abandoning or completely revamping the treaties by which ISDS was created.

In this book, I explain the rise and accumulation of foreign investor protections and how they have become part of an architecture of global inequality. I examine how ISDS treaties were invented in the 1960s as a substitute for colonial rule and how they grew, mostly in the 1990s, into a complex web of constraints for most countries. I also show how the treaties were designed and activated by ISDS lawyers in favour of investors, and identify some of the leading lawyers who led this process in their powerful role as arbitrators. In deciding early ISDS cases, the lawyers and arbitrators were so creative as to be like legal wizards casting spells from old scrolls. By 2000, they had triggered a boom in investor claims that has become a lucrative revenue stream for corporations and law firms. For many countries trying to exercise their sovereignty by regulating the wealthy, however, ISDS has created a vexing array of new risks and potentially devastating costs.

The context of global inequality

The rise of global inequality since the 1970s roughly coincides with the ascendance of foreign investor protections. Extreme disparities of wealth did not directly create the protections, just as the protections are not the leading cause of the inequality. Yet inequality is reflected brightly in the protections, especially in their favouring of the wealthy over everyone else. Pro-investor favouritism is the legal foundation of ISDS treaties, making it vital to highlight the context of global inequality before turning to the protections themselves.

As of 2017, about 255,000 people, each with over USD 30 million in net wealth, had acquired combined wealth of $31.5 trillion, exceeding the combined wealth of 80 per cent of the world's adult population, about four billion people.[4] Fewer than fifty individuals collectively owned as much as the poorest half of humanity.[5] From 1980 to 2016, the wealthiest 0.1 per cent of the world population obtained twice as much income growth as the bottom 50 per cent.[6] It is estimated that, over the next twenty years, 701 ultra-rich individuals will leave over USD 3 trillion to their

[4] Wealth-X, *World Ultra Wealth Report 2018* (Wealth-X 2018) 3–4; Credit Suisse Research Institute, *Global Wealth Report 2018* (2018) 20; Credit Suisse Research Institute, *Global Wealth Databook 2018* (2018) Table 3-1.

[5] DA Vázquez Pimentel, I Macías Aymar, and M Lawson, *Reward Work, Not Wealth: Methodology Note* (Oxfam International 2018) 6.

[6] F Alvaredo and others, *World Inequality Report 2018* (World Inequality Lab 2017) 40.

heirs.[7] A pertinent question for present purposes is whether these individuals are so vulnerable or so helpful to others that they deserve the most powerful protections in international law, protections unavailable to all others.

One thousand large multinationals, each consisting of networks of companies under some central direction, dominate the global economy and national economies. The ten largest ones, such as Exxon, Shell, and Wal-Mart, have collective revenue exceeding the combined revenue of 180 states.[8] Just one hundred multinationals were responsible for 71 per cent of global industrial greenhouse gas emissions between 1988 and 2015.[9] Governments may sometimes condemn this concentration of wealth and call for it to be shared more widely. Yet many seem intent to expand ISDS and thus, whether or not knowingly, to fortify a deep inequality under the law.

As 'foreign investors', multinationals own far more than other investors. Like the ultra-wealthy individuals who occasionally sue in their own name, multinationals are the investors that can bring ISDS claims carrying billion-dollar risks for countries. Moreover, ISDS arbitrators have tended to interpret the treaties in pro-investor ways more often in cases brought by very large corporations.[10] Based on such interpretations, multinationals have a much higher 'win' rate in ISDS than other claimants.[11]

By concluding ISDS treaties, it is said, countries will make themselves more attractive to investors. The more a country concedes to the protections, the more they will benefit from investment, growth, jobs, and so on. Beyond these economic concerns, it is also said that the more countries constrain their institutions to the power of international arbitrators, the more they will advance the rule of law. Leaving aside the issue of whether these claims about ISDS are supported by enough evidence to justify the concessions ISDS entails for countries, one should

[7] UBS and PricewaterhouseCoopers (n 2) 24; J Stadler and others, *New Visionaries and the Chinese Century: Billionaires' Insights 2018* (UBS and PricewaterhouseCoopers 2018).

[8] Global Justice Now, 'Ending Corporate Impunity: The Struggle to Bring about a Binding UN Treaty on Transnational Corporations and Human Rights', Raw data on 2017 revenues of governments and corporations (2018). The concentration of corporate ownership in 2018 had reportedly increased by 48 per cent since 1996, based on the Herfindahl-Hirschman index: S Fleming, 'Corporate Power on the Agenda at Jackson Hole' *Financial Times* (London, 17 August 2018).

[9] P Griffin, *The Carbon Majors Database: CDP Carbon Majors Report 2017* (Carbon Disclosure Project 2017) 14.

[10] I refer here to corporations with over USD 10 billion in annual revenue, relying on the methodology and data discussed in G Van Harten, 'Arbitrator Behaviour in Asymmetrical Adjudication (Part Two): An Examination of Hypotheses of Bias in Investment Treaty Arbitration' (2016) 53 Osgoode Hall LJ 540, supplemented by further analysis in March 2016 by statistician Heather Krause, who found a significant tendency of such corporations to benefit from pro-claimant interpretations by ISDS arbitrators (rather than more restrictive alternatives adopted by other arbitrators) across 347 arbitrator-specific interpretations in 35 cases brought by extra-large corporations compared to 654 arbitrator-specific interpretations in 88 cases brought by other claimants). The project covered arbitrator interpretations of fourteen disputed legal issues under ISDS treaties for all known cases up to May 2012.

[11] Such corporations obtained a cumulative 'win' rate in ISDS of 71 per cent (through the jurisdictional and merits stages of a claim) across 48 cases, compared to 42 per cent for other claimants across 166 cases: Van Harten and Malysheuski (n 1) 8–9.

acknowledge that the treaties have a stated purpose and a potentially compelling justification.

Yet ISDS is also an extraordinary tool for safeguarding wealth. For ultra-wealthy litigants, it is the power to bring or credibly threaten a legal assault on a country whose institutions or officials are acting undesirably from the investor's point of view. ISDS gives an exceptional level of force to arbitrator decisions that a state's conduct was not 'fair and equitable', did not give 'full protection and security', or denied full compensation for 'indirect' expropriation of investor assets, for example.[12] It is justifiable to call ISDS a Bill of Rights for the global rich. As one practitioner described the power of ISDS lawyers and arbitrators:[13]

> Imaginative counsel can construct a [fair and equitable treatment] claim out of virtually any set of facts, provided there is some governmental action in the picture, and any number of experts can be lined up to calculate the millions or even billions in profits that the business would have made if only it had been treated fairly by the host state. With the right tribunal and a state caught off guard or otherwise unable to manage the situation, the stage could be set for an award that transforms a bad investment into a windfall ...

If the investor convinces the arbitrators that a country's laws, policies, or court judgments violated one of the treaty's protections, the investor usually wins compensation. Where the affected wealth is great, the owed compensation can be enormous. Thus, even an abstract risk of ISDS liability may deter a country from regulating in ways that would benefit or protect its citizens, communities, and environment (this type of deterrence, often called regulatory chill, is discussed in Chapter 6, 'Intimidating Sovereigns'). Many ISDS treaties are worded so loosely that they let investors bring claims even when those investors are 'foreign' only in a formal legal sense: after setting up a holding company in the opposite country under the treaty, the corporation has thus 'nationality shopped' its way into ISDS.[14]

Alongside global wealth there is immense poverty, with billions of people facing destitution or economic decline. The number of hungry worldwide, for example, rose in 2017 to about 821 million, one in nine people.[15] Among children under five

[12] Any standard text on international investment law provides an overview of the foreign investor protections, albeit always with some level of fealty to the treaties and without highlighting that they serve primarily to protect the ultra-wealthy; eg A Newcombe and L Paradell, *Law and Practice of Investment Treaties: Standards of Treatment* (Kluwer Law International 2009). More specialized books address specific protections, again usually with some level of admiration for the arbitrators' pro-investor turn in the law; eg A Diehl, *The Core Standard of International Investment Protection: Fair and Equitable Treatment* (Kluwer Law International 2012).

[13] G Kahale III, 'ISDS: The Wild, Wild West of International Law and Arbitration', Brooklyn Lecture on International Business Law, Brooklyn Law School (3 April 2018) 18.

[14] BP Ebert, *Forum Shopping in International Investment Law* (Mohr Siebeck 2017).

[15] United Nations (UN) [Food and Agriculture Organization (FAO) and others], *The State of Food Security and Nutrition in the World 2018: Building Climate Resilience for Food Security and Nutrition* (FAO 2018) xii.

years old, 151 million—22 per cent in the world—were 'stunted' by malnutrition.[16] Among adults, 750 million could not read or write, close to one billion lack access to electricity, and two billion rely on a drinking water source contaminated with faeces.[17] Half the world population lacks access to essential health care, 100 million are pushed into extreme poverty each year due to health expenses, and 8.6 million die each year from inadequate health care.[18]

These millions or billions of the world's people cannot afford to bring ISDS claims and none will ever get funding to do so from hedge funds and other speculators, as foreign investors increasingly do.[19] They must respond to encroachments on their lives and property in national forums that often also favour the wealthy. Moreover, all of them are simply barred from using ISDS since they do not own significant assets abroad and thus are not 'foreign investors' under the treaties. All domestic investors are likewise ineligible for the protections offered to foreign investors in ISDS. For every country, the great majority of the population assumes the costs and risks of ISDS treaties, without obtaining equivalent access to an international tribunal to protect their own livelihood or land when threatened by a government or a multinational.[20] When they encounter an ISDS treaty, it is typically because the treaty has been used to challenge a law, regulation, or other decision in their country that might otherwise have protected them—over the objections of a foreign investor.

This contrast between the wealthy and everyone else returns us to how ISDS backs inequality and augments the power of corporations in relation to government. In most policy realms (such as taxation, financial regulation, or corporate law), the wealthy are assisted by rules that favour them, often after the rules were shaped by politicians, media, lawyers, or lobbyists they funded or hired.[21] The

[16] ibid 13.

[17] UN Educational, Scientific and Cultural Organization (UNESCO) Institute for Statistics, 'Literacy Rates Continue to Rise from One Generation to the Next', Fact Sheet No 45 (2017) 1; International Energy Agency, *World Energy Outlook 2018: Electricity Database* (2018); WHO, 'Drinking-Water' (*WHO*, 7 February 2018) <https://www.who.int/news-room/fact-sheets/detail/drinking-water> accessed 14 January 2020.

[18] WHO and International Bank for Reconstruction and Development/World Bank, *Tracking Universal Health Coverage: 2017 Global Monitoring Report* (WHO 2017) vii and ix; ME Kruk and others, 'Mortality Due to Low-Quality Health Systems in the Universal Health Coverage Era: A Systematic Analysis of Amenable Deaths in 137 Countries' (2018) 392 The Lancet 2203, 2207.

[19] FJ Garcia, 'Third Party Funding as Exploitation of the Investment Treaty System', Boston College Law School Faculty Paper (2018); B Güven and L Johnson, 'The Policy Implications of Third-Party Funding in Investor–State Dispute Settlement', Columbia Center on Sustainable Investment Paper (2019).

[20] A Arcuri, 'The Great Asymmetry and the Rule of Law in International Investment Arbitration' in L Sachs, L Johnson, and J Coleman (eds), *Yearbook on International Investment Law and Policy 2018* (OUP 2019) 6; M Boase, 'A Genealogy of Censurable Conduct: Antecedents for an International Minimum Standard of Investor Conduct' in SW Schill, CJ Tams, and R Hofmann (eds), *International Investment Law and History* (Edward Elgar 2018) 322–23.

[21] See eg J Mayer, *Dark Money: The Hidden History of the Billionaires behind the Rise of the Radical Right* (Anchor Books 2016); Oxfam, 'An Economy for the 1%: How Privilege and Power in the Economy Drive Extreme Inequality and How This Can Be Stopped', Oxfam Briefing Paper (18 January 2016).

special contribution of ISDS to this favouritism is to tighten in place a skewed structure and to fortify the concentrated wealth it generates. ISDS treaties allow the conversion of vast wealth into intense pressure on countries to accept the social or environmental harms emanating from that wealth. The pressure is not to tax, not to regulate, not to disapprove, not to disrupt.

An overview of foreign investor protections

ISDS treaties take three forms. The most common is bilateral investment treaties (or BITs), also called 'foreign investment promotion' treaties, 'economic cooperation' treaties, and so on. They are bilateral since they are between two countries. The first few were signed in the late 1960s and they proliferated rapidly in the 1990s and early 2000s, with approximately 2,300 now in force.[22] A second form of the treaties is investment chapters in 'free trade' deals, where investor protections and ISDS are brought into a larger trade agreement.[23] This linking of trade and ISDS was a product of US trade negotiating strategy in the 1980s, first realized in the North American Free Trade Agreement of 1994. Now several dozen 'free trade' agreements contain ISDS provisions. The third form of the treaties is a multilateral agreement (other than a trade agreement) that authorizes ISDS. The clearest example is the Energy Charter Treaty, signed in 1994 among European and former Soviet bloc countries. In each of these forms of the treaties, the key element is that countries agree, in ways that are difficult to reverse, to allow investors from one country under the treaty to bring ISDS claims against another.

From the start, the treaties were designed to favour foreign investors.[24] Their lopsidedness can be traced to the 1960s, when European trade officials and business lobbies searched for ways to protect European firms in former colonies, as direct rule was being resisted and overthrown.[25] Newly independent countries, for their part, often wanted a better deal in the global economy, based on more control over their territory, natural resources, labour conditions, and markets.[26] Where they had the bargaining power to do so, officials from the former European colonial powers typically insisted on a model of generous protections for the investors, who at the time came overwhelmingly from the European side. In the 1990s, the treaties were eventually activated by specialist lawyers, and interpreted by specialist arbitrators, to allow wide-ranging claims by investors based on vaguely worded

[22] UN Conference on Trade and Development (UNCTAD) International Investment Agreements Navigator: <https://investmentpolicy.unctad.org/international-investment-agreements> accessed 14 January 2020.

[23] There are approximately 100 such agreements in force; ibid.

[24] T St John, *The Rise of Investor–State Arbitration* (OUP 2018) 9; Boase (n 20) 351–54.

[25] K Miles, *The Origins of International Investment Law: Empire, Environment and the Safeguarding of Capital* (CUP 2013) 78–89.

[26] N Gilman, 'The New International Economic Order: A Reintroduction' (2015) 6(1) Humanity 1.

standards of protection. The treaties were also interpreted to allow investors to win compensation orders that could be enforced internationally by piggybacking on treaties that were originally designed for contractual arbitration. Yet, unlike a contract between an investor and a state, ISDS treaties omit any right of the state to sue an investor for not meeting some agreed standard of conduct under the treaty. Their legal asymmetry serves to protect investors from countries without protecting countries, or anyone else, from investors.

ISDS has profound implications for the sovereign as the legal representative of its people. It allows a foreign investor to trigger a transfer of authority from the country's institutions, especially its courts, to international arbitrators.[27] The transfer is far-reaching because the investor can use ISDS to attack virtually anything the state has done in its sovereign role. The claim must be based on one of the various protections for investors in the treaty, but these are broadly worded and thus offer myriad ways for arbitrators to decide on the boundaries and costs of sovereignty. When a tribunal rules against a country, usually it orders compensation retrospectively. The arbitrators' orders can reach astronomical amounts and are more enforceable than court decisions. In this last respect, the treaties direct courts in many countries to enforce ISDS awards by seizing assets of the losing country in order to make it pay. Thus, they use the courts of one state to discipline another state.

Weaknesses of common arguments for ISDS

How does one justify providing a variety of exceptionally enforceable protections for the ultra-wealthy? One should expect the promoters of ISDS, themselves often lawyers and arbitrators in ISDS, to focus on making a strong case for this explicit discrimination in international law. Yet they have often resorted instead to disregarding or misrepresenting arguments against ISDS, shifting the burden of proof to those who object to special protections for the wealthy, calling for overwhelming evidence of the harms of ISDS (while assuming claims of its benefits are true), or simply seeking to discredit ISDS critics.[28]

Probably the most longstanding and commonplace argument for ISDS is that foreign investor protections will attract investment to a country (or, more coyly,

[27] *BG Grp, Plc v Republic of Argentina*, 134 S Ct 1198 (2014) (US) (Roberts, CJ, dissenting) 10 ('Substantively, by acquiescing to arbitration, a state permits private adjudicators to review its public policies and effectively annul the authoritative acts of its legislature, executive, and judiciary').

[28] R Tansey, *Blaming the Messenger: The Corporate Attack on the Movement for Trade Justice* (Corporate Europe Observatory and LobbyControl 2017). On the familiarity of the tactics, see ME Mann, 'The Serengeti Strategy: How Special Interests Try to Intimidate Scientists, and How Best to Fight Back' (2015) 71 Bull Atomic Scientists; T Cave and A Rowell, *A Quiet Word: Lobbying, Crony Capitalism and Broken Politics in Britain* (The Bodley Head 2014); Y Saloojee and E Dagli, 'Tobacco Industry Tactics for Resisting Public Policy on Health' (2000) 78(7) Bull WHO 902.

that it will 'improve the investment climate'), especially if the country has weak national institutions.[29] The problem with this argument is that it was long assumed true without evidence, and that subsequent investigation has not yielded compelling evidence to support it.[30] The claim dates to before the earliest of ISDS treaties in the late 1960s and early 1970s, but from the start it was unsupported by evidence, at least in the public sphere.[31] By the late 1990s, when systematic research on whether the treaties worked as advertised started to be done, the bulk of the treaties were locked in. The argument seems to have been more a pitch or an after-the-fact justification than a studied rationale, yet it survives because a pretext, repeated often enough as a statement of fact, is hard to disprove.

There is also a deeper problem with this argument for ISDS. Even if it were shown that ISDS regularly attracts investment to countries accepting it, this finding would also reveal just how much the concentration of wealth and mobility of capital have weakened states,[32] by intensifying competition among them for private investment to such a degree that they have sacrificed principles of equality under the law, democracy, and judicial independence in order to favour multinationals and billionaires. In any gilded age, the extremely wealthy control the resources on which most others depend. When countries concede core elements of their sovereignty in a bid for more of these resources, it seems the law has been rewritten too strongly in favour of the wealthy and compromised the protections needed by others.

[29] eg IFI Shihata, 'The Settlement of Disputes regarding Foreign Investment: The Role of the World Bank, with Particular Reference to ICSID and MIGA' (1986) 1 Am U Int'l L Rev 97, 98; UT Isayev, 'Session VII: Foreign Investment during the Transition: How to Attract It, and How to Make the Best Use of It', Presentation to the International Monetary Fund–Kyrgyz Republic Conference on Challenges to Economies in Transition: Stabilization, Growth, and Governance (Bishkek, 27–28 May 1998) 3–4; SD Franck, 'Foreign Direct Investment, Investment Treaty Arbitration, and the Rule of Law' (2007) 19 Global Bus Dev't LJ 337, 338; Y Fortier, 'Investment Protection and Rule of Law: Change or Decline?' British Institute of International and Comparative Law, 50th Anniversary Event Series (17 March 2009) 8; UNCTAD, *The Role of International Investment Agreements in Attracting Foreign Direct Investment to Developing Countries*, UNCTAD Series on International Investment Policies for Development (UN 2009) 111–12; CN Brower and SW Schill, 'Is Arbitration a Threat or a Boon to the Legitimacy of International Investment Law?' (2009) 9 Chi J Int'l L 471, 477; JR Markusen, 'Commitment to Rules on Investment: The Developing Countries' Stake' (2001) 9 Rev Int'l Pol Econ 287; SW Schill, 'Fair and Equitable Treatment under Investment Treaties as an Embodiment of the Rule of Law', NYU School of Law Institute for International Law and Justice Working Paper 2006/6 (2006) 32 and 36.

[30] M Hallward-Driemeier, 'Do Bilateral Investment Treaties Attract Foreign Direct Investment? Only a Bit ... and They Could Bite', World Bank Policy Research Working Paper (2003); KP Gallagher and MBL Birch, 'Do Investment Agreements Attract Investment? Evidence from Latin America' (2006) 7 J World Invest Trade 961; E Aisbett, 'Bilateral Investment Treaties and Foreign Direct Investment: Correlation versus Causation' in KP Sauvant and LE Sachs (eds), *The Effect of Treaties on Foreign Direct Investment: Bilateral Investment Treaties, Double Taxation Treaties, and Investment Flows* (OUP 2009) 395; A Berger and others, 'More Stringent BITs, Less Ambiguous Effects on FDI? Not a Bit!', World Trade Organization Staff Working Paper ERSD-2010-10 (2010); LNS Poulsen, 'The Importance of BITs for Foreign Direct Investment and Political Risk Insurance: Revisiting the Evidence' in KP Sauvant (ed), *Yearbook on International Investment Law and Policy 2009–2010* (OUP 2010) 539–74.

[31] St John (n 24) 154–56.

[32] S Strange, *The Retreat of the State* (CUP 1996); BA Simmons, 'Bargaining over BITs, Arbitrating Awards: The Regime for Protection and Promotion of International Investment' (2014) 66 World Pol 12.

A second argument for ISDS, related to the first, is that investors require durable protections for their 'sunk' costs of investment.[33] The argument in turn is that a government must make credible commitments to those who control capital in exchange for their financing of long-term projects.[34] This argument is not a complete justification for the treaties, since the treaties apply to all foreign-owned assets, not just those with sunk costs. Thus, the argument distracts somewhat from the larger issue of states having reconfigured their institutional processes to favour the ultra-wealthy, whose assets (sunk or not) pose the greatest risks for states in ISDS. Yet, even if the treaties were limited to assets actually shown to have been sunk, the treaties would still make countries highly dependent on the super-rich for the welfare of their people. What can one say about a bargain by which a country, in exchange for hosting profit-seeking activity, has to give long-term commitments to indemnify investors against risks arising from the country's exercise of sovereignty? The problem with this argument for ISDS is that it does not acknowledge how foreign investors can have too much bargaining power because of global inequality.

Foreign investors, like anyone else, deserve protection under the law. Like anyone else, they must accept the prospect of encroachment on their property for the state to exist and to govern. Today's ISDS treaties go well beyond merely protecting investors and balancing their interests against those of others. They commit the state to an extraordinary level of publicly funded security for foreign investors that could never be extended to all because doing so would bankrupt the state. The fact that investors take long-term risks is not a sufficient justification for them to receive extraordinary protection. Would not a victim of execution or torture have a more important long-term interest in their life or security than a tycoon does in the value of his assets? Do victims of environmental harm have less interest in the ability of their government to regulate polluters than an oil company does in maintaining its revenue stream? ISDS treaties over-protect investors at the expense of others. If investors do suffer abuse, there are less discriminatory and more targeted ways for them to be protected by relying on markets and risk insurance; that is, by expecting foreign investors to negotiate adequate protections in their contracts with state entities, to purchase private or public risk insurance, and to use national laws and courts unless they are shown not to offer justice.[35]

A third argument for ISDS is that foreign investors cannot rely on national institutions and therefore require ISDS to protect them, especially from corrupt or

[33] Brower and Schill (n 29) 477–83 (Brower is a leading ISDS hawk, as described below, and his former intern, Schill, later became an ISDS arbitrator).

[34] Markusen (n 29).

[35] eg K Gordon, 'Investment Guarantees and Political Risk Insurance: Institutions, Incentives and Development', OECD Investment Policy Perspective 2008 (OECD 2008); D Ayine and others, 'Lifting the Lid on Foreign Investment Contracts: The Real Deal for Sustainable Development', Sustainable Markets Briefing Paper No 1 (International Institute for Environment and Development 2005).

inefficient courts.[36] Certainly, national institutions are very weak in some countries. This limitation creates a need to improve institutions for everyone, not just certain investors.[37] ISDS treaties reserve their powerful protections for wealthy companies and individuals. They omit domestic investors, thus distorting markets. They omit other foreigners, such as migrants or refugees, who may also be mistreated in the country where they reside. The treaties also ignore the victims of foreign investors themselves. None of these others have international protections that are enforceable in ISDS or any similarly powerful means of dispute resolution. This gap exposes a key problem with the claim that ISDS remedies weak institutions. In fact, ISDS allows foreign investors to protect themselves from weak institutions, while relying on those same weak institutions to win benefits and avoid accountability at the expense of others.[38]

The treaties are likewise far too sweeping in their rejection of national institutions. Typically, they give foreign investors the power to invoke ISDS without regard for the strength of a country's courts or government. Yet national courts are often far superior to ISDS in terms of their independence, fairness, and openness. This implicit condemnation of national institutions is a departure from international law. Both in customary international law and in other treaties that allow international claims on behalf of private actors, it must be first shown that there was something wrong with a country's courts before an international claim can go ahead against the country.[39] This logic of mutual sovereign respect is absent in ISDS, as foreign investors have been relieved completely from the usual duty to exhaust the available local remedies. In turn, they have been granted a power to filter their relationship with national laws and institutions. They can sidestep the courts, bring parallel claims, and use a range of complex routes of lawyering that are closed to others in the pursuit of public compensation. ISDS emerges as a mechanism to protect the rich and powerful even more, while making it harder for sovereigns to hold these actors accountable for misconduct.

A fourth argument for ISDS is that it ensures or promotes the rule of law and good governance.[40] These values are obviously important, albeit vague as criteria by which to evaluate a treaty. It is revealing that they are also not used by ISDS promoters to evaluate ISDS itself, which appears to fall well short of satisfying either principle. For example, the tribunals that hear ISDS claims are not courts and, depending on the rules under which the investor brings the claim, their decisions

[36] C Schreuer, 'Interaction of International Tribunals and Domestic Courts in Investment Law' in AW Rovine (ed), *Contemporary Issues in International Arbitration and Mediation: The Fordham Papers 2010* (Brill 2011) 71 (Schreuer is an ISDS arbitrator).

[37] UN, *The Sustainable Development Goals Report 2018* (UN 2018) 12.

[38] eg S Imai, L Mehranvar, and J Sander, 'Breaching Indigenous Law: Canadian Mining in Guatemala' (2007) 6 Indigenous LJ 101; JM Luiz and M Ruplal, 'Foreign Direct Investment, Institutional Voids, and the Internationalization of Mining Companies into Africa' (2014) 49 Emerging Markets Fin Trade 113.

[39] G Van Harten, *Investment Treaty Arbitration and Public Law* (OUP 2007) 110–13.

[40] Schill (n 29).

are either completely or very heavily insulated from judicial review. Typically, an ISDS tribunal has three arbitrators, one appointed by the investor, another by the sued country, and a third by agreement of the investor and the country or, failing that, by an outside body.[41] The arbitrators operate on a for-profit basis since they are appointed case by case and paid by the claim. All have an apparent interest to favour investors, since only investors can bring the claims and, the more claims that are brought, the more opportunities arise for arbitrators. By using for-profit arbitrators instead of judges in this context, the treaties remove longstanding institutional safeguards that define independent courts. These safeguards include security of tenure for the judge, a set salary that does not depend on the frequency of claims, prohibitions on outside work by the judge, and an objective method of assigning cases to the judges. Such safeguards have long bolstered the rule of law and good governance where private parties sue sovereigns.[42] How is it that ISDS can drop them while promoting the same values?

If these arguments do not provide a compelling basis for the special protections for foreign investors, why were ISDS treaties pushed by powerful countries? I suspect the most likely explanation is that officials and lobbyists in powerful countries were focused on protecting the wealth of 'their' investors, with much less concern for how the protections affected other constituencies. To do so, they sought to constrain governments in newly independent countries from expropriating, regulating, or otherwise interfering with the assets of colonial-era companies. Even if acquired by conquest, foreign-owned property was to be sacrosanct. Eventually, the logic of protecting wealth by suppressing sovereignty would be extended to all countries.

The ISDS industry

ISDS would not have exploded without a powerful legal industry behind it. Most clearly, the industry consists of specialist lawyers, arbitrators, and experts, some of whom had previously worked in national trade departments or international economic organizations. The business model of the industry is rooted, very simply, in the power of arbitrators to require a state and its population to pay compensation. Those working in the industry have 'invested', career-wise, in the litigation of ISDS disputes. The deeper a claimant's pockets and the more valuable its assets, the more a case can be made for financing an ISDS claim in the hope of winning

[41] Rarely, the tribunal consists of a single arbitrator appointed by agreement of the parties or by an outside body.

[42] G Van Harten, 'A Case for an International Investment Court', Society of International Economic Law Inaugural Conference Paper (2008).

compensation. Sometimes billions in compensation and tens of millions in legal fees are at stake.

Pioneering members of the ISDS industry laid the foundations for its growth in a series of little-known claims and rulings in the 1990s. In this gestational period, specialized lawyers filed the first claims in each of today's leading ISDS forums: the International Centre for Settlement of Investment Disputes, the Permanent 'Court'[43] of Arbitration (PCA), and the Stockholm Chamber of Commerce. A string of innovative rulings followed, in which the arbitrators developed the theory of the 'asymmetrical' sovereign consent (whereby an ISDS treaty is said to establish the country's advance agreement to be sued by an unknown class of foreign investors, without the need for a more specific expression of consent by the country in relation to the actual investor that has initiated the 'dispute' by bringing an ISDS claim). Further, they accepted broad conceptions of 'investment' and novel arguments for nationality shopping; they allowed claims by minority shareholders for the whole company in which they owned shares; and they introduced far-reaching, exaggerated ideas of protection for investors such that the basic tenets of the treaties (eg 'fair and equitable treatment', 'full protection and security', and protection from 'indirect' expropriation) could be applied in ways that heavily favour the wealthy. By 2000, a legal platform had been erected, with little discussion beyond the specialists, for the steady stream of ISDS claims and awards that has followed.[44]

Most of the early ISDS claims in the 1990s were brought by entrepreneurial lawyers on behalf of small companies. In the 2000s, the treaties evolved into a mainstay for big law firms that regularly represent multinationals. More ISDS claims led to more arbitrator appointments, and most arbitrators endorsed investor-friendly interpretations of the treaties, which encouraged more claims. Over the course of about a hundred ISDS rulings from the early 1990s to 2010, arbitrators consolidated the structure of foreign investor privilege by taking an expansive view of their powers, of state obligations, and of investor entitlements to compensation. Consciously or not, the arbitrators sent signals to corporate lawyers, and ultimately to multinationals and billionaires, about the promise of ISDS as a source of compensation and a potential weapon to use against countries.

At the centre of this emergent power was a group of repeat players, some having started up in the exploratory cases of the 1990s and others in the early 2000s' boom. They often played multiple roles in ISDS as counsel, expert witness, treaty negotiator, World Bank official, and so on, and they promoted the treaties publicly and professionally. Yet their most significant role by far was that of arbitrator, which

[43] I use scare quotes because the PCA is not a court with judges, but rather a house for arbitration.

[44] One step not taken by any tribunal, in any known award up to 2000, was to order compensation in excess of USD 20 million. That milestone was passed in 2003 when the *CME* tribunal ordered the Czech Republic to pay about USD 395 million (including pre-award interest). *CME v Czech Republic*, Awards (13 September 2001; 14 March 2003).

empowered them to rule on claims, resolve ambiguity in the treaties, and order states to pay compensation.

To isolate the repeat players who, in their role as arbitrators, appear to have contributed the most to ISDS expansion, I reviewed all ISDS awards between 1990 and 2010 to track how the arbitrators resolved contested legal issues and whether they tended to favour expansive or restrictive approaches to textual ambiguity. A small group stood out for their pro-investor impact on the law, most clearly Yves Fortier, Francisco Orrego Vicuña, Charles Brower, Marc Lalonde, Stephen Schwebel, and Gabrielle Kaufmann-Kohler. I highlight these individuals periodically throughout the book to stress the role of arbitrator agency in transforming international law to favour the wealthy. I also discuss their influence in promoting ISDS, with two examples of misleading advocacy from Fortier and Orrego Vicuña, in the Appendix of the book. Shining a light on these repeat arbitrators helps to reveal how ISDS was established by a small group of legal specialists. They are a micro-level part of the story of how foreign investor protections were invented as a framework to constrain former colonies, how they were activated decades later and promoted on misleading terms, how they give an extraordinary array of advantages to the wealthy, and how they are now used with devastating effect against countries and their people. The trouble with foreign investor protections should be a concern for all those wishing to stem the extreme concentration of global wealth and give countries viable pathways to overcome our many public health, environmental, and economic challenges.

2
Origins of ISDS Treaties

Investor–state dispute settlement (ISDS) treaties are extraordinary because they allow private actors to sue countries on an open-ended basis, while reserving this right to owners of international wealth. In contrast, countries signing the treaties have no parallel right to sue investors who wrongly harm individuals, communities, or the environment. How did such lopsided treaties come to be? Originally, the treaties were adopted by former European colonial powers as a means to constrain the newly won sovereignty of former colonies. No longer able to rely on military force to protect the assets of European companies operating abroad, the colonial powers, with guidance from World Bank officials, turned to ISDS treaties for robust legal protection.[1] Thus the retreat of colonialism was far from absolute. Indeed, the treaties created in its wake have eventually become a conditioning framework for all countries, including the colonial powers themselves.[2]

The first ISDS treaties were signed as long ago as the late 1960s, but they expanded only gradually. Scattered countries negotiated a few dozen in the 1970s and a few hundred more in the 1980s. The treaties received little attention beyond trade officials and specialist lawyers.[3] They were not studied or debated publicly to test whether they worked as advertised for investment-seeking countries or whether they might undermine the ability of governments to regulate. Then, in the 1990s, more than 1,000 of the treaties were rapidly concluded, setting the stage for today's ISDS litigation boom.

From a legal perspective, the treaties are extraordinary in part because they can and have been used to fit the innovation of an open-ended sovereign acceptance of arbitrator power into the traditional idea of mutual consent to arbitration. In ISDS, the 'mutual' consent is said to be between a state and an unknown investor, even though the investor does not consent in the same way, or even at the same time, as the sovereign.[4] This peculiar legal device was the genesis of ISDS as a supreme

[1] T St John, *The Rise of Investor–State Arbitration* (OUP 2018); K Miles, *The Origins of International Investment Law: Empire, Environment and the Safeguarding of Capital* (CUP 2013) 78–89.

[2] R Grinspun and R Kreklewich, 'Consolidating Neoliberal Reforms: "Free Trade" as a Conditioning Framework' (1994) 43 Stud Pol Econ 33.

[3] St John (n 1) ch 6.

[4] J Paulsson, 'Arbitration without Privity' (1995) 10 ICSID Rev—FILJ 232. For a discussion of how the state's consent under the ICSID Convention could be withdrawn prior to an investor claim, see MC Porterfield, 'Aron Broches and the Withdrawal of Unilateral Offers of Consent to Investor–State Arbitration' *Investment Treaty News* (11 August 2014), citing A Broches, 'Selected Essays: World Bank, ICSID, and Other Subjects of Public and Private International Law' (M Nijhoff 1995) 447 and 453.

institution to protect foreign investors from countries. When enterprising lawyers realized the potential of ISDS, premised on this theory of the asymmetrical sovereign consent, it led to a series of claims and rulings against countries, and ultimately transformed international law. In this chapter, I highlight the institutional foundations of ISDS and explain how the treaties became a platform from which the wealthy can challenge sovereigns and everyone represented by them.

Links to post-colonial violence

When the first wave of ISDS treaties came in the late 1960s and 1970s, most were between a Western European country and a former colony, usually said to be developing.[5] The stronger country in this relationship faced no real prospect of being sued by anyone from the weaker country. Its relative safety made it easier to write the treaties in favour of foreign investors. That choice was made primarily by officials of the country from which the investors came and to which, at the time, most of their revenues returned. Occasionally in this early period, when ISDS was still dormant, the treaties were extended to relations among developing or transition countries themselves, albeit still based on the models of Western European and World Bank officials. For former colonies, the treaties were usually presented by such officials as a tool to attract investment and develop their economies.

It appears that the first ISDS treaty was signed in 1968 between the Netherlands and Indonesia. The treaty was called an 'Agreement on economic cooperation'[6] and it laid out now-familiar protections for foreign investors, meaning, in reality, Dutch investors in their former colony. The protections included, for example:[7]

- a commitment to ensure 'fair and equitable treatment' for 'investments, goods, rights and interests';
- a commitment to 'freedom of transfer' for 'net profits, interests, dividends, royalties, depreciation of capital assets and any current income, accruing from investment activities'; and
- a commitment to 'just compensation' for any direct or indirect expropriation (called 'deprivation' at the time) of investments, goods, rights, or interests.

[5] Up to 1980, thirty-eight (86 per cent) of forty-four bilateral investment treaties fit this model; author's analysis in 2018 using UN Conference on Trade and Development (UNCTAD) International Investment Agreements Navigator: <https://investmentpolicy.unctad.org/international-investment-agreements> accessed 14 January 2020.

[6] The full name was the 'Netherlands and Indonesia Agreement on economic cooperation (with protocol and exchanges of letters dated on 17 June 1968)', signed on 7 July 1968, registered with UN Treaty Section on 4 November 1971, Treaty No 11386 (13 UNTS 38).

[7] ibid Articles 5, 6, and 7.

To an extent, these protections mimicked the Western powers' commercial treaties from the quasi-colonial period of the nineteenth and early twentieth centuries.[8] Yet the 1968 treaty was innovative as it combined broad protections for investors with the power of ISDS. Thus, the protections were matched with a power of investors to bring claims directly against the state, allowing for enforcement beyond state-to-state processes of dispute settlement.

Interestingly, the 1968 treaty was not as lopsided in favour of investors as most ISDS treaties have later become. The asymmetrical sovereign consent had not yet been perfected, since the treaty allowed both the investor and the state to sue each other. According to the treaty, Indonesia and the Netherlands 'shall assent to any demand' by a national of the other country—and 'any such national shall comply with any request' by the country—'to submit, for conciliation or arbitration, to the Centre established by the [ICSID] Convention ... any dispute that may arise in connection with the investment'.[9] Thus, the pioneering treaty was balanced, at least formally, where today's treaties are not. Even so, Indonesia's government took a fateful step in consenting to ISDS, just as the Dutch government was the first to use ISDS to support its corporate owners of assets in a former colony. It is therefore important to consider the context for the deal, which shows how early ISDS treaties were often concluded against a backdrop of violent reaction to nationalist or socialist governments in former colonies.

Japan occupied the Dutch colony of Indonesia during the Second World War. After Japan's defeat, the Netherlands re-occupied Indonesia, trying to re-establish the colonial administration of the Dutch East Indies Company. With US support, the Netherlands fought, and ultimately lost, a brutal colonialist war between 1946 and 1949.[10] Newly independent Indonesia was then led by the nationalist leader Sukarno until 1965, when Sukarno was overthrown in a military coup. Again with US support, the new government of General Suharto carried out a horrific purge in which at least half a million people, labelled as communists, were murdered.[11] A few years after seizing the sovereign pen in this way, Suharto's government then signed its pioneering ISDS treaty with the Netherlands.

Like other early ISDS treaties, the Netherlands–Indonesia treaty lay dormant for several decades. Suharto meanwhile became one of the most corrupt Western-backed despots in history, reportedly stealing USD 15–25 billion over the course of

[8] M Sornarajah, *The International Law on Foreign Investment* (CUP 2010) 180–82; KJ Vandevelde, 'A Brief History of International Investment Agreements' (2005) 12 UC Davis J Int'l L and Pol 157, 162–66.

[9] Netherlands–Indonesia BIT (n 6) Article 11.

[10] B Luttikhuis and AD Moses, 'Mass Violence and the End of the Dutch Colonial Empire in Indonesia' (2012) 14 J Genocide Res 257.

[11] PD Scott, 'The United States and the Overthrow of Sukarno, 1965–1967' (1985) 58 Pacific Affairs 239; J Kim 'US Covert Action in Indonesia in the 1960s: Assessing the Motives and Consequences' (2002) 9 J Int'l Area Stud 63, 76–9; K McGregor, 'Mass Violence in the Indonesian Transition from Sukarno to Suharto' (2013) 15 Global Dialogue 134.

his rule.[12] He was finally overthrown in 1998 in a national uprising sparked by the Asian financial crisis. Soon after emerging from dictatorship, Indonesia faced a raft of actual or threatened ISDS claims by multinationals. The claims and threats came mostly as the Indonesian government tried to unwind projects approved in the Suharto era. Awakened to the constraints imposed by ISDS, in 2014 Indonesia cancelled its treaty with the Netherlands (a 1994 version that had modified the 1968 one) but remains bound by other ISDS treaties dating from the Suharto era.[13]

The original ISDS treaty is thus hard to see as an expression of national self-determination by a former colony. It emerged from a period of extreme violence in the service of national kleptocracy and foreign looting. Not all early ISDS treaties are linked so closely to repression of nationalism or socialism, but nearly all emanated from a former colonial power or from the World Bank and all have a proximity to the history of colonial occupation and its aftermath. Italy followed the Netherlands in 1968 and 1969, respectively, by signing treaties with two countries that won their independence (from France) in 1960: the first was Gabon, where a few months before the president had declared a one-party state, and the second was Chad, then also under authoritarian rule.[14] The Netherlands then raced ahead between 1970 and 1972, concluding five more ISDS treaties with Uganda, Kenya, Malaysia, Morocco, and Singapore, all governed at the time by a one-party or authoritarian leadership. Between 1972 and 1975, France signed its first wave of ISDS treaties with Tunisia, the Congo, Serbia, Egypt, Morocco, and Singapore, and Belgium followed in 1974 and 1977 by signing treaties with South Korea and Egypt. In 1975, the UK signed its first treaty (with Egypt), followed in 1976 by treaties with Singapore, South Korea, Romania, and Suharto's Indonesia. Sweden signed its first in 1978 and Germany did so in 1979. In a twist that is not well explained, the treaties also began to expand among developing countries (and one Soviet bloc country, Romania, although its treaties sought to limit the use of ISDS to disputes over expropriation only), starting with a Kuwait–Tunisia treaty in 1973, South Korea–Tunisia in 1975, Egypt–Romania in 1976, Egypt–Japan in 1977, and Pakistan–Romania in 1978.

Even so, by the end of the 1970s, only about four dozen ISDS treaties had been signed. The countries with the most were France, Netherlands, and the UK (with thirteen, nine, and seven, respectively), joined by Egypt and Romania (with seven each).[15] Tellingly, it is the latter two countries that are today among the twenty

[12] 'Suharto Tops Corruption Rankings' *BBC News* (25 March 2004) http://news.bbc.co.uk/2/hi/3567745.stm.

[13] Indonesia has terminated many of its Suharto-era ISDS treaties. The most threatening still in force, as of 31 July 2019, appear to be those with Australia, Sweden, and the UK; author's analysis using the UNCTAD International Investment Agreements Navigator (n 5).

[14] The listing of ISDS treaties in this paragraph relies on the UNCTAD International Investment Agreements Navigator (n 5).

[15] These numbers should be taken as approximate, since new treaties from this period continue to be rediscovered and added to databases such as the UNCTAD International Investment Agreements Navigator (n 5).

most-sued countries in ISDS, whereas the former three have hardly ever been sued, reflecting how they limited their own risk by avoiding ISDS treaties with other major capital exporting countries.[16] Yet ISDS itself remained unused after the first decade of the treaties, and was barely known beyond the officials promoting it and the lawyers gathering around it.

Building momentum

The number of ISDS treaties grew more rapidly in the 1980s, driven as usual by capital exporting countries. The UK signed twelve such treaties in the early years of Margaret Thatcher's tenure between 1980 and 1982.[17] Finland signed its first treaty in 1980, albeit with Egypt, which by then had seven treaties of its own, and Switzerland did so in 1981. The United States, under the Reagan Administration, signed its first in 1982 with Panama, when that country was governed by a military junta led in part by Manuel Noriega, who was on the Central Intelligence Agency (CIA) payroll at the time.[18] China signed its first treaty the same year with Sweden, although the treaty limited ISDS to disputes over expropriation, like Romania's early approach and (from the mid-1980s) that of other Soviet bloc countries.[19] By 1990, all of the major Western countries had signed at least one ISDS treaty: Norway in 1984, Austria and Denmark in 1985, Australia and New Zealand in 1988 (both with China), Portugal in 1988, and Spain and Canada in 1989. Thus, the treaties were pushed along by the usual capital exporters, led by the UK, France, and the Netherlands. Indeed, by 1990, just ten European former colonial powers had signed 67 per cent of all 221 ISDS treaties; adding the United States, Japan, and other Western countries, just nineteen leading capital exporters had signed over 80 per cent of the treaties by that year.[20] The major capital exporters thus pushed treaties that privileged the wealthy, presumably motivated by the interests of Western companies that still owned the bulk of the world's foreign-owned assets.

[16] Author's analysis from own data and UNCTAD Investment Dispute Settlement Navigator: <https://investmentpolicy.unctad.org/investment-dispute-settlement> accessed 14 January 2020.

[17] The country-by-country tallies of ISDS treaties in this paragraph and the rest of this section rely on the UNCTAD International Investment Agreements Navigator (n 5).

[18] PD Scott and J Marshall, *Cocaine Politics: Drugs, Armies, and the CIA in Central America* (University of California Press 1991) 66–67; W Blum, *Killing Hope: US Military and CIA Interventions since World War II* (Black Rose Books 1998) 306.

[19] A Reinisch, 'How Narrow are Narrow Dispute Settlement Clauses in Investment Treaties?' (2011) 2 J Int'l Disp Settlement 115, 117. The author, who is an ISDS arbitrator, also surveys interpretive techniques used by arbitrators to avoid limitations on state consents to ISDS.

[20] Among the ten former European colonial powers: United Kingdom (thirty-seven), France (thirty-one), Netherlands (twenty), Belgium/Luxembourg (sixteen), Germany (fourteen), Italy (thirteen), Sweden (ten), Denmark (four), Portugal and Spain (one each). Among other capital exporters: United States (ten), Switzerland (eight), Finland (five), Norway (three), Japan (three), and Australia, Austria, Canada, and New Zealand (one each). The remaining forty-one treaties were between two developing or transition countries.

Those who benefited from colonialism, one could say, did not relinquish the gains easily.

In contrast, most other countries appear to have had little or no interest in ISDS treaties. Most had not signed a single one by 1990; among those that did, over 80 per cent signed just one or two of them.[21] With little success, World Bank officials had lobbied governments to consent to ISDS for two decades. A majority of countries in each of Africa, Asia, Latin America, and the Caribbean, and the South Pacific—as well as the Soviet bloc—had no ISDS treaties at all.[22] In Africa, the significant non-participants included Algeria, Nigeria, South Africa, and Tanzania; in Asia and the Middle East, they included India, Iran, Iraq, Saudi Arabia, Uzbekistan, and Vietnam; in Latin America, they included Argentina, Brazil, Colombia, Mexico, Peru, and Venezuela. A modest majority of Middle Eastern, and of Central or Eastern European, countries had signed an ISDS treaty by 1990, but most had only one or two. Among all developing or transition countries, China led with twenty treaties, but all of these limited the scope of ISDS in the manner of the Romanian model. China was followed by Sri Lanka[23] (with sixteen treaties), Hungary (with fifteen), Romania (with thirteen), South Korea (with twelve), Tunisia (with eleven), Egypt (with eleven), Malaysia (with ten), and Poland (with ten).[24] Besides the outlier of Romania, which had concluded its first ISDS treaties in the mid-1970s, Soviet bloc countries began signing only after 1985. Most importantly, as the Soviet Union was collapsing, Russia rapidly signed treaties with the UK, Germany, France, the Netherlands, and Canada in 1989.

By 1990, just thirteen developing or transition countries[25] accounted for most of the forty-one ISDS treaties signed by such countries.[26] The other developing

[21] Among 170 non-Western countries (excluding Japan), seventy-three (44 per cent) had signed one ISDS treaty by 1990 and most (forty-four) had signed only one or two.

[22] Among *African* countries: twenty-one of fifty countries had an ISDS treaty by 1990, led by Tunisia (eleven), Morocco (six), Ghana and Senegal (five each), Cameroon (four), and the Congo (three). Among *East, Central, and South Asian* countries: fourteen of thirty-two countries had an ISDS treaty, led by China (twenty); Sri Lanka (sixteen); South Korea (twelve); Malaysia (ten); Bangladesh, Pakistan, and Singapore (five each); and the Philippines (three). Among *Middle Eastern* countries, ten of seventeen countries had an ISDS treaty, led by Egypt (eleven), Kuwait (seven), Turkey (six), and Yemen (four). Among *Latin American and Caribbean* countries, fifteen of thirty-nine countries had an ISDS treaty, led by Panama (five), Bolivia (four), Haiti (three), and Uruguay (three). Among *South Pacific* countries: none of fourteen countries had an ISDS treaty. Among *Central/ Eastern/Southern European* countries: thirteen of twenty-one countries had an ISDS treaty, led by Hungary (fifteen), Romania (thirteen), Poland (nine), Bulgaria (eight), Russia (five), and Serbia (three).

[23] The first ISDS treaty claim, *AAPL v Sri Lanka*, was filed in 1987 under the UK–Sri Lanka treaty of 1980. The tribunal's ruling in 1990 was the first under any ISDS treaty but was hardly noticed beyond the specialist lawyers, like a drop of rain before a shower.

[24] Only four others had more than five ISDS treaties by 1990: Bulgaria (eight), Kuwait (seven), Morocco (six), and Turkey (six).

[25] The thirteen such countries include all those with more than five ISDS treaties each by 1990: China, Bulgaria, Egypt, Hungary, Kuwait, Malaysia, Morocco, Poland, Romania, South Korea, Sri Lanka, Tunisia, and Turkey.

[26] More specifically, these forty-one treaties were signed by at least one of the thirteen developing or transition countries, and eighteen were between two of these thirteen countries.

or transition countries that had signed an ISDS treaty by 1990 appear to have responded to a Western country's treaty programme or, less often, to one of the thirteen developing or transition countries that were actively signing. After 1990, however, the treaties entered a new stage as opposition was weakened by debt crises, by the collapse of import-led development in Latin America, and by the fall of the Soviet Union. Latin America and the Soviet Union had led post-war opposition to the concessions of sovereignty to foreign investors but, by the 1990s, they were at the point of surrender.

From decolonization to ISDS

Stephen Schwebel has been a repeat player and a leading pro-investor hawk among ISDS arbitrators. Aged seventy-one when he entered ISDS arbitration in 2001, Schwebel's earlier career provides a personal link to the history of Western reaction to self-determination in the former colonies. His first job after law school was with the corporate law firm White and Case, where he worked in the 1950s as a lawyer on a team representing oil giant Aramco in a contract-based arbitration with Saudi Arabia.[27] Schwebel described the experience as having 'triggered an interest, which has remained with me to this day, in international arbitration'.[28] In the 1960s and 1970s, he held an academic position and worked in the US government and, in the latter capacity, took part in legal battles over economic aspects of decolonization, including the negotiations that led to the United Nations (UN) resolution on permanent sovereignty of natural resources of 1962.[29] Schwebel described this resolution as being 'of intense interest and concern to capital exporting states like the United Kingdom and the United States, and the great companies that made these investments' since the resolution 'attempted to codify the international law governing foreign investment of a long-term kind in natural resources'.[30] He described the resolution as 'remarkably balanced' after a 'very intense' negotiation, noting that Soviet bloc countries 'bitterly opposed' it as 'a sell out to capitalism'.[31]

In contrast, Schwebel lamented that later UN resolutions—such as the Charter of Economic Rights and Duties of States in 1974, for which Schwebel chaired the US negotiating team—'became more and more one-sided, and asserted the total dominance of national law and the exclusion of international law in the treatment and taking of foreign investment'.[32] Using his language, perhaps these later resolutions

[27] L Dingle and D Bates, 'A Conversation with Judge Stephen M Schwebel' (*University of Cambridge Squire Law Library*, 13 May 2009) <https://www.squire.law.cam.ac.uk/eminent-scholars-archivejudge-stephen-m-schwebel/conversation-judge-stephen-m-schwebel> accessed 14 January 2020.

[28] ibid 8.

[29] United Nations, *Resolution on Permanent Sovereignty over Natural Resources*, GA Res 1803, UN GAOR, 17th Sess, Supp No 17, UN Doc A/5217 (1962) 15, 57 AJIL 710.

[30] Dingle and Bates (n 27) 12.

[31] ibid 12.

[32] ibid 12.

could be called a 'sell out' to sovereignty and self-determination. Schwebel's sympathies evidently did not lie with countries that had overcome colonialism, only to find their governments constrained by a version of international law that favoured the former colonial powers and their 'great companies'. Schwebel denounced these later UN resolutions as part of an 'extremist trend', by which a state 'can treat foreign investment as it likes and certainly no better than it treats its own national investors'.[33] Here, Schwebel labelled it 'extremist' for developing countries to seek simply to limit the international minimum standard of treatment for foreign investors to the principle of non-discrimination with a country's own investors. His comment suggests a bias in favour of the interests of Western multinationals, consistent with Schwebel's later hawkish record as an ISDS arbitrator.

Institutional foundations

Decolonization obviously presented a grave risk for those whose revenue streams flowed from colonialism. To guard against the risk, Western officials pushed for stronger foreign investor protections at the UN and other multilateral forums. They met with success most clearly at the World Bank, which in the 1960s created a forum to resolve disputes between investors and countries, especially newly independent ones. The forum was the International Centre for Settlement of Investment Disputes (ICSID), established in Washington under the ICSID Convention of 1965.

Today, ICSID is one of the leading arbitration houses for ISDS,[34] but in its first three decades ICSID was little known and lightly staffed. It was led by Aron Broches, who described himself as 'the principal negotiator and draftsman' of the ICSID Convention.[35] Earlier in his career, Broches had been part of the Netherlands' delegation to the UN Monetary and Financial Conference in Bretton Woods, New Hampshire, in 1944, where the World Bank and the International Monetary Fund were established. Soon after, he was hired as a lawyer at the Bank, rising to become its general counsel from 1959 to 1979.[36] During this period, he emerged as the most prominent among a network of officials who endorsed ISDS as part of a mission to protect foreign (especially Western) investors, purportedly for 'development'.[37]

33 ibid 12.

34 S Dezalay and YM Dezalay, 'Professionals of International Justice: From the Shadow of State Diplomacy to the Pull of the Market of Arbitration' in J d'Aspremont and others (eds), *International Law as a Profession* (CUP 2017) 325–32.

35 RW Oliver, 'A Conversation with Aron Broches', California Institute of Technology, Division of the Humanities and Social Sciences (7 November 1985) 7–8.

36 AR Parra, 'Remembering Aron Broches' (*Investment Claims*, 14 October 2016) <https://oxia.ouplaw.com/page/icsid-aron-broches> accessed 14 January 2020.

37 S George and F Sabelli, *Faith and Credit: The World Bank's Secular Empire* (Penguin 1994) 7 ('The Bank resembles the Church ... Both believe themselves invested with a mission, both (the Church

Thus, Broches worked with the Bank's President in the early 1960s to push through a proposal to create ICSID, which was approved by the Bank's Executive Directors in 1965. He then served as ICSID's Secretary General from 1967 to 1980, and after became a prominent early ISDS lawyer and arbitrator.[38] In these latter roles, he was a member of the investor's legal team in the ground-breaking ISDS case of *SPP v Egypt* (where the investor sued under the host state's ICSID-influenced national investment law).[39] He also represented the International Council for Commercial Arbitration—an arbitration industry organization—at the inter-governmental discussions toward the United Nations Commission on International Trade Law (UNCITRAL) model law on international commercial arbitration, which guided legal reforms in many countries to preclude review of arbitration awards in national courts.[40] Above all, soon after leaving the World Bank, Broches quickly became an august promoter of the curious idea of the state's 'advance' or 'general' or 'asymmetrical' consent to ISDS in investment treaties, which is the founding concept of today's special protections for foreign investors and of the corresponding costs for many others.

Under Broches' leadership, ICSID avidly promoted ISDS treaties as a new way for countries to bind their sovereignty in favour of investors, beyond the old way of doing so by signing contracts with investors. In the case of the treaties, it was said, a country could agree in advance to arbitration claims brought by any foreign investor—'foreign investors' being a potentially huge class of unknown litigants who own assets in the country. In turn, any member of this owner class could force the sovereign to answer to arbitrators for anything the investor alleged was not 'fair and equitable', did not ensure 'full protection and security', and so on. The country committed up front to arbitration without knowing anything about the specific dispute and investor, the individual arbitrators, or, often, which forum would be used for the arbitration. From the other side, investors obtained the right to bring claims against the country after a dispute had arisen, and largely according to how the investor itself defined the dispute. In the early 1990s, ISDS arbitrators began to confirm the theory, long cultivated by Broches, that the unilateral and open-ended consent of the sovereign in the treaties was part of a 'mutual' agreement to arbitrate with whichever investor later brought a claim.[41] This innovation

historically, the Bank at present) have set themselves against the state. Both celebrate the poor rhetorically while refraining from actually improving their capacity to change their earthly lot.').

[38] Parra, 'Remembering' (n 36) 2–3.

[39] A Broches, 'Bilateral Investment Protection Treaties and Arbitration of Investment Disputes' in JC Schultsz and AJ van den Berg (eds), *The Art of Arbitration* (Kluwer 1982). On *SPP v Egypt*, see Chapter 3, 'Activation of the Treaties'.

[40] G Van Harten, *Investment Treaty Arbitration and Public Law* (OUP 2007) 53 (n 51), citing eg L Biucovic, 'Impact of the Adoption of the Model Law in Canada: Creating a New Environment for International Arbitration' (1998) 30 Can Bus LJ 376, 381.

[41] Paulsson (n 4); Van Harten, *Investment Treaty Arbitration and Public Law* (n 40) 63–70.

crystallized an underlying asymmetry in favour of the wealthy and made possible today's ISDS boom.

ISDS treaties use an arbitration process that was borrowed from investor–state contracts. For decades before the treaties, and extending far back into the history of colonial and quasi-colonial rule, these contracts often protected Western companies by referring contractual disputes—between the company and a relative weak country—to a forum that was structured in the company's favour.[42] However, investor–state contracts also had a much narrower scope for ISDS than the treaties, since the contract was limited to a known investor and a specific agreement with that investor. Alternatively, powerful countries sometimes used historical 'claims commissions' to protect investors by creating an arbitration tribunal to hear investor claims against the weaker country, usually in the wake of a war or revolution, or to legitimize a conquest and annexation of the weaker state's territory.[43] Like modern ISDS treaties, the historical claims commissions were structured so that companies from the powerful country did most of the suing and the weaker country did most of the paying. Yet even this process was a more limited concession of a country's sovereignty than today's treaties because the country's consent to arbitrate was limited to a particular period and the cause of the disputes was known, at least approximately, when the consent was given. In defence of the weaker countries, they also often conceded their sovereignty in this way under the threat of armed invasion or blockade.[44] Most of today's treaties were signed without such pressure, but they go much further in their constraints on sovereignty.

ISDS favours the wealthy in ways that an independent judicial process never could. In most forms of investor–state arbitration (whether under a treaty or a contract), the investor picks one arbitrator, the country picks another, and, if they do not agree, a designated body chooses the presiding arbitrator. Arbitration is thus consensual but also mandatory, especially when the sovereign's consent to arbitrate comes before the actual dispute has arisen. By giving such a consent in a treaty, the sovereign accepts the power of a designated body to force arbitrators upon them. Usually, this power is held by the World Bank (which operates politically in the orbit of the United States) or by the Permanent 'Court' of Arbitration (similarly in the orbit of the Western Europeans, especially the Netherlands).[45] Under

42 AFM Maniruzzaman, 'The Pursuit of Stability in International Energy Investment Contracts: A Critical Appraisal of the Emerging Trends' (2008) 1 J World Energy L & Bus 121; L Cotula, *Investment Contracts and Sustainable Development: How to Make Contracts for Fairer and More Sustainable Natural Resource Investments* (International Institute for Environment and Development 2010).

43 Miles (n 1) 55–69; A Powers, 'Settlement Colonialism: Compensatory Justice in United States Expansion, 1903–1941' (PhD thesis, Columbia University, 2017).

44 An example is the Venezuelan claims commission of the early 1900s; M Hood, *Gunboat Diplomacy 1895–1905* (George Allen & Unwin 1975) 187–88; G Morón, *A History of Venezuela* (George Allen & Unwin 1964) 185–87; St John (n 1) 57–58; Miles (n 1) 55–69.

45 On the World Bank and ICSID, see G Van Harten, 'Investment Treaty Arbitration, Procedural Fairness, and the Rule of Law' in S Schill (ed), *International Investment Law and Comparative Public Law* (OUP 2010) 645–47. The PCA is run conventionally by officials from the government of the

some treaties, the power is even held by a private business organization such as the International Chamber of Commerce.[46] For the main houses, business has grown mightily as a result of the explosion of ISDS claims.[47]

For this coercive force to support the arbitrators' power, all ISDS treaties must have a basic foundation with at least three components. First, an outside body must have the authority to impose arbitrators on countries. Second, someone must approve and apply procedures for the arbitrations. Third, a mechanism is needed to endorse and enforce the arbitrators' rulings in national courts. In this last respect, ISDS treaties relied initially on the ICSID Convention of 1965 and then also on the New York Convention of 1958.[48] The latter convention was originally established to enforce awards in commercial arbitration, but, in the 1970s and 1980s, ISDS treaties extended it to arbitrations against sovereigns.[49] Usually, this three-pronged foundation for arbitrator power is provided by one or more arbitration houses named in the ISDS treaty, although the houses ultimately trace their power to the authority of national courts to seize a sued country's assets in the court's territory. Beyond this ultimate role of the courts, virtually all aspects of the ISDS process have been transferred to arbitration. Thus, the treaties piggyback on courts while also diminishing them. Critically, they substitute arbitrators for judges to boost the position of foreign investors in their relations with the sovereign.

International Centre for Settlement of Investment Disputes

ICSID is the leading house for ISDS today. The World Bank began working to create it in the 1960s, as the United States and Western Europeans shifted their proposals for stronger foreign investor protections out of the United Nations. At the Bank, unlike the UN, the former colonial powers could control outcomes more conclusively through their dominance of the Bank's wealth-based voting system. Many countries that opposed the capital exporters at the UN were not even World Bank members. At the Bank, the investor-friendly proposals focused on creating a forum for ISDS and removing obstacles to enforcement of the awards. Individual

Netherlands whose 'Dutch' investors—often holding companies for investors from the United States or elsewhere—have brought more known treaty claims than any country except the United States.

[46] ibid 647–48.

[47] ICSID staff grew by about 350 per cent between 2004 and 2018. The PCA staff grew by about 500 per cent between 2005 and 2018. D Gaukrodger, 'Appointing Authorities and the Selection of Arbitrators in Investor–State Dispute Settlement: An Overview', Organisation for Economic Co-operation and Development Consultation Paper (2018) 27 and 30.

[48] Convention on the Settlement of Investment Disputes between States and Nationals of Other States (ICSID Convention) signed 18 March 1965, entered into force 14 October 1966 (4 ILM 524); United Nations Convention on the Recognition and Enforcement of Foreign Arbitral Awards (the New York Convention) signed 10 June 1958, entered into force 7 June 1959 (330 UNTS 3).

[49] Van Harten, *Investment Treaty Arbitration and Public Law* (n 40) 50–58.

countries could then be pressed to consent to arbitration at ICSID based on generous investor protections.

Even so, many countries that were members of the Bank still opposed its proposal for ICSID. Developing country representatives must have known they could not out-vote the West. Moreover, most had only recently won their independence, they lacked domestic capital, and their export-based economies depended on access to Western markets. Yet, when the Bank's president, George D Woods, proposed a draft ICSID Convention at the Bank's annual meeting in 1964 (going so far as to 'recommend ... and urge [the Bank's governors'] unanimous approval' of the draft[50]), twenty-one developing countries bravely opposed it.[51] These included Iraq, the Philippines, and all nineteen Latin American countries at the meeting.[52] Speaking in opposition, Félix Ruiz of Chile informed the Bank's officials and other delegates that Latin American countries already gave foreign investors 'the same rights and protection as their own nationals', prohibited discrimination, and required compensation for expropriation. The proposal for ICSID, he said, would give foreign investors 'the right to sue a sovereign state outside its national territory, dispensing with the courts of law' and would 'confer a privilege on the foreign investor, placing the nationals of the country concerned in a position of inferiority'.[53] Unsurprisingly, these prescient objections did not deter ICSID's capital exporting champions, but they at least recorded how today's controversies over ISDS were embedded in its history from the start.[54]

Soon after the Bank adopted the ICSID Convention, ICSID's staff began proselytizing for ISDS. They pressed developing countries to agree to contracts, treaties, or domestic laws[55] that would give foreign investors the ability to sue the country at ICSID, where the make-up of tribunals could be controlled by the Bank's President or his appointees.[56] Developing countries were told that their concession

50 International Bank for Reconstruction and Development and International Development Association, 'Annual Address by George D Woods, President of the Bank and its Affiliates', 1964 Annual Meetings of the Boards of Governors (Tokyo, 7–11 September 1964) 11.

51 R Broad, 'Remembering the "Tokyo No" Fifty Years Later' (*Triple Crisis*, 5 December 2014) < http://triplecrisis.com/remembering-the-tokyo-no-fifty-years-later/> accessed 14 January 2020.

52 The nineteen Latin American countries were Argentina, Bolivia, Brazil, Chile, Colombia, Costa Rica, Dominican Republic, Ecuador, El Salvador, Guatemala, Haiti, Honduras, Mexico, Nicaragua, Panama, Paraguay, Peru, Uruguay, and Venezuela. AR Parra, *The History of ICSID* (OUP 2012) 66–67.

53 Excerpt from statement of Felix Ruiz, Governor for Chile (9 September 1964) quoted in ibid 67.

54 Most of the objecting countries eventually conceded to ratify the Convention in the 1990s, when so many of ISDS treaties were signed, or more recently, as in the case of Haiti, Iraq, and Mexico. Bolivia, Ecuador, and Venezuela subsequently withdrew from the Convention in the mid-to-late 2000s and Brazil and the Dominican Republic never joined it.

55 Shortly after ICSID was created, its staff took the idea of consent beyond investment contracts—which had been the focus of the discussions to create ICSID—and pushed for asymmetrical sovereign consents to ISDS in treaties. St John (n 1) 151–52 and 196–207.

56 ICSID Convention (n 48) Articles 38 and 52(3). The Bank's President himself is effectively chosen by the US Administration, whose nominee has never been rejected by the Bank's Board, based on a post-war 'gentleman's agreement' with the Europeans. On the most recent US nomination of the Bank's President: R Costa, 'Trump Will Nominate David Malpass, a Treasury Official, to Lead World Bank' *The Washington Post* (Washington, DC, 4 February 2019); A Lowrey, 'The US Doesn't Deserve the World Bank Presidency' *The Atlantic* (12 February 2019).

of sovereignty to ISDS was a way to attract investment, but the more direct effect was to protect Western-owned assets.

Other arbitration houses

After ICSID, other arbitration houses were eventually brought into the treaties. This multiplication of forums aided investors further, by giving them more choice of where and how to sue a country. For example, ICSID has authority over claims under an ISDS treaty only if both of the treaty partners—the investor's 'home' country and the sued country—have ratified the ICSID Convention.[57] To avoid this legal obstacle, Western European governments began to incorporate other houses into their ISDS treaties; a France–Syria treaty in 1977 appears to have been the first to add the Paris-based International Chamber of Commerce (ICC) as an ISDS forum, opening the door to investor claims at the ICC where ICSID was unavailable.[58] The ICC calls its house a 'Court' of International Arbitration, but its members are not actually judges. They are arbitrators, picked for the role by ICC business officials.

The innovations continued to the point that most ISDS treaties now allow foreign investors to choose among several arbitration houses when filing a claim. In 1978, ICSID added an 'Additional Facility', which enabled ICSID to administer ISDS cases even if the sued country was not a party to the ICSID Convention.[59] In 1982, a UK–Belize treaty seems to have been the first to allow ISDS claims under the UNCITRAL arbitration rules,[60] which, in a complicated twist, empower the Permanent 'Court' of Arbitration (PCA) in The Hague to choose, in each individual case, who has the power to impose arbitrators if the parties do not agree who to appoint.[61] Now the ISDS boom has transformed the role of the PCA, which had nearly run out of work in its conventional business of inter-state arbitration.[62] Similarly, Belgium's mid-1980s treaties with Hungary and Poland appear to have been the first to introduce the Stockholm Chamber of Commerce (SCC) as an

[57] ICSID Convention (n 48) Article 25(1).

[58] France–Syria investment treaty, signed 28 November 1977, Article 8. In 1983, a United States–Haiti investment treaty, signed 13 December 1983, in Article VII(3)(a), adopted the ICC as its sole forum for ISDS. The treaties are available from UNCTAD International Investment Agreements Navigator (n 5).

[59] ICSID, *Rules Governing the Additional Facility for the Administration of Proceedings by the Secretariat of the International Centre for Settlement of Investment Disputes*, revised 1 January 2003 and 10 April 2006 (original rules 1978) 1 ICSID Rep 213. Claims at ICSID under the Additional Faculty Rules, like claims under all arbitration rules other than the ICSID Rules, are subject to domestic court enforcement under the New York Convention, rather than the ICSID Convention.

[60] UK–Belize investment treaty, signed 28 November 1977, Article 8(2)(c), UNCTAD International Investment Agreements Navigator (n 5).

[61] United Nations, *Arbitration Rules of the United Nations Commission on International Trade Law*, UN GA Res 31/98, UN GAOR, 31st Session, Supp No 17, UN Doc A/31/17, c V, s C (1976) Article 6(2).

[62] Dezalay and Dezalay (n 34) 325–27 and 332–36. See n 47 below on the growth in staff at the PCA since the mid-2000s.

alternative to ICSID, the ICC, or UNCITRAL/PCA.[63] The SCC has since become a mainstay for ISDS claims under the Energy Charter Treaty (ECT) and against former Soviet countries. Vitally, by including any arbitration house in an ISDS treaty, countries allow the house to change the rules that govern investor claims after the treaty has been locked in for countries. Thus, they allow an international organization, or even a private business organization, to decide how the wealthy should be able to seek public compensation from countries.

Above all, the multiplication of arbitration houses appeases investors, especially those most able to finance claims. It does so by pressuring each house to favour investors, lest the law firms that represent deep-pocketed investors shift to other forums. In the early ISDS treaties, investors could only bring claims at ICSID, but over time they were given the right to pick among various combinations of ICSID, the ICSID Additional Facility, UNCITRAL/PCA, the ICC, and the SCC. The first treaty I have found giving investors this right to choose is the Belgium–Hungary treaty of 1986,[64] which allows for a choice between ICSID, the ICC, and the SCC, but also limits ISDS to expropriation disputes. In 1987, Belgium signed a treaty with Malta giving similar options to investors (substituting UNCITRAL/PCA for the SCC), but without limiting ISDS to expropriation disputes.[65] By the end of the 1980s, various treaties gave this flexibility to investors, such as the United States–Poland investment treaty of 1990.[66] The same flexibility was included in the North American Free Trade Agreement (NAFTA), where investors could choose between ICSID, the ICSID Additional Facility, and UNCITRAL/PCA,[67] and also in the ECT, which added the SCC to the list.[68]

Thus, the treaties create an alphabet soup of rules and houses in the course of enabling investors to adjust the process by which their protections are defined. Investors can decide who will pick arbitrators if the sued country does not appoint its arbitrator or does not agree with the investor about the presiding arbitrator. They can alter the level of openness in the proceedings (the ICC and SCC are especially secretive) and the likelihood that other parties will be allowed to participate in the proceedings, even to the point of often being able to block openness and participation entirely. They can choose the process for review and enforcement of tribunal's rulings. Perhaps most importantly, investors can exploit the incentives

[63] Belgium–Hungary investment treaty, signed 14 May 1986, Article 9(2)(a); Belgium–Poland investment treaty, signed 19 May 1987, Article 9(2)(a). Both treaties are available from UNCTAD International Investment Agreements Navigator (n 5).

[64] Belgium–Hungary investment treaty (n 63).

[65] Belgium–Malta investment treaty, signed 5 March 1987, Article 8(3), UNCTAD International Investment Agreements Navigator (n 5).

[66] United States–Poland investment treaty, signed 21 March 1990, Article IX(3), UNCTAD International Investment Agreements Navigator (n 5).

[67] North American Free Trade Agreement (NAFTA) signed 17 December 1992, entered into force 1 January 1994 (32 ILM 296 and 605) Article 1120(1).

[68] Energy Charter Treaty (ECT) (annex 1 of the Final Act of the European Energy Charter Conference) signed 17 December 1994, entered into force 16 April 1998 (34 ILM 373) Article 26(4).

of all the houses to compete for claims, as I discuss further in Chapter 5, 'Special Access to Public Funds'.[69] This flexibility and competition builds redundancy into the state's retreat, helping investors to avoid reforms in one ISDS forum by shifting claims to another.

The great expansion

It took over two decades, up to 1990, for countries to sign a few hundred bilateral investment treaties. From 1990 to 1997, they signed over 1,000 more, such that, by 2000, there were about 1,500 such treaties. That is a big number, yet it only covered about 8 per cent of the bilateral relations among all countries.[70] Today, there are about 2,300 ISDS treaties in force, covering 13 per cent of these relations. To extend ISDS to all foreign investors in all countries would require roughly 19,000 bilateral treaties. This patchiness of the existing treaty coverage helps to explain the ongoing efforts of major capital exporters to incorporate ISDS into new trade agreements and multilateral treaties.[71]

Not surprisingly, the US government played a critical if somewhat belated role in the treaties' expansion. First, it adopted a model bilateral investment treaty in the early 1980s that expanded on Western European BIT models.[72] Then, US

[69] As an indication of the incentives, the PCA charges a fee of EUR 2000 to designate or act as appointing authority for a claim under the UNCITRAL rules and fees of EUR 250 per hour for work by the Secretary General or Deputy Secretary General and EUR 125 to 175 per hour for work by legal staff. The PCA also rents out its hearing space for EUR 1000 per day and its 'entire suite' for EUR 1750 per day. For its part, ICSID charges a fee of USD 42,000 at the time of a claim and annually thereafter; USD 25,000 for a claim or annulment application; and USD 10,000 for a claim to a new tribunal after annulment. ICSID arbitrators are paid at least USD 3,000 per day plus expenses. PCA, 'Schedule of Fees and Costs' (*PCA*, undated) <https://pca-cpa.org/fees-and-costs/> accessed 14 January 2020; ICSID, 'Schedule of Fees' (*ICSID*, 1 July 2017) <https://icsid.worldbank.org/en/Pages/icsiddocs/Schedule-of-Fees.aspx> accessed 14 January 2020

[70] The figure of 8 per cent was calculated by dividing the number of existing ISDS treaties at the relevant time by the approximately 19,000 treaties needed to cover all bilateral relationships among the world's 195 countries.

[71] The figure does not account for nationality shopping, which I roughly estimate would increase ISDS coverage by 20 per cent, ie to about 10 per cent coverage of bilateral relationships among countries. The estimate is derived from incidental data on nationality shopping in G Van Harten and P Malysheuski, 'Who Has Benefited Financially from Investment Treaty Arbitration? An Evaluation of the Size and Wealth of Claimants', Osgoode Hall Law School Legal Studies Research Paper No 14 (2016) 7–8.

[72] The main expansion was to include 'market access' (also known as 'pre-establishment national treatment') for foreign investors, by which US investors would typically gain a general right to buy assets in the other country while the US, in a schedule of exceptions, would maintain its authority to protect its own economy—in major sectors such as banking, energy, natural resources, and transportation—from purchase by investors from the other country. The United States began applying its more expansive model in treaties with Panama in 1982, Senegal and Haiti in 1983, and the Democratic Republic of Congo in 1984. By the time the NAFTA negotiations began in 1988, the United States had signed ten such treaties with countries in the Caribbean and Africa. By comparison, European countries negotiated ISDS treaties with protections that applied after the foreign investor was admitted to the country,

negotiators succeeded in their efforts to add ISDS to trade agreements, beginning with NAFTA in 1992[73] and expanding in the early 2000s to trade agreements with Vietnam, Singapore, Chile, and Morocco.[74] The Western Europeans did something similar by incorporating ISDS into the ECT, which targeted former Soviet bloc countries, in 1994.[75] Both NAFTA and the ECT were vital to ISDS expansion. In NAFTA, ISDS was embedded into a much larger structure of trade commitments, making it harder for countries to extricate themselves from ISDS. In the ECT, ISDS was built into a regional agreement that included many major economies, albeit only for the energy sector. Both agreements were negotiated before the boom in ISDS litigation began in the late 1990s, and both are very rare historical examples of major Western countries catching each other in the ISDS net. Thus, they were the first signals of the climax of foreign investor protections: to apply them to all countries.

With help from specialist lawyers, the treaties of the 1990s laid the basis for an ISDS litigation explosion. Of nearly 1,000 known claims by investors today, the great majority trace to a treaty signed in the early or mid-1990s. Most governments thus appear to have conceded their sovereignty to ISDS arbitrators without knowing how they would use their power and with only a vague hope that the treaties would bring investment. If it was a lapse of judgement, however, it was also understandable at a time when ISDS was still dormant. Only a few ISDS rulings were issued between 1990 and 1995, they were investor-friendly and creatively reasoned, and they deserved closer attention than they received from those outside the specialized field. Yet they were also kept confidential or under the radar. The big reveal came with the first wave of NAFTA claims, accounting for nine of the eighteen ISDS treaty claims between 1996 and 1998.[76] The NAFTA claims, alongside the Organisation for Economic Co-operation and Development's (OECD's) proposed Multilateral Agreement on Investment in 1998, attracted intense public

but not before. To get 'market access' for their investors, European countries came to rely in the 2000s on so-called Economic Partnership Agreements (EPAs) and, more recently, on a series of European Union trade agreements. G Van Harten, 'Investment Provisions in Economic Partnership Agreements' (*Social Science Research Network*, 1 March 2008) <https://papers.ssrn.com/sol3/papers.cfm?abstract_id=1461110> accessed 14 January 2020.

[73] NAFTA (n 67).

[74] These four US trade agreements were signed, respectively, in 2000, 2003, 2003, and 2004. Australia kept ISDS out of its trade agreement with the United States in 2004; K Tienhaara and P Ranald, 'Australia's Rejection of Investor–State Dispute Settlement: Four Potential Contributing Factors' *Investment Treaty News* (12 July 2011).

[75] ECT (n 68).

[76] The remaining nine claims from 1996 to 1998 were brought under bilateral investment treaties. Before 1996, there had been four other claims under bilateral investment treaties, one of which, *Saar Papier v Poland*, did not become public until 2004. Therefore, NAFTA accounted for 36 per cent of all treaty claims by the end of 1998 and was the only treaty to have generated more than one claim by that time. NAFTA was also the first treaty to generate more than one claim. (Here I include a NAFTA 'notice of intent' to bring a claim as a 'claim'.)

opposition,[77] but by then most of today's treaties had been locked in, usually for a minimum term of between ten and thirty-five years. Thus, ISDS was quietly activated well before the costs and risks to countries were debated publicly.

Canada and the United States have played a leading role in the retreat of sovereignty through ISDS. Canada in particular is the only major developed country to have accepted ISDS with the United States, having taken this step in NAFTA.[78] An earlier trade agreement between Canada and the United States in 1989 was controversial in Canada, but did not include ISDS.[79] NAFTA then introduced ISDS in a novel investment chapter that was mostly transplanted from the US model bilateral investment treaty. For the United States too, this step was a remarkable concession of sovereignty. By putting ISDS into a trade deal, the United States effectively created a permanent forum to protect multinationals, even in countries that have well-established courts and democracies, including the United States itself. It seems that US officials were motivated to take this step out of an excessive focus on foreign investor protection in the aftermath of the Iranian revolution of 1979. The US negotiating team for NAFTA investment chapter included Daniel M Price, then deputy general counsel for the US Trade Representative.[80] Earlier in his career, Price had been a junior lawyer in the US state department, where he represented US interests in the litigation of investor claims at the Iran–United States claims tribunal. This tribunal offered an additional prototype for US officials when pushing for ISDS in NAFTA.[81] The remarkable thing is that NAFTA ISDS is much more generous to multinationals than the Iran–United States claims tribunal had been. It is forward-looking instead of limited to past events, it includes a much wider range of investor protections, and it applies to relations among countries that had not been at war or experienced a revolution for many generations.[82] Canada and the United States (and Mexico) thus relinquished more to each other's corporations and billionaires than Iran had done to US investors in 1981, while under extreme pressure from a superpower.

NAFTA points to how ISDS treaties differ greatly from each other in their impact. As a source of claims against countries, for example, just forty-eight of the treaties—led by NAFTA and the ECT—have generated more claims than all other

[77] Organisation for Economic Co-operation and Development (OECD), *The MAI Negotiating Text* (OECD 1998). eg M Barlow and T Clarke, *MAI: The Multilateral Agreement on Investment and the Threat to Canadian Sovereignty* (Stoddart 1997).

[78] Australia, Japan, and New Zealand were poised to follow suit in 2016 under the proposed Trans-Pacific Partnership until the Trump Administration pulled out of that deal.

[79] Canada–United States Free Trade Agreement, signed 2 January 1988, entered into force 1 January 1989 (27 ILM 293).

[80] Price went on to become a private ISDS lawyer and arbitrator.

[81] One of the leading ISDS hawks, Charles Brower, had been a US.-picked judge at the Iran–United States claims tribunal.

[82] Mexico nationalized US-owned land and other assets during its revolution of 1910–20, leading to a United States–Mexico claims commission of the time; the United States and Canada (then a British colony) fought a war during 1812–14.

ISDS treaties combined.[83] Indeed, only a few hundred of the 2,300 ISDS treaties in force have led to a known claim, and only a few dozen have led to more than one claim. Just twelve of the treaties had led to about 87 per cent of total compensation ordered by ISDS treaty tribunals as of the spring of 2015.[84] Simply, many ISDS treaties are between countries whose economies do not have enough foreign-owned assets to justify claims, even if the treaties may still deter governments behind the scenes. Not surprisingly, the most dangerous ISDS treaties for any country are those with a major economic power. A treaty with one of the leading capital exporters is especially menacing because it extends ISDS to wealthy companies and tycoons whose litigation threats are more credible.[85] To free itself from ISDS, any country must above all withdraw from these most dangerous treaties.

An incomplete network

Most countries have now concluded at least one ISDS treaty, covering some part of the country's foreign-owned economy. ISDS thus constrains the governments of most people, although not fully and to varying degrees. For example, Colombia has about one dozen ISDS treaties in force, covering investors from the United States, China, Japan, the UK, Spain, Switzerland, and Canada. Colombia has thus immersed itself in ISDS risk.[86] In contrast, Vanuatu is unconstrained by ISDS, having signed two treaties, with China and the UK, neither of which is in force.[87] Most

[83] This figure is derived from a review of 491 ISDS treaty claims as of 21 February 2017. Of these claims, seventy-three were brought under NAFTA, fifty-six under the Energy Charter Treaty, sixty-eight under sixteen US bilateral investment treaties or the United States–Central America–Dominican Republic Free Trade Agreement, thirty-three under eighteen of the Netherlands' bilateral investment treaties, and thirty-four under eleven other bilateral investment treaties, including those of Canada–Venezuela, France–Argentina, France–Egypt, Germany–Argentina, Germany–Czech Republic, Germany–Egypt, Spain–Argentina, Spain–Egypt, Spain–Venezuela, UK–Argentina, and UK–Venezuela, for a total of 264 claims.

[84] These treaties included Belgium–Argentina, France–Argentina, Germany–Argentina, Moldova–Kazakhstan, Netherlands–Czech Republic, Netherlands–Venezuela, Sweden–Romania, Turkey–Kazakhstan, UK–Argentina, United States–Argentina, United States–Ecuador, and United States–Venezuela, under which a total of USD 6.347.8 billion (not including pre-award interest) or USD 8.0116 billion (including pre-award interest) was ordered, amounting to 88 per cent and 87 per cent, respectively, of the total compensation of USD 7.191 billion and 9.164 billion as of spring 2015. The data is in Van Harten and Malysheuski (n 71) 3–5; the analysis excludes the USD 50 billion award in the *Yukos v Russia* claims [*Yukos Universal Limited (Isle of Man) v Russia* (Award, 30 November 2009)] which by itself generated about 86 per cent of the total compensation ordered.

[85] In 2018, the leading capital exporters were the United States, China (including Hong Kong), the Netherlands, the UK, Japan, Germany, and France (based on total outward foreign investment stock of the country's nationals). UNCTAD, *World Investment Report 2019* (UN 2019) 216–19. One could add Canada and Australia to the list, due to the resource industry's apparent proclivity for ISDS. K Mohamadieh and D Uribe, 'The Rise of Investor-State Dispute Settlement in the Extractive Sectors: Challenges and Considerations for African Countries', South Centre Research Paper (2016) 6–8.

[86] UNCTAD International Investment Agreements Navigator (n 5).

[87] ibid.

developing and transition countries are more like Colombia and, until recently, most Western countries were more like Vanuatu, except for NAFTA and the ECT.[88] Put differently, the governments of most people in developing and transition countries are heavily constrained by ISDS, while most in the developed world have remained relatively free of such constraints.

From this picture, one sees that ISDS is far from a global institution. It does not apply everywhere, protecting all foreign-owned assets. A few countries have avoided or withdrawn from the treaties. None has signed a treaty with all other countries. The network has gaps and is at risk of a reversal, if more countries withdraw from their treaties. This possibility helps explain the push by corporate lobbies and trade officials to negotiate new treaties that would expand and solidify foreign investor protections.

What would happen if ISDS was expanded to the point that it applied to all? A good indication comes from the experience under NAFTA and the ECT, which, unlike other ISDS treaties, have long exposed Western countries to claims by each other's investors. Today, these two treaties by themselves account for 20–25 per cent of all known claims under all of the treaties.[89] In the case of NAFTA, each country has been sued between twenty and forty times (with Canada facing about twice as many claims as the United States or Mexico).[90] In the case of the Energy Charter Treaty, the first claims were brought by Western European corporations against former Soviet bloc countries, but by the mid-2000s the corporations began targeting Western European countries too. Since 2009, Western European countries, especially Spain and Italy, have faced at least sixty-nine claims.[91] Incidentally, beyond the officials and lawyers who took part in their negotiation, both NAFTA and the ECT appear to have received no attention from governments or the public when they were negotiated. It is, of course, at least as threatening to sovereignty for a developing country to be constrained by ISDS as it is for a Western country. The importance of NAFTA and the ECT is that they reveal the growth potential of ISDS if it were expanded to the world. As an educated guess, if Western countries opened themselves fully to claims by each other's investors, I would expect the number of ISDS claims roughly to quadruple to 300 per year.[92] The number would

[88] Another qualifier is that many Western countries have concluded an ISDS treaty with China, which now has much more potential for claims in both directions than a typical bilateral investment treaty does, especially under China's 'going out' policy. H Wang, 'A Deeper Look at China's "Going Out" Policy', Centre for International Governance Innovation Commentary (2016).

[89] I base the 25 per cent figure on the data in Van Harten and Malysheuski (n 71). Data from the UNCTAD Investment Dispute Settlement Navigator (n 16) generates a proportion a figure of 19.5 per cent as of June 2019, but without counting NAFTA 'notices of intent' as claims (as I do, partly because they sometimes lead to settlements).

[90] Virtually all claims against Canada and the United States have been brought by the other's companies, and virtually all claims against Mexico have been brought by US companies.

[91] UNCTAD Investment Dispute Settlement Navigator (n 16).

[92] I base this estimate on a comparison of the rate of claims against Canada and the United States under NAFTA, and against Western European countries under the ECT (albeit only in the energy sector), to the rate of claims in ISDS generally.

grow higher still if other countries also expanded their exposure. Importantly, this number does not account for settlements, which appear to exceed known claims by a significant factor.[93] Sovereignty has taken major blows from ISDS in many countries, but it may not survive at all if ISDS is globalized.

Conclusion

ISDS treaties originated in decolonization. Former colonial powers wanted to protect their corporations' wealth in newly independent countries, and the treaties were a means to constrain self-determination. They grew slowly in the 1970s and 1980s and rapidly in the 1990s. A new ISDS industry began to grow too in the 1990s, pursuing an opportunity, which arbitrators helped create, to feed on the carcass of the pre-ISDS sovereign. Institutions like ICSID, the PCA, and the SCC sought to attract the claims that brought business to the house. By 2000, the ongoing boom in ISDS litigation had begun.

If ISDS continues to expand, it will eventually make all countries semi-independent. The logic of foreign investor protections is ultimately to trust no people to govern themselves where it threatens the assets of the ultra-wealthy. That is also the logic of unequal globalization. It extends special privileges to investors, no matter where or how they come to own assets, and it allows corporate lawyers to act as supreme judges, by using vague laws to issue rulings that create public debt and discredit the sovereign. Faced with the mobility and obscurity of capital, many countries that signed ISDS treaties to win the favour of investors are now paying a high price.

93 See Chapter 6, 'Intimidating Sovereigns'.

3
Activation of the Treaties

Investor–state dispute settlement (ISDS) is something of a rags-to-riches story. In the 1970s, a handful of ISDS claims were filed at the World Bank's new International Centre for Settlement of Investment Disputes (ICSID), but they were based on contracts, not treaties. International law specialists seem not to have been aware, or to have believed, that the treaties gave such far-reaching powers to arbitrators as they regularly exercise today. It was thought, for example, that a more specific statement of consent by the state was needed, beyond the usual language in the treaties, for investor claims to be valid and actionable.[1]

The inauspicious start to ISDS came in 1987 when a UK company brought the first ISDS treaty claim against Sri Lanka. The arbitrators decided in the investor's favour in 1990.[2] In doing so, they forced their way through some vexing obstacles to arrive at an acceptance of sovereign consent, as I explore in this chapter. Yet this landmark ruling did not attract wide attention.[3] A second ISDS treaty claim was filed in 1992, another in 1993, another in 1995, and then five more in 1996.[4] The 1990s were thus an incubation period for claims and rulings. One might also call it the product development phase of the ISDS industry. Enterprising lawyers saw the potential of the treaties, if interpreted liberally, and looked for clients. Some lawyers became the arbitrators who quietly handed a string of victories to claimants, just as hundreds of new treaties were being signed by governments.

In each of the first ten ISDS rulings, which trickled out between 1990 and 1999, the tribunal dismissed the sued country's objections to the tribunal's authority and ordered compensation for the investor or, more rarely, the tribunal's initial ruling

[1] See eg M Sornarajah, *The Pursuit of Nationalized Property* (Martinus Nijhoff 1986) 38–39 (noting that a mere reference to ICSID in an investment treaty did not give ICSID jurisdiction over investor claims. Some clauses in the treaties authorized claims only with the further and specific consent of the country, others required the country to consider the claim sympathetically, and others required it to consent to ICSID at the investor's request [thus making it a violation of the treaty for the country to refuse, but without creating jurisdiction for an investor–state tribunal under the treaty]).

[2] *Asian Agricultural Products Ltd (AAPL) v Sri Lanka* (Award, 27 June 1990) 30 ILM 577.

[3] LNS Poulsen, *Bounded Rationality and Economic Diplomacy: The Politics of Investment Treaties in Developing Countries* (OUP 2015) 37, 135, and 138–39.

[4] The claims are known because of the rulings in *Saar Paper Vertriebs GmbH v Poland* (Awards, 17 August 1994 and 16 October 1995); *American Manufacturing & Trading Inc v Republic of Zaire* (Award, 21 February 1997) 36 ILM 1534; *Goetz (Antoine) v Burundi (No 1)* (Award, 10 February 1999); *Sedelmayer (Franz) v Russian Federation* (Award, 7 July 1998); *Signa v Canada* (Notice of intent, 4 March 1996); *Fedax NV v Republic of Venezuela* (Award, 11 July 1997) 37 ILM 1378; *Metalclad Corpn v United Mexican States* (Award, 30 August 2000) 40 ILM 36; and *Vivendi v Argentina (No 1): Compañia de Aguas del Aconquija SA & Vivendi Universal v Argentina* (Award, 21 November 2000).

set the stage for a concessionary or confidential settlement by the country.[5] Not a single investor lost a case until November 1999, when a NAFTA tribunal dismissed a US investor's claim based on a more respectful view of the role of domestic courts.[6] By then, arbitrators had ruled against a country on every continent other than Australia and Antarctica. They had disciplined an impoverished, war-torn country (the Congo) that did not even participate fully in the arbitration, and they had assumed the authority to review the national parliament of a wealthy, stable G-7 country (Canada). By 2000, the litigation boom was underway as ten more tribunals issued rulings that year, compared to eleven in the previous decade.[7]

Five of the earliest rulings are reviewed in this chapter, while others are left for later chapters. The purpose in each case is to show how arbitrators made dubious interpretations of the treaties, reflecting a consistent disrespect for sovereignty. Each was thus a stepping-stone to activating arbitrator power. Indeed, some of the rulings read as if the tribunal, or its majority, was intent on finding a way to claim authority over the sovereign.

Discovering the general consent

A country cannot be sued in international law without first having consented to the court's or tribunal's authority to hear the claim.[8] Most countries are cautious about giving such consent.[9] Further, longstanding principles in international law require a state's consent to be given clearly; where a treaty or contract is ambiguous,

[5] Referring to the date of the tribunal's award on jurisdiction (often combined with its award on the merits), the rulings emerged in this order: *AAPL* (n 2); *Saar Papier* (n 4); *American Manufacturing* (n 4); *Fedax* (n 4); *Ethyl Corpn v Canada* (Award, 24 June 1998) 38 ILM 708; *Sedelmayer* (n 4); *Lanco International Inc v Republic of Argentina* (Award, 8 December 1998) 40 ILM 457; *Goetz (No 1)* (n 4); *Wena Hotels Ltd v Arab Republic of Egypt* (Award, 25 May 1999) 41 ILM 881; and *Lemire (Joseph Charles) v Ukraine (No 1)* (Award, 18 September 2000) [7] (indicating the date of the tribunal's decision on jurisdiction as 24 September 1999). Three of these cases (*Ethyl*, *Lanco*, and *Lemire*) ended in a settlement; the other seven ended in an order of compensation for the investor.

[6] *Azinian (Robert) v United Mexican States* (Award, 1 November 1999) 39 ILM 537.

[7] The ten rulings in 2000, seven of which led to an order of compensation, were *Maffezini (Emilio Agustín) v Kingdom of Spain* (Award, 25 January 2000) 16 ICSID Rev 212; *Pope & Talbot Inc v Government of Canada* (Award, 26 January 2000); *Waste Management Inc v United Mexican States (No 1)* (Award, 2 June 2000) 40 ILM 56; *Metalclad* (n 4); *Olguín (Eudoro Armando) v Republic of Paraguay* (Award, 26 July 2001); *Swembalt AB Sweden v Latvia* (Award, 23 October 2000); *SD Myers Inc v Government of Canada* (Award, 13 November 2000) 40 ILM 1408; *Vivendi (No 1)* (n 4); *Gruslin (Philippe) v Malaysia* (Award, 27 November 2000) 5 ICSID Rep 484; and *Feldman Karpa (Marvin Roy) v United Mexican States* (Award, 6 December 2000) 18 ICSID Rev 469. The eleven rulings in the 1990s were those listed in n 5 and n 6 above.

[8] MO Hudson, *International Tribunals* (Carnegie Endowment for International Peace and the Brookings Institution 1944) 67–69.

[9] For instance, only seventy-three countries have accepted the general jurisdiction of the International Court of Justice (ICJ) to hear claims against them (ICJ, 'Declarations Recognizing the Jurisdiction of the Court as Compulsory' (*ICJ*, undated) <https://www.icj-cij.org/en/declarations> accessed 14 January 2020). Of the five permanent members of the UN Security Council—China, France, Russia, the United Kingdom, and the United States—only the United Kingdom has done so.

courts have tended to err in favour of preserving sovereignty.[10] Thus, in the case of ISDS, foreign investor claims became possible only after arbitrators decided that the treaties, after decades of dormancy, contained sovereign consents to the arbitrators' authority to hear such claims. It was not at all straightforward for arbitrators to take this step.

For about two decades after the first ISDS treaties, lawyers did not bring any claims based on the idea of an asymmetrical sovereign consent. Throughout the 1970s, all ISDS claims at ICSID came from consents by a country (or an investor) in contracts that explicitly allowed either side to sue the other. The same was true in the 1980s for all ICSID claims except two. The first of the exceptional claims was filed under Egypt's domestic law on foreign investment; the second was the *AAPL v Sri Lanka* claim, filed under the UK–Sri Lanka investment treaty on 8 July 1987.[11]

AAPL owned a shrimp farm in Sri Lanka which the Sri Lankan military had destroyed, saying it was being used by local Tamil Tiger rebels. The investor disputed the point and sued under the treaty. A tribunal was established and two of the arbitrators decided that Sri Lanka had not done enough to protect the investor, breaching the treaty.[12] They ordered USD 610,000 in compensation. The dissenting arbitrator criticized the other two for having gone too far in scrutinizing decisions of battlefield commanders in a context of civil war.[13]

Though it attracted little attention, the decision was very significant. It showed how arbitrators could interpret an ISDS treaty in a way that allowed investor claims without the country having consented specifically to the arbitration. It is hard to know fully how the tribunal reached this landmark result; the only official information that is public comes from the treaty and the tribunal's ruling in June 1990. The submissions to the tribunal from the government and the investor, and any other documents or testimony put to the tribunal, have never been made public.

According to the treaty, both Sri Lanka and the UK:[14]

[10] The principle of respect for sovereignty was well established when the treaties were put in place: eg World Trade Organization (Appellate Body), *EC Measures Concerning Meat and Meat Products (Hormones)* (Decision, 16 January 1998) [165] (note 154) citing R Jennings and A Watts (eds), *Oppenheim's International Law*, vol I (9th edn, Longman 1992) 1278:

> The principle of in dubio mitius applies in interpreting treaties, in deference to the sovereignty of states. If the meaning of a term is ambiguous, that meaning is to be preferred which is less onerous to the party assuming an obligation, or which interferes less with the territorial and personal supremacy of a party, or involves less general restrictions upon the parties [to the treaty].

The principle has since been near-universally disregarded by ISDS tribunals; G Van Harten, *Sovereign Choices and Sovereign Constraints: Judicial Restraint in Investment Treaty Arbitration* (OUP 2013) 56 and 90–91.

[11] *Southern Pacific Properties (Middle East) Ltd (SPP) v Arab Republic of Egypt* (Award, 14 April 1988) 3 ICSID Rep 131; *AAPL* (n 2).

[12] *AAPL* (n 2) [85–86].

[13] ibid (dissenting opinion of SKB Asante).

[14] UK–Sri Lanka investment treaty, signed 13 February 1980, Article 8(1), UN Conference on Trade and Development (UNCTAD) International Investment Agreements Navigator: <https://investmentpolicy.unctad.org/international-investment-agreements> accessed 14 January 2020.

> hereby consents to submit to [ICSID] ... for settlement by ... arbitration under the [ICSID] Convention ... any legal dispute arising between the Contracting Party and a national or company of the other Contracting Party concerning an investment of the latter in the territory of the former.

The first-order question was whether this clause allowed UK-based investors in general to bring an ICSID case against Sri Lanka or, alternatively, whether it merely set up some pending authority of ICSID over arbitrations under agreements that had a clearer consent to arbitrate both by the country and a specific investor. Today, we know that ISDS arbitrators have answered resoundingly in favour of the theory of the general consent of sovereigns, but in 1987 it was an open and vitally important issue whether the UK–Sri Lanka treaty crossed the threshold for establishing sovereign consent.

Remarkably, Sri Lanka seems not to have argued the point at all. There is no evidence in the tribunal's ruling that Sri Lanka's lawyers denied that the treaty allowed the tribunal to hear claims in general by UK investors. The tribunal simply reported that the government and the investor, at the first hearing, 'declared that they were satisfied that the Tribunal had been properly constituted' based on the ICSID Convention.[15] Thus, Sri Lanka's legal team appears to have limited itself to second-order arguments about the content of the investor's entitlement to 'full protection and security' under the treaty, and ultimately lost the case.

Sri Lanka was represented in this respect by a law firm called Coudert Brothers.[16] The same firm acted for the investor in the earlier ICSID case of *SPP v Egypt*.[17] Both *AAPL* and *SPP* are legal landmarks in the retreat of the state, due to the tribunals' acceptance of the theory of the asymmetrical sovereign consent under a treaty and a domestic law, respectively.[18] Woodhouse notes that most of the firm's lawyers in these cases 'went on to have careers as leading counsel and arbitrators' in ISDS.[19] For example, Paul Friedland was 'involved in both cases' and became global head of the mega-firm White and Case.[20] Thus, one of the top lawyers for multinationals today participated in the genesis of ISDS litigation more than thirty years ago.

On the *AAPL* tribunal, the key decision maker appears to have been Ahmed El-Kosheri. As presiding arbitrator, he joined the tribunal's investor-side arbitrator to

15 *AAPL* (n 2) [60].

16 S Woolhouse, 'Seats of Corporate Convenience and International Investment Law' (PhD thesis, University of Waterloo 2016) 154–55.

17 *SPP* (n 11). The SPP arbitration team included the late Peter Munk, owner of SPP, who went on to found Barrick Gold, which became the largest gold mining company in the world and the largest company in Canada by capitalization. The *SPP* claim was filed in 1984. E Reguly, 'Peter Munk: The Extraordinary Life of a Business Legend, Philanthropist and National Champion' (*Globe and Mail*, 29 March 2018); S Saunders, 'Barrick Gold Founder Peter Munk Leaves a Tarnished Legacy' (*NOW Magazine*, 25 April 2018).

18 Woolhouse (n 16) 154–57.

19 ibid 155.

20 ibid 155.

issue the majority award against Sri Lanka. Until his recent death, El-Kosheri was an Egyptian commercial arbitrator.[21] He worked at the International Chamber of Commerce (ICC) from 1994 to 2009, including for ten years as vice-president of the ICC's International 'Court' of Arbitration. His Cairo-based former firm advertises itself as a leading Arab World firm in corporate law, privatization, telecommunications, arbitration, foreign investments, international business transactions, and oil and gas.[22] It caters to multinationals such as AT&T, Caterpillar, Enron, Lockheed Martin, and Philip Morris. It thus seems fair to describe El-Kosheri as a lawyer from the corporate world of arbitration who, in *AAPL*, presided over a ruling that sparked the ISDS transformation of international law in favour of the wealthy and to the detriment of sovereignty. Incidentally, El-Kosheri's firm reports that he also took part in the *SPP v Egypt* case, though he is not listed as counsel or arbitrator in public documents for that case.[23]

One must stress the boldness of the *AAPL* tribunal's acceptance of the theory of the asymmetrical consent. A key impediment to this theory arose from the so-called 'choice-of-law' question.[24] International arbitrators cannot apply any source of law they please to decide a dispute. They are supposed to apply the law that was chosen by the disputing parties. The *AAPL* claim in particular was brought under the ICSID Convention, which says that arbitration tribunals must decide disputes 'in accordance with such rules of law as may be agreed by the parties'.[25] The 'parties' here clearly refers to the state and the investor appearing before the arbitrators. The ICSID Convention then says that, if the parties have not agreed on the choice of law, the tribunal must apply the law of the country that is involved in the dispute and any applicable rules of international law.[26] In *AAPL*, the tribunal did not apply Sri Lankan law and the applicable rules of international law.[27] Therefore, it must have applied some law that had been agreed by the disputing parties, Sri Lanka and the investor, as the choice of law. No other option was possible under the ICSID Convention.

This issue of the applicable law posed a challenge to the whole idea of the asymmetrical sovereign consent. How could Sri Lanka and APPL have chosen to apply some specific law to their relationship if they never actually agreed with each

[21] A El-Kosheri, 'Curriculum Vitae' (*Kosheri, Rashed & Riad*, undated) <http://www.krr-law.com/assets/det-ver-of-dr-ahmed-cv.pdf> accessed 14 January 2020.

[22] Kosheri, Rashed & Riad, 'Company Profile' (*Kosheri, Rashed & Riad*, undated) < http://www.krr-law.com/#companyprofile > accessed 14 January 2020.

[23] Kosheri, Rashed & Riad, 'Founders' (*Kosheri, Rashed & Riad*, undated) <http://www.krr-law.com/#founders> accessed 14 January 2020.

[24] A Redfern and A Hunter, *Law and Practice of International Commercial Arbitration* (Sweet & Maxwell 2004) ch 2.

[25] Convention on the Settlement of Investment Disputes Between States and Nationals of Other States (ICSID Convention) signed 18 March 1965, entered into force 14 October 1966 (4 ILM 524), Article 42(1).

[26] ibid Article 42(1).

[27] *AAPL* (n 2) [19].

other—with knowledge on both sides that the other side existed at the time of their agreement—to arbitrate disputes to ICSID? According to theory of the asymmetrical consent, Sri Lanka gave its consent in general to investor claims under the treaty, such that any UK investor could later consent to arbitration of a dispute simply by bringing a claim. Yet how could this mismatch of general and specific consents also create an agreement on Sri Lanka's and AAPL's choice of the applicable law?[28]

The *AAPL* tribunal's majority—El-Kosheri and the investor-side arbitrator—overcame this impediment by a kind of legal wizardry. They ruled that 'the choice-of-law process would *normally materialize* after the emergence of the dispute, *by observing and construing the conduct of the Parties* throughout the arbitration proceedings'.[29] This statement is vague at best. Frankly, I doubt it would pass muster in a school yard game, let alone a serious forum. How can an agreement 'materialize' in a 'normal' way by 'observing and construing' the conduct of a country and a company? Agreements are indicated by words describing what the parties offered and accepted with each other. Here, there were no words to indicate the parties' agreement on the applicable law to govern disputes between them. In turn, there was good reason to doubt that Sri Lanka had agreed in the treaty to allow claims based on an asymmetrical consent. How could it have done so if, according to the ICSID Convention, such claims are premised on a direct agreement between the investor and the country and there is none?

The *AAPL* arbitrators skirted these details. They decided instead to rely on their own observations of 'conduct' to satisfy the ICSID Convention's requirement for an agreement on the choice of law. They likewise assumed the power to 'materialize' agreements without any written version of them. Based on such reasoning, countries were taken to have conceded sovereignty in a profound way—by authorizing arbitrators to review any investor claim against the country's laws and institutions—without even having recorded the necessary agreement, with the other party, on the law that the arbitrators should apply. The reasoning was also inconsistent with the position in international law that a state's consent to a tribunal's authority has to be clear. Where the *APPL* arbitrators should have taken care to preserve sovereignty, they sacrificed it and, in doing so, helped to found a new era of arbitrator power.

ICSID responded approvingly, by promoting the *APPL* tribunal's innovative approach. It published the tribunal's award in the ICSID journal on foreign investment law aimed at specialized lawyers in the field. ICSID also published a 'note' by

[28] As NB Ziadé, 'Some Recent Decisions in ICSID Cases' (1991) 6 ICSID Review—FILJ 514, 514–15pointed out, 'the parties (i.e. the investor and the host State) had had no opportunity to exercise the prior choice of law' under Article 42(1) of the ICSID Convention 'due to the fact that the case was instituted on the basis of a bilateral investment treaty'.

[29] *AAPL* (n 2) [20] (emphasis added). The dissenting arbitrator would have subjected the dispute to the national law of the sued country: *AAPL* (n 2) (dissenting opinion) 577.

one of its staff lawyers (who had also been secretary to the tribunal in *SPP v Egypt*), Nassim G Ziadé.[30] In the note, Ziadé called it a 'point of interest' in the *AAPL* award that, '[h]itherto, in the overwhelming majority of ICSID cases, consent to ICSID jurisdiction has resulted from arbitration clauses contained in investment agreements [ie contracts with specific consent to arbitration by the sovereign] concluded between foreign investors and the host State'.[31] Ziadé reported that *APPL* was 'the first ICSID case where the jurisdiction of a tribunal has been based on consent expressed in a bilateral investment treaty' and highlighted that '[m]any bilateral investment treaties contain similar provisions'.[32] Ziadé also declared boldly that investment treaties '*establish* the *unconditional* consent of each contracting State to submit investment disputes to … arbitration before ICSID upon a request from an investor who is a national of the other contracting State'.[33] To support this claim, Ziadé merely cited ICSID's former leader Aron Broches, saying Broches' theory of the general consent 'seems to have been accepted by the parties, the majority award and the dissenting opinion' in *AAPL*.[34] ICSID thus endorsed the arbitrators' activation of a system that ICSID had facilitated for decades under Broches' direction.

Ousting the courts

Saar Papier v Poland was the second ruling under an ISDS treaty. The investor had sued Poland in 1992 under a Germany–Poland investment treaty that was concluded in 1989. In 1995, the tribunal ordered Poland to pay about USD 2.2 million in compensation to the investor.[35] However, none of the documents, including the ruling, were made public at the time and the case remained secret until 2004, when a specialized news reporter disclosed it after he 'pieced together' information on the case 'through interviews with the parties or their legal representatives, following the discovery of the proceedings in German courts'.[36] Thanks to this investigation, the tribunal's reasoning could be reviewed but, as in *AAPL*, the parties' submissions and other key records have never been disclosed.

Much like *AAPL*, the arbitrators in *Saar Papier* split two-to-one, with the presiding and the investor's arbitrator green-lighting the investor's claim. The

[30] *SPP* (n 11).

[31] Ziadé (n 28). Ziadé also highlighted *SPP* (n 11), where ICSID arbitrators decided they had authority to hear investor claims 'founded on investment legislation promulgated by the host State' rather than a specific consent in a contract.

[32] Ziadé (n 28).

[33] ibid (emphasis added).

[34] ibid (emphasis added). A Broches, 'Bilateral Investment Protection Treaties and Arbitration of Investment Disputes' in JC Schultsz and AJ van den Berg (eds), *The Art of Arbitration* (Kluwer 1982).

[35] *Saar Papier* (16 October 1995) (n 4) [103].

[36] LE Peterson, 'Early Investment Arbitrations against "Improper" Use of Environmental Laws Uncovered' *Investment Law and Policy Weekly News Bulletin* (International Institute for Sustainable Development, 5 January 2004).

claim was innovative because it targeted Poland's 'administrative and judicial process' in circumstances where the investor had not gone to Poland's national courts before suing under the treaty.[37] Further, the treaty in this case seemed to require investors to pursue a resolution in the national courts before bringing an ISDS claim.[38] Thus, the case marks the beginning of the arbitrators' now commonplace reflex of interpreting ambiguity in the treaties in ways that allow investors to avoid national courts.

The tribunal's decision was also exceptionally poorly explained. Its reasons consisted of just nine pages, less than two of which address the essential issue of whether the claim should be allowed to go ahead at all. Had Poland even objected to the theory of the asymmetrical consent? The tribunal's majority stated obliquely that Poland 'entered a plea of lack of jurisdiction' but 'does not contest the existence and validity of the arbitration agreement as such'.[39] Even so, Poland clearly raised major objections to the tribunal's authority. First, Poland stressed that the treaty only allowed for investor claims against an expropriation, nationalization, or 'equivalent' measures, not against other decisions of Polish authorities.[40] Here, the investor had challenged a customs order blocking the company from importing waste paper into Poland from Germany. Polish customs officials had taken their decision based on a Polish law that barred imported waste in general. How could that decision be 'equivalent' to expropriation? Second, Poland argued that the treaty, based on a translation of its Polish-language official text, gave the Polish ordinary courts the role of deciding the 'legality' of the purported expropriation or equivalent measure and the amount of compensation owed, if any.[41] This precondition for an ISDS claim—referral to the courts to determine these critical issues—had not been met by the investor.

The tribunal's majority curtly rejected both of Poland's objections, saying the treaty 'does not give any indication what "equivalent measures" might be' and that an import prohibition could be 'equivalent' to an expropriation.[42] Yet the majority

[37] *Saar Papier* (17 August 1994) (n 4) [18].

[38] Germany–Poland investment treaty, signed 10 November 1989, UNCTAD International Investment Agreements Navigator (n 14) Article 4(2) ('The legality of any such expropriation, nationalization or comparable measure and the amount of compensation shall be subject to review by due process of law') and Article 11(2). See also n 41.

[39] *Saar Papier* (17 August 1994) (n 4) [8] and [14].

[40] ibid [17]; ibid (dissenting opinion of Tadeusz Szurski) [3a].

[41] Germany–Poland investment treaty (n 38) Articles 4(2) and 11(2). According to the dissenting arbitrator (n 41 at [1]), the treaty stated in Article 4(2) that '[t]he legality of expropriation, nationalization or measures equivalent in their effect as well as the amount of compensation is subject to examination in the ordinary court proceedings'. Also, the reference in Article 11(2) to a six-month cooling-off period prior to a claim being permitted under the treaty referred to disputes arising from the matters in Article 4(2), the legality of which, according to the dissenting arbitrator, 'were subjected to examination in the ordinary court proceedings in the host state'; *Saar Papier* (16 October 1995) (n 4) (dissenting opinion of Tadeusz Szurski) [2]. Here, the dissenting arbitrator said that he was quoting 'the exact translation of the Polish text of the Treaty' which, according to Article 14 of the treaty, 'has the same binding force as the "German" text'.

[42] *Saar Papier* (17 August 1994) (n 4) [17].

had itself managed the proceedings in a way that heightened any uncertainty about this issue under the treaty. Over the objections of Poland's arbitrator, the majority arbitrators *declined even to review* the evidence presented by the disputing parties, especially that of the investor.[43] Instead, as Poland's arbitrator put it, the majority chose to hear the claim 'based exclusively on allegations of the claimant, without evaluation of documents filed by the claimant to substantiate those allegations'.[44] It appears that Saar Papier did not even have to give evidence, as the company claimed, that it was previously allowed to import waste paper from Germany.[45] If Saar Papier had challenged the customs order through the 'clearly established' procedures in Polish law, the dissenting arbitrator said, then the legality of the customs order 'would have been clarified quickly'.[46]

Normally under international law, one must first seek justice in a country's courts, and do so competently, before claiming a denial of justice by the country.[47] That is a laudable principle of respect for courts and sovereigns in general. In *Saar Papier*, the tribunal's majority merely noted that the investor claimed to have been 'wronged by the way Poland's administrative and judicial process worked' and that the tribunal 'need not distinguish between the various branches of the government within Poland'.[48] The treaty 'was set up to resolve disputes between investors and the host country as a whole' and the question of whether the investor was wronged by Poland 'is the very question that the Arbitral Tribunal will have to decide' (even if the investor skipped going to court).[49] Thus, in a roundabout way, the majority avoided the treaty's requirement, at least in its Polish-language version, for investors to seek relief in the courts first. More broadly, it upended the principle of exhaustion of local remedies in customary international law. The national courts therefore could not play their usual role of analysing and deciding the dispute before it reached the international level, and the tribunal was able to evaluate the investor's allegations lopsidedly or, as the majority arbitrators put it, 'in the light most favourable to claimant'.[50] The decision showed how easily ISDS arbitrators would allow investors to skirt national courts, as a step towards assuming the power to review sovereigns and compensate the companies that brought the claims.[51]

[43] *Saar Papier* (17 August 1994) (n 4) (dissenting opinion of Tadeusz Szurski) [3].
[44] ibid [3].
[45] ibid [3c].
[46] *Saar Papier* (16 October 1995) (n 4) (dissenting opinion of Tadeusz Szurski) [4].
[47] C Eagleton, *The Responsibility of States in International Law* (NYU Press 1928) 79, 96, and 100; P Okawa, 'Admissibility and the Law on International Responsibility' in MD Evans (ed), *International Law* (2nd edn, OUP 2006) 493–94.
[48] *Saar Papier* (17 August 1994) (n 4) [18].
[49] ibid [18].
[50] ibid [15].
[51] The presiding arbitrator, whose vote presumably swung the tribunal against Poland, was Pierre Karrer. He had been a full-time international commercial arbitrator since 1976. Although the tribunal's explanation is sparse on the point, one can gather how Karrer came to be appointed as presiding arbitrator from the fact that the investor filed its claim (the first known treaty claim) under the United Nations Commission on International Trade Law (UNCITRAL) arbitration rules, which authorize Permanent 'Court' of Arbitration (PCA) officials to decide who can impose an arbitrator on one or both

Disciplining a poor country

The third claim under an ISDS treaty was filed in 1993. It targeted an impoverished, war-torn country, the Democratic Republic of the Congo, whose people had endured a barbaric history of colonialism.[52] The claim arose in the turmoil of the dying years of the military dictatorship of Mobutu Sese Seko, established in the 1960s after the country's post-independence leader, Patrice Lumumba, was overthrown and murdered in post-colonial interventions by Belgium and the United States.[53] Mobutu had led the national military at the time and, with Central Intelligence Agency (CIA) funding, seized power and then ruled the country, renamed Zaire in 1971, for over three decades.[54] In this period, the Congo sank deeply into debt to private creditors and the International Monetary Fund (IMF), losing billions to capital flight abroad.[55] By the early 1990s, the army, after going unpaid, rebelled and looted several cities.[56] The rebellion was a prelude to Mobutu being pushed from power in 1996 in an armed uprising supported by Rwanda and other countries.[57]

ISDS first appeared in the Congo in 1984, when Mobutu's government became one of the first to commit its country to an ISDS treaty with the United States. The treaty entered into force in 1989 and, in 1993, a US company called American Manufacturing invoked it to claim compensation for damage to its property in the course of the army's rebellion. The tribunal agreed to hear the claim, endorsing the theory of the general consent[58] and showing how ISDS could be used to discipline a country whose government was unable even to participate effectively in the proceedings. On this latter point, for example, ICSID intervened to appoint the Congo's arbitrator after the government failed to appoint. The tribunal's members

disputing parties. The ruling notes that Karrer was chosen as presiding arbitrator by the Arbitration Institute of the Stockholm Chamber of Commerce. Therefore, it appears that officials at one arbitration house, the PCA, gave officials at another, the Stockholm Chamber of Commerce (SCC), the power to appoint the arbitrators and that the latter picked Karrer, a repeat player in commercial arbitration, as presiding arbitrator. PA Karrer, 'Curriculum Vitae' (*Pierre Karrer*, undated) <http://www.pierrekarrer.com/curriculum.html> accessed 14 January 2020; *Saar Papier* (17 August 1994) (n 4) [2].

52 A Hochschild, *King Leopold's Ghost: A Story of Greed, Terror, and Heroism in Colonial Africa* (Mariner Books 1998).

53 W Blum, *Killing Hope: U.S. Military and CIA Interventions Since World War II* (Black Rose Books 1998) 157–59.

54 B Berkeley, 'Zaire: An African Horror Story' *The Atlantic* (August 1993).

55 L Ndikumana and JK Boyce, 'Congo's Odious Debt: External Borrowing and Capital Flight in Zaire' (1998) 29 Dev Change 195.

56 W Breytenbach and others, 'Conflicts in the Congo: From Kivu to Kabila' (2010) 8 African Security Rev 33; JJ Quinn, 'Diffusion and Escalation in the Great Lakes Region: The Rwandan Genocide, the Rebellion in Zaire, and Mobutu's Overthrow' in SE Lobell and P Mauceri (eds), *Ethnic Conflict and International Politics: Explaining Diffusion and Escalation* (Palgrave Macmillan 2004).

57 WG Thom, 'Congo–Zaire's 1996–97 Civil War in the Context of Evolving Patterns of Military Conflict in Africa in an Era of Independence' (1999) 19 J Conflict Stud; Quinn (n 56).

58 *American Manufacturing* (n 4) [5.20] and [5.23].

split two-to-one as the Congo's ICSID-appointed arbitrator criticized the majority's award of USD 9 million as exceeding 'by far' both 'the injuries actually suffered' by the investor and 'the profits including the interests it could have reasonably expected', and favoured a much smaller award of USD 4 million.[59]

Whatever the amount of compensation, it should have been clear to the tribunal that the Congo's government, in chaos at home, could not respond effectively in the arbitration (held at the World Bank's offices in Paris). At first, the government did not even reply to the investor's request for arbitration in 1993. ICSID's Secretary General then intervened by recommending two individuals for the World Bank President to appoint as the presiding arbitrator and as the Congo's arbitrator.[60] Based on this thin layer of consent by the Congo, the tribunal declared itself constituted in August 1993, just as the Congo was beset by widespread violence.[61] That month, for example, the *Atlantic* reported how armed forces had pillaged the country's major cities in September 1991, leading to 200 deaths, and then again pillaged Kinshasa in January 1993, but '[t]his time Mobutu's elite troops intervened, grabbing their share and then summarily executing hundreds of rank-and-file looters'.[62] This same violence triggered American Manufacturing's ISDS claim, which blamed the government for not protecting the investor's factory and inventory. One might logically have asked whether an investor who decides to invest in a conflict-ridden dictatorship is in a credible position to request public compensation when its facilities are later destroyed in an armed uprising. No such question appears in the tribunal's ruling, however. Nor did the tribunal discuss the impact of the public in the Congo, who ended up owing compensation to American Manufacturing. Yet the *Atlantic*'s report gives an idea:[63]

> The losers in all this, needless to say, are the long-suffering Zairean people. Last year inflation soared to more than 6,000 percent. Unemployment is at 80 percent. Gross domestic product has by some estimates been contracting by as much as 30 percent a year since the *pillage*. Hospitals and schools have repeatedly shut down … Many Zaireans eat just one meal a day, some only one every other day. The public-service sector has largely stopped functioning. Tax collection has ceased—except for the 'direct taxation' of army shakedowns. The country's banking system has all but collapsed. The nation of nearly 40 million … is heading deeper into anarchy by the day.

Ignoring or ignorant of this context, the tribunal pushed ahead with the ISDS proceedings in the absence of the sued government. After the tribunal was established,

[59] ibid (dissenting opinion of Kéba Mbaye).
[60] ibid [2.03].
[61] ibid [2.04].
[62] Berkeley (n 54).
[63] ibid.

the government did manage to make submissions objecting to the tribunal's authority in May 1993 and then again in July 1994. The government argued, according to the tribunal's brief summary,[64] that the claimant should have tried other means to settle the dispute, including diplomacy, and that it was 'only after all these means had failed' that the investor should be able to use ICSID.[65] That position seems broadly consistent with a principle of respect for sovereignty;[66] the tribunal wholly rejected it.[67] As the government also explained, its earlier failures to reply to the investor's claim 'were due to the "*unfortunate and disastrous*" consequences triggered by the disturbances in the country'.[68] Other than reproducing this statement, however, the majority said nothing at all about the dire issues facing the country, merely delaying the proceedings by a month in response to the government's lack of participation.

The hearing in Paris ultimately took place in December 1994, after the tribunal denied a request from the Congo to delay it by another month.[69] At the hearing, the government did not make any submissions and was represented, as the tribunal put it dismissively, 'in the person of a Counsellor of the Embassy without nomination, authorization or accreditation of any kind'.[70] The tribunal later offered to hold another hearing, but only if the Congo paid the arbitrators' additional fees and expenses.[71] As context for that request, the Congo's per capita GDP at the time was about USD 2500, while the fees for the arbitrators would have amounted to several thousand USD per day.[72] The Congo's government offered no reply to the tribunal's offer, and so the additional hearing never happened. As a result, no defence at all was given on the merits, and no evidence was submitted, for the Congo.

Much like *AAPL v Sri Lanka*, it was doubtful whether the ISDS treaty in *American Manufacturing* even contained a consent to arbitrate by the Congo. Article VII of the treaty said: 'Each Party hereby consents to submit investment disputes to [ICSID] for settlement by ... binding arbitration',[73] but added in the next paragraph: 'If the dispute cannot be resolved through consultation and negotiation, then the dispute shall be submitted for settlement *in accordance with the applicable dispute-settlement*

64 None of the parties' submissions in the case were released by the tribunal.
65 *American Manufacturing* (n 4) [3.10].
66 See n 10.
67 *American Manufacturing* (n 4) [5.28].
68 ibid [4.06] (citing a letter from the government dated 30 May 1994).
69 ibid [3.22].
70 ibid [3.23].
71 ibid [3.25].
72 GDP per capital data for 1994 taken from Trading Economics, 'Republic of the Congo GDP per Capita' (*Trading Economics*, undated) <https://tradingeconomics.com/republic-of-the-congo/gdp-per-capita> accessed 14 January 2020. The arbitrators did not report their rates in the ruling, but in their final decision they did order the government to pay USD 104,828.96 to the investor, amounting to 'half of the costs of the proceeding for which advance payments have been made' by the investor, in addition to the order of USD 9 million in compensation for the investor.
73 United States–Congo investment treaty, signed 3 August 1984, Article VII (para 2), UNCTAD International Investment Agreements Navigator (n 14).

procedures upon which the Parties to the dispute may have previously agreed.'[74] It seems therefore that the treaty allowed for arbitration only if the Congo had 'previously agreed' with the investor to 'applicable dispute-settlement procedures'. That condition of consent is what one would usually expect in contractual arbitrations at ICSID. Yet, for arbitrations based on the novel idea of asymmetrical sovereign consent, it was hard to see what procedures could have been 'previously agreed' by the Congo and American Manufacturing: the company was not even a party to the treaty in which the Congo's consent was supposed to have been given, and where any previously agreed dispute settlement procedures would presumably need to be found. The tribunal dodged this major obstacle to its authority by saying:[75]

> [i]t appears clearly that if Zaire and the United States agree that the disputes of the type which is submitted to the Tribunal could be brought before ICSID, they have thus, each on its part, accepted the competence of ICSID to be eventually proceeded against by a national of the other co-contracting State.

Thus, the treaty's apparent call for 'the Parties to the dispute' (as opposed to the countries that signed the treaty) to have previously agreed to the relevant procedures was shunted aside, in favour of the innovation of the asymmetrical consent. For the tribunal, it was enough that the Congo had agreed with the United States to allow for claims at ICSID, even if the Congo had also agreed with the United States that such claims should be conditioned on a previous agreement between the Congo and the investor.

Having taken the treaty in this investor-friendly direction, the arbitrators went on to award compensation to American Manufacturing, explaining that the company's factory had been wrecked by soldiers and that the Congo was responsible, whether or not the soldiers acted under government orders.[76] According to the tribunal, the Congo had not shown (at the hearing where it did not participate!) that it took adequate steps to protect the factory.[77] In an earlier submission to the tribunal, the government argued that it did not compensate anyone in the country for the widespread violence and thus did not discriminate against the investor, but the tribunal decided that equal treatment was not enough; the lack of compensation for American Manufacturing violated the treaty's minimum protections for foreign investors.[78] It seemed that the tribunal might also acknowledge that the investor should be held responsible for its decision 'to invest in a country such as Zaire' as opposed to 'constructing a castle in Spain or a Swiss chalet in Germany',[79]

[74] United States–Congo investment treaty (n 73) Article VII (para 3) (emphasis added).
[75] *American Manufacturing* (n 4) [5.20].
[76] ibid [6.09], [6.13], and [7.06].
[77] ibid [6.07], [6.09], and [6.23].
[78] ibid [6.10], [6.24], and [6.25].
[79] ibid [7.15].

but the tribunal instead awarded bountiful compensation. Moreover, the majority arbitrators did not explain how they tallied up the award of USD 9 million, even when the Congo's arbitrator called for an award of less than half that amount (and an expert appointed by the tribunal to assess the investor's losses similarly arrived at USD 4.45 million).[80]

Like other early awards, *American Manufacturing* offered a stepping-stone for more ISDS litigation. The tribunal signalled that investors could be indemnified, in effect, against predictable violence in a war-torn country. It did so where many others—who lost their livelihoods and loved ones without access to an international tribunal and compensation—would obviously have to help cover the bill for the investor's losses as well as the arbitrators' fees.

Ruling on sovereign debt

Filed in 1996, *Fedax v Venezuela* was the first claim to target a Latin American country.[81] This 'first' was significant because, for much of the twentieth century, Latin American countries had opposed the colonial powers' assertion of absolute protections for foreign investors in international law. The Latin American position reflected the writings of a nineteenth-century Argentine jurist, Carlos Calvo, whose 'Calvo doctrine'—now habitually denigrated by ISDS promoters—condemned the use of force to protect foreign investors; required foreign investors, upon entering a state's territory, to respect local laws and subject themselves to domestic courts; and limited foreign investor protections under international law to the same protections as domestic investors.[82] In contrast, the major capital exporters called for an international minimum standard of treatment for foreign investors, albeit a more limited one than what we see today in ISDS. For much of the twentieth century, the two sides clashed over the content of international law, especially over the legal consequences of expropriation and the physical security of foreign investors.[83] By the early 1990s, though, most Latin American countries had relinquished the Calvo doctrine by concluding ISDS treaties with requirements for states to provide generous compensation for direct or indirect expropriations, 'fair

[80] ibid [7.19]; ibid (dissenting opinion of Kéba Mbaye).

[81] *Fedax* (n 4).

[82] C Calvo, *Le Droit International* (5th edn, A Rousseau 1896) 118–64; A Hershey, 'The Calvo and Drago Doctrines' (1907) 1 AJIL 26; DR Shea, *The Calvo Clause* (University of Minnesota Press 1955) 9–21.

[83] For instance, League of Nations Conference for the Codification of International Law, Responsibility of States for Damage Caused in their Territory to the Person or Property of Foreigners, League of Nations Conference for the Codification of International Law, Bases of Discussion, vol 3, LN Doc C.75.M.69.1929.V (1929) 15; EM Borchard, 'The "Minimum Standard" of the Treatment of Aliens' (1940) 38 Mich L Rev 445, 445–47 and 450–51; Sornarajah (n 1) 29.

and equitable treatment', and 'full protection and security' for foreign investors.[84] ISDS arbitrators later took these protections further still, to the point that, as I discuss in later chapters, the treaties are now used to give much more favourable treatment to foreign investors than anyone else in host or home country alike.[85]

Against this backdrop of debates over international law, the *Fedax* claim marked a turning point for Latin America. It was filed under the Netherlands–Venezuela investment treaty of 1991.[86] Importantly, it did not involve a farm, factory, or other physical assets (as typically associated with the concept of foreign direct investment)[87] but rather six promissory notes that entitled the bearer, in this case a company in the Netherlands Antilles tax haven, to a share of Venezuela's sovereign debt.[88] This 'foreign investment' had been bought from the Venezuelan government by a Venezuelan company which later endorsed them to the tax haven company.[89] From the arbitrators' ruling, it is unclear whether the same individuals owned or controlled both companies but, regardless, by extending the idea of 'investment' to promissory notes, the arbitrators asserted an even broader power to decide disputes than in other ISDS cases to that point, with potentially major implications for sovereign debt.

Normally, disputes over sovereign debt are resolved in courts. Sovereign debt contracts usually designate the law and courts of a creditor-friendly jurisdiction (such as New York state or England) as the forum for dispute resolution under the contract.[90] Alternatively, where a country defaults on its sovereign debt and the default affects many creditors, the default would usually be worked out in negotiations managed by the IMF and the US treasury, in consultation with the relevant banks and other creditors.[91] Both of these conventional forums—court proceedings and work-out negotiations—become more complicated where ISDS expands into sovereign debt, and creditors, especially vulture funds, suddenly acquire new rights as 'investors'.[92] ISDS can then be used to frustrate a government's ability to respond to

[84] D Schneiderman, 'Investment Rules and the New Constitutionalism' (2000) 25 Law & Social Inquiry 757, 768.

[85] S Montt, *State Liability in Investment Treaty Arbitration: Global Constitutional and Administrative Law in the BIT Generation* (Hart Publishing 2009) 21–23.

[86] Netherlands–Venezuela investment treaty, signed 22 October 1991, UNCTAD International Investment Agreements Navigator (n 14).

[87] International Monetary Fund (IMF), *Balance of Payments Manual* (6th edn, IMF 2009) 100–10; A Maffry, 'Direct Versus Portfolio Investment in the Balance of Payments' (1954) 44 American Econ Rev 614.

[88] *Fedax* (n 4) [13].

[89] ibid [13] and [16].

[90] J Schumacher, C Trebesch, and H Enderlein, 'Sovereign Defaults in Court', European Central Bank Working Paper No 2135 (2018) 4–5; G Weisz, NE Schwarzkopf, and M Panitch, 'Selected Issues in Sovereign Debt Litigation' (1991) 12 U Pa J Int'l Bus L 1.

[91] IMF, 'Sovereign Debt Restructuring—Recent Developments and Implications for the Fund's Legal and Policy Framework', IMF Policy Paper (2013).

[92] KP Gallagher, 'The New Vulture Culture: Sovereign Debt Restructuring and Trade and Investment Treaties', IDEAs Working Paper No 02/2011 (2011) 15–27; M Guzman and JE Stiglitz, 'Creating a Framework for Sovereign Debt Restructuring That Works' in M Guzman, JA Ocampo, and JE Stiglitz

economic crisis and to help speculators move money in and out of countries at the expense of financial stability. They become a tool to reshape debtor–creditor relations in the international financial system. The IMF recognized the risks posed by ISDS in 2012, when its executive directors expressed the view that, even though national capital controls may be 'an appropriate policy response' in a sovereign debt crisis, they 'could still violate a member's obligations under other international agreements' if the other agreements do not have 'temporary safeguard provisions compatible with the Fund's approach'.[93] In more direct language, ISDS treaties conflict with the important goal of regulating hot money to guard against the collapse of a country's economy.

Arbitrators need not have assumed this new power over sovereign debt. In *Fedax*, Venezuela argued that the promissory notes should not qualify as 'investment' and were not covered by the ICSID Convention, making the ISDS claim invalid.[94] Under the Netherlands–Venezuela investment treaty, Venezuela argued, 'investment' meant 'the laying out of money or property in business ventures, so that it may produce a revenue or income' and the purported investment here was apparently just a paper transfer of assets from a company in Venezuela to one in the Netherlands Antilles.[95] The tribunal rejected this prudent position on the basis that the promissory notes were not 'purely commercial' and therefore covered by the ICSID Convention.[96] According to the tribunal, the notes had five 'basic features' of investment: 'a certain duration', 'a certain regularity of profit and return', 'assumption of risk', 'a substantial commitment', and 'a significance for the host State's development'.[97] These features came to be known as the *Fedax* criteria, although, like many investor-friendly positions, the tribunal in fact borrowed them from Christoph Schreuer, an investment law expert and later ISDS arbitrator.[98] As criteria, they are highly flexible and rarely applied to bar investor claims. Yet some future ISDS tribunals found even these features too limiting, such that they ignored them or reframed them as mere guidelines when assessing whether to allow a claim.[99]

(eds), *Too Little, Too Late: The Quest to Resolve Sovereign Debt Crises* (Columbia University Press 2016) 10–12.

93 IMF, 'The Liberalization and Management of Capital Flows: An Institutional View', IMF Policy Paper (14 November 2012) 42.
94 *Fedax* (n 4) [19].
95 ibid [1], [17], and [19].
96 ibid [15]. Ironically on this point, sovereign debt contracts are often classified as 'commercial' in national courts to avoid conventional principles of sovereign immunity that would otherwise protect the debtor country; eg *Trendtex Trading Corpn v Central Bank of Nigeria* [1977] QB 529, 557–58 (CA); GR Delaume, 'Sovereign Immunity and Transnational Arbitration' (1987) 3 Arb Int'l 28, 28–29.
97 *Fedax* (n 4) [43], citing C Schreuer, *The ICSID Convention: A Commentary* (CUP 2001) 372.
98 C Schreuer, *The ICSID Convention: A Commentary* (CUP 2001) 372, cited in *Fedax* (n 4) [43]. I discuss Schreuer further in Chapter 7, 'Fault Lines and the Future of ISDS'.
99 For examples, see Van Harten, *Sovereign Choices* (n 10) 92 (note 94) and 103 (note 160).

Beyond this issue of what constitutes 'investment', Venezuela's wider objections to the tribunal's authority remain a mystery. The parties' submissions are not public, so one must rely on the tribunal's statements in its ruling to glean what Venezuela argued, and all the tribunal reported was that, at its first session in Washington DC, Venezuela raised 'objections to the jurisdiction of [ICSID] and to the competence of the Tribunal, both orally and in a written submission'.[100] Moreover, once the tribunal decided to hear the claim, Venezuela then simply conceded the case by confirming that its public authorities had approved payment of the promissory notes, with interest, and by agreeing to cover half the cost of the arbitration.[101] The tribunal issued a ruling based on these commitments, indicating the specific amount Venezuela should pay and noting 'with satisfaction' that *Fedax* was the first ICSID case where the sued country 'is a prominent member of the Latin American region'. For the tribunal, this Latin American development showed 'the evolution that the legal treatment of foreign investments has had in this region as elsewhere in the world'.[102] In other words, the Calvo doctrine was dying and the arbitrators saw its demise as an achievement.

Importantly, *Fedax* is the first case in which we encounter the leading (Chilean) ISDS hawk Federico Orrego Vicuña as the presiding arbitrator. One might ask, how could this individual, who was a former high-level official in the Augusto Pinochet dictatorship, come to have the power to judge Venezuela as an international arbitrator? The *Fedax* ruling is ambiguous about Orrego Vicuña's appointment, stating only that he was chosen by the World Bank President '[a]fter consultation with the parties' and 'in accordance with the parties' agreement'.[103] This 'agreement' appears simply to have been that the World Bank should make the appointment where the parties could not otherwise agree, meaning that the World Bank preferred Orrego Vicuña for the role.[104]

Power over Parliament

Around the same time as *Fedax*, ISDS burst onto the scene in North America with the *Ethyl* ruling against Canada.[105] Ethyl Corporation, a chemicals manufacturer, brought its claim under NAFTA in 1997. The claim reportedly shocked Canadian government officials.[106] Even today, the treaties are often presented only

[100] *Fedax* (n 4) [9].
[101] *Fedax NV v Republic of Venezuela* (Award, 9 March 1998) 37 ILM 1391, [27] and [34].
[102] ibid [36].
[103] *Fedax* (n 4) [9]. The World Bank President made the appointment, as usual under the ICSID Convention, in his *ex officio* role as Chair of ICSID's Administrative Council.
[104] ibid [6]–[7].
[105] *Ethyl* (n 5).
[106] This statement is based on several confidential interviews with government insiders; G Van Harten and DN Scott, 'Investment Treaties and the Internal Vetting of Regulatory Proposals: A Case Study from Canada' (2016) 7 J Int'l Disp Settlement 92, 110–11.

as safeguards against expropriation in developing countries; with *Ethyl*, their constraints were revealed as extending to developed countries too.[107] Indeed, in *Ethyl*, the target was the national parliament of a well-established Western democracy and, in the ensuing battle, the company won decisively.

Ethyl Corporation was one of the first large multinationals to sue under an ISDS treaty.[108] It brought its claim after a law was proposed to ban a gasoline additive called MMT, which Ethyl manufactured.[109] The proposed ban responded to concerns from the automobile industry that MMT disrupted that industry's new emissions control systems. Public health researchers also expressed concerns about health risks linked to inhalation of MMT in gasoline fumes. These risks were uncertain (as they had also been for the leaded gasoline additives that MMT replaced once they were banned in the 1970s after decades of work by public health researchers and advocates). At the time of Ethyl's ISDS claim, MMT was a particular problem in Canada because it was prohibited or kept out of use in nearly all US states due to health or environmental concerns.

For Ethyl, the NAFTA lawsuit was just one tactic in a larger lobbying effort. The company had pushed for years for MMT to be approved in the United States, after having long opposed earlier efforts to ban leaded additives, which Ethyl also manufactured. Canadian regulators rashly approved MMT in the 1980s, but moved in the 1990s toward a ban based on mounting evidence of MMT's risks. By then, Ethyl could invoke its NAFTA right to sue Canada in ISDS, and it did so before the law was even in force. Ethyl was represented by an enterprising Canadian lawyer, Barry Appleton, who, ironically, had earlier warned of the dangers of foreign investor protections for Canadian social programmes and sovereignty.[110] Since those well-justified warnings over twenty years ago, Appleton has represented investors in numerous ISDS cases and advocated against proposed reforms of the treaties.[111]

[107] R Grinspun and R Kreklewich, 'Consolidating Neoliberal Reforms: "Free Trade" as a Conditioning Framework' (1994) 43 Stud Pol Econ 33.

[108] The other was the French multinational Vivendi. My threshold for 'big' is a company with over USD 1 billion in annual revenue.

[109] Bill C-29, leading to the *Manganese-Based Fuel Additives Act*, SC 1997, c 11.

[110] See eg B Appleton, 'Municipalities and the MAI', Brief by Appleton and Associates (1998); testimony of B Appleton in British Columbia Legislature, *Report on the Multilateral Agreement on Investment: Transcripts of Proceedings* (1998). See also M Dobbin, *The Myth of The Good Corporate Citizen* (James Lorimer & Co 2003) 119; S Shrybman, Letter to DR Cass and LV Fortier re: *United Parcel Service of America Inc v Government of Canada* (*ICSID*, 3 November 2005) <http://icsidfiles.worldbank.org/icsid/ICSIDBLOBS/OnlineAwards/C5546/DC8845_En.pdf> accessed 14 January 2020.

[111] See eg B Appleton, 'The Song is Over: Why It's Time to Stop Talking about an International Investment Arbitration Appellate Body' (2013) 107 ASIL Proc 23. Appleton also co-chaired the Investment Treaty Working Group of the International Arbitration Committee of the American Bar Association Section on International Law, which produced a timely attack on the EU's proposals for ISDS reform in October 2016: Investment Treaty Working Group of the International Arbitration Committee of the American Bar Association Section on International Law, 'Initial Task Force Discussion Paper: Executive Summary & Conclusions and Recommendations', Discussion Paper (2016).

We know more about *Ethyl* than other ISDS cases because most of the documents were uncovered by researchers and eventually published by governments. One can see from the documents how far Ethyl went in its challenge to Canada's proposed law, seeking an astonishing USD 201 million in compensation to cover its claimed lost profits, expected costs of reducing its operations in Canada, and alleged losses to its worldwide sales 'due to other countries relying on' Canada's approach.[112] However, the *Ethyl* tribunal never actually ruled on this aspect of the claim because, once the tribunal decided it had the power to review the proposed law, Canada agreed to a concessionary settlement with Ethyl. I discuss this settlement as an example of regulatory chill in Chapter 6, 'Intimidating Sovereigns'.

In objecting to the tribunal's authority, Canada's main argument was that the dispute related more to 'trade' than 'investment' and should therefore be dealt with by NAFTA's country-to-country processes of dispute settlement, not the ISDS mechanism in NAFTA's investment chapter. According to Canada, the proposed law emerged from the federal government's power to regulate import and trade in MMT (and these 'trade' issues were covered by other trade-related chapters of NAFTA).[113] Echoing this view, Mexico submitted to the tribunal that Ethyl should not be allowed to use ISDS 'to launch what is in reality a challenge against a trade measure in the guise of an investment dispute'.[114] Both NAFTA countries therefore offered the arbitrators a straightforward reason to dismiss Ethyl's claim.

The arbitrators rejected this argument in favour of an expansive approach to their authority. They stressed that they saw no reason for caution, even in circumstances of an attack on a national law. According to the tribunal, it was 'appropriate first to dispense with any notion' that NAFTA's ISDS mechanism 'is to be construed "strictly"'.[115] The arbitrators also went out of their way to disapprove of Canada having seemed 'at least to hint at such a principle'.[116] Apparently, they found it audacious for a government to suggest that an international tribunal should err in favour of protecting a country's sovereignty when a treaty is unclear about the extent of the country's consent to arbitration. Here, the tribunal cited a ruling by an earlier ICSID tribunal as purported support for the view that NAFTA should be construed so as 'to respect the common will of the parties'.[117] Yet the earlier ICSID tribunal had been empowered under a contract, not a treaty, making the *Ethyl* ruling especially dubious. Under a contract, the 'parties' whose 'common will' authorizes the arbitration would always include the investor as a party to the contract with the sued country. In ISDS under a treaty, though, the 'common will of the parties'

[112] *Ethyl Corpn v Canada* (Statement of claim, 2 October 1997) [51].
[113] *Ethyl* (n 5) [62].
[114] ibid [48]. Mexico could make this argument because, under NAFTA, the other states parties (ie those which have not been sued) have an express right to make submissions to a tribunal.
[115] *Ethyl* (n 5) [55].
[116] ibid [55 (note 20)].
[117] ibid [55], citing *Amco Asia Corpn v Indonesia* (Award, 25 September 1983) 23 ILM 351.

always excludes the investor, since an investor is not a sovereign and so can never be a party to the treaty in which two or more countries have consented to ISDS. By citing a contract-based case, therefore, the *Ethyl* tribunal conveniently confused an investor's specific consent under a contract with a country's general and asymmetrical consent under a treaty.[118] These two forms of consent are as different as a private company is from an elected legislature. One pursues profit for its shareholders, the other makes policy decisions on behalf of a population; one decides based on ownership, the other based on citizenship. By contorting the 'common will of the parties', the *Ethyl* arbitrators substituted a company for a sovereign, marrying in an obscure way their dubious power and the inequality of the treaties.

Having asserted their authority by downgrading sovereignty, the tribunal then had to determine what 'common will' of the parties should guide their interpretation of NAFTA. Absurdly, it did so by disregarding the views of Canada (notably the only disputing party that was actually a party to the treaty) and of Mexico (one of the other two parties to the treaty), both of which had told the arbitrators to dismiss Ethyl's trade-related claim on the basis that it was not authorized for ISDS at all.[119] The tribunal lamented that Canada 'cites no authority ... as to why the two [parts of NAFTA—on trade and on investment] necessarily are incompatible'.[120] Yet it is hard to know what 'authority' Canada could possibly cite for this point, since *Ethyl* was the first ISDS claim under NAFTA.[121] Further, the tribunal complained that Canada 'confines itself' to the NAFTA text, even though the text of any treaty is clearly a primary indicator of the 'common will of the parties' to that treaty.[122] Here, the NAFTA text stated that '[i]n the event of any inconsistency between this Chapter [the investment and ISDS chapter of NAFTA] and another Chapter, the other Chapter shall prevail to the extent of the inconsistency'.[123] Admittedly, this provision is not entirely clear in its instruction that arbitrators should reserve trade-related disputes for dispute settlement processes in NAFTA's trade-related chapters. Yet any tribunal inclined to respect sovereignty would give the article very close attention. The *Ethyl* arbitrators discarded it on the basis that Canada 'indicated at the Hearing on jurisdiction that this [provision] was not "an issue that was absolutely critical to be disposed of at [the relevant] hearing"' and then concluded lamely that the question 'must abide another day'.[124]

This particular objection to the tribunal's authority was not the only obstacle in the way of Ethyl's claim. For example, NAFTA provides for a six-month cooling off

[118] For a more detailed discussion, see G Van Harten, *Investment Treaty Arbitration and Public Law* (OUP 2007) 62–70.
[119] *Ethyl* (n 5) [48] and [62].
[120] ibid [63].
[121] ibid [63].
[122] ibid [63].
[123] North American Free Trade Agreement (NAFTA) signed 17 December 1992, entered into force 1 January 1994 (32 ILM 296 and 605) Article 1112.
[124] *Ethyl* (n 5) [64].

period before an investor can initiate ISDS against a country's 'measure'.[125] Ethyl had not waited the six months; indeed, at the time of its claim, the proposed law on MMT was not even in effect. As the purpose of a cooling-off period would seemingly be to let the investor and government discuss the pending dispute before moving to arbitration, Canada argued that Ethyl's claim was premature.[126] The arbitrators rejected this concern, speculating that they did not think Canada would repeal or amend the law anyway.[127] On the contrary, after the tribunal issued its ruling on jurisdiction, Canada did in fact withdraw the law as part of its settlement with Ethyl. Thus, the arbitrators cast aside the treaty's cooling-off provision based on a dubious claim and creatively assumed the power to review proposed as well as actual laws.

The *Ethyl* case was a starting point for two of the leading ISDS hawks: Charles Brower and Marc Lalonde. The former was the investor's arbitrator; the latter was Canada's. The presiding arbitrator was Karl-Heinz Bockstiegel, who was chosen, according to the tribunal, by the ICSID Secretary General 'after first ascertaining that neither Party [i.e. Canada and Ethyl] would have any objection to such appointment'.[128] As in many ISDS cases, it is hard to know how the Secretary General wielded its appointment power and to what extent the parties had any real choice in the matter.[129] In any event, all three individuals went on to become repeat players in ISDS and all three have tended towards investor-friendly interpretations, especially Brower and Lalonde.[130]

Conclusion

The earliest ISDS cases are exceptional because they were written on blank slates. Arbitrators delivered liberal interpretations, paving the way for an expansionist ISDS movement in which the fortunes of investors and arbitrators are closely aligned. Ambiguity in the treaties facilitated this bold assumption of power over public budgets, putting the policy choices of countries in jeopardy. By 2000, arbitrators had validated the theory of the asymmetrical sovereign consent. They had pushed aside the courts, even when the treaty appeared to endorse their role. They had espoused a loose view of 'investment' and ruled on claims against decisions by legislatures, courts, and governments. As discussed in Chapter 4, they had extended the treaties to assets only indirectly or partially owned by a foreign investor,

125 NAFTA (n 123) Articles 1101(1) and 1120(1).
126 *Ethyl* (n 5) [13], [45], and [65].
127 ibid [85].
128 ibid [11].
129 G Van Harten, 'Leaders in the Expansive and Restrictive Interpretation of Investment Treaties: A Descriptive Study of ISDS Awards to 2010' (2018) 29 EJIL 507, 523–25.
130 See the Appendix of this book.

and they had taken expansive approaches to a range of investor protections. Not all of the early arbitrators endorsed investor-friendly approaches, but most did, and that was enough to keep hope alive for those financing the litigation.

Thus, ISDS was activated in the 1990s through a series of pro-claimant innovations. By the time it became notorious for draining public coffers and intimidating regulators, it was too late for most countries to avoid the ISDS web. Nearly all the early cases involved small or unknown companies. Some were not publicly disclosed for years, and governments later reported they had been in the dark about how the treaties were being used.[131] By the late 1990s, the foundation was laid for an explosion of litigation. At this stage, the first wave of NAFTA claims against developed countries was perhaps the most eye-opening, although undoubtedly the most abused early target was Argentina. That country faced a shocking wave of claims in the early 2000s after a dire economic crisis, as foreign investors sought to sue their way out of the foreseeable costs of their investment risks. Eventually, countries in every inhabited region of the world would be sued under ISDS treaties signed in the 1990s. Since the rush of treaties began to ebb around 1996, investors have brought nearly 1,000 claims compared to four before that year.[132]

[131] See eg Department of Trade and Industry (South Africa), 'Bilateral Investment Treaty Policy Framework Review', Government Position Paper (2009) 5.

[132] UN Conference on Trade and Development (UNCTAD) Investment Dispute Settlement Navigator: <https://investmentpolicy.unctad.org/investment-dispute-settlement> accessed 9 November 2019 (reporting 983 treaty-based ISDS cases as of 31 July 2019). The four pre-1996 cases were *AAPL* (in 1987), *Saar Papier* (in 1992), *American Manufacturing* (in 1993) and *Goetz* (in 1995) (all n 4).

4
The Most Powerful Protections

It would be absurd to say people should be protected by law if they are foreign and if they own assets, but not otherwise. This absurdity is the conceptual foundation of ISDS. The treaties give broad and powerful protection to foreign investors, but not to others, many of whom are far more vulnerable.

True, some legal protections are inherently and justifiably limited according to nationality or wealth. Citizenship rights turn on nationality, for example, and property rights require ownership of something. Yet in ISDS the rights are to 'fair and equitable treatment' or 'full protection and security' or 'no-less-favourable' treatment—none of which require the rights holder, by definition, to be foreign and wealthy. Such broadly framed rights should in principle belong to everyone based on our common interests in life, liberty, security, work, privacy, voting, and so on. For such guarantees from the sovereign, the law should protect all, subject to the need to balance one person's interests against another's and against those of the community.

Instead, ISDS treaties, by their unique combination of features, give foreign investors the most powerful protections, by far, of any private actor in international law. The protections go well beyond those available for victims of torture or rape, for example, who rely on relatively weak international safeguards to protect them from abuse by states and corporations alike.[1] If one considers that foreign investors as a group include the wealthiest organizations and people in the world, the treaties effectively reserve the most powerful protections for the least vulnerable actors. They write inequality firmly into the law, for countries to observe and respect.

Moreover, the treaties establish these exceptional protections for foreign investors without creating corresponding responsibilities for them to respect a country's laws and people. Often, they also allow investors to avoid national courts and adjust their nationality to access ISDS, while closing the ISDS process to all

[1] G Echeverria, 'Redressing Torture: A Genealogy of Remedies and Enforcement' (2006) 16 Torture 152; HM Smith, 'Sex Trafficking: Trends, Challenges, and the Limitations of International Law' (2011) 12 Human Rights Rev 271; RM Latore, 'Coming Out of the Dark: Achieving Justice for Victims of Human Rights Violations by South American Military Regimes' (2002) 25 BC Int'l Comp L Rev 419; L van den Herik and JL Černič, 'Regulating Corporations under International Law: From Human Rights to International Criminal Law and Back Again' (2010) 8 J Int'l Crim Justice 725; JA Zerk, *Multinationals and Corporate Social Responsibility: Limitations and Opportunities in International Law* (CUP 2009) ch 3; and Oxford Pro Bono Publico, 'Obstacles to Justice and Redress for Victims of Corporate Human Rights Abuse', Comparative submission prepared for Professor John Ruggie (UN Secretary General's Special Representative on Business and Human Rights) (3 November 2008).

but the investor and the sued country's national government. Anyone else, even if affected profoundly by the claim, is excluded from the arbitration, usually completely and always unfairly (including, in the latter case, where affected 'third parties' are given limited ISDS participation rights as 'amicus'). In ISDS, it is as if all those impacted by the important relationships among corporations and governments were by default wiped from the legal picture. In turn, investors can attack countries without having to face others whose knowledge or arguments might undermine the investor's claim. Even worse, the investor can make gross allegations against others who are not allowed to respond, and ISDS arbitrators can decide against those others without ever hearing from them. It is an understatement to call such a process unequal and unfair.

Rights without responsibilities

The treaties frame foreign investor protections broadly in two key ways. First, they use vague language to describe the protections, referring to 'fair and equitable treatment', 'full protection and security', or 'indirect expropriation' for example. This ambiguity has helped hawkish arbitrators to interpret the treaties in investor-friendly ways, raising the odds of countries having to pay compensation and intensifying the pressure on governments to appease the wealthy. Second, the treaties allow investors to challenge a very wide array of sovereign decisions, including the laws, regulations, policies, orders, bylaws, requirements, and practices of all those exercising the state's authority at all levels of government.[2] Investors could challenge a country's constitution and demand compensation if it were applied in ways they do not want. Thus, ISDS creates a new institutional layer in the governing apparatus of states, especially with respect to public budgets. Put differently, ISDS allows foreign investors to shift authority away from all of a sovereign's other institutions and assign it instead to arbitrators—arbitrators who are unlikely to be expert in the relevant area of domestic law and policy, but are nevertheless given the authority to determine the legitimacy of laws and policies that protect businesses, workers, consumers, depositors, shareholders, children, the sick, the environment, or any number of matters having very little to do with the specialized field of international investment law.

ISDS promoters sometimes reject these criticisms, claiming that the treaties do not give any protections or rights to foreign investors beyond what all investors

[2] This scope of coverage is defined expressly in some ISDS treaties (eg North American Free Trade Agreement (NAFTA), signed 17 December 1992, entered into force 1 January 1994 (32 ILM 296 and 605), Article 201(1)), and it applies generally under ISDS treaties based on the principle of the state as a unified entity in international law. International Law Commission, 'Draft Articles on Responsibility of States for Internationaly Wrongful Acts', *Report of the International Law Commission on the Work of Its Fifty-Third Session*, UN GAOR, 56th Sess, Supp No 10, annex, UN Doc A/56/10 (2001) 35.

otherwise have in domestic law.[3] If that were true, one may ask why ISDS lawyers put so much effort into promoting and using the treaties, and why major corporations are willing to finance ISDS claims. Above all, this pro-ISDS argument fails because the treaties give investors the power to challenge decisions that could never be challenged under a country's own laws. Most obviously, they allow investors to attack laws passed by a country's highest legislature and endorsed by its highest court. Such laws are the clearest expression of a country's authority to govern its territory; law making is the heart of sovereignty.[4] By allowing investors to challenge them in an exceptionally powerful way at the international level, the treaties clearly grant them a status beyond anyone else's in domestic law.

Meanwhile, the treaties do not go on to create investor responsibilities that are actionable in the manner of their protections.[5] For instance, they do not create obligations for investors to respect national and international labour standards or to comply with taxation rules when a country's institutions do not or cannot enforce them. A government cannot bring an ISDS claim against an investor where the investor is alleged to have defrauded, abused, or murdered its citizens. Indeed, it is doubtful that a government could bring such a counterclaim, even when the investor invokes an ISDS treaty to challenge how the country's criminal or anti-fraud laws have been applied to the investor. With such a lopsided arrangement, the wealthy obtain a suite of special protections, without actionable responsibilities to go along with them.

Pro-investor expansiveness

The early case of *Metalclad v Mexico* revealed the sheer breadth of foreign investor protections, once they are interpreted expansively by arbitrators.[6] *Metalclad* was a

[3] See eg US Chamber of Commerce, '13 Myths about Investment Agreements and Investor–State Dispute Settlement (ISDS)' (*US Chamber of Commerce*, 13 April 2015) <https://www.uschamber.com/sites/default/files/13_myths_about_investment_agreements_and_isds.pdf > accessed 14 January 2020 ('US law affords greater protections to assure fair and equitable treatment of foreign investors than any international investment treaty'; 'since 2004, the US Model BIT [bilateral investment treaty] has expressly stated that investment agreements do not create greater rights for foreign investors than those enjoyed by domestic investors'); G Van Harten, 'Comments on the European Commission's Approach to Investor–State Arbitration in TTIP and CETA', Osgood Legal Studies Research Paper No 59 (2014) 3 (reproducing the European Commission's statement in a public consultation document that '[i]nvestment protection provisions consist of a limited number of standards guaranteeing that governments will respect certain fundamental principles of treatment' that 'are reflected in the rights that democratic governments grant to their own citizens and companies').

[4] Legal Information Institute, 'Sovereignty' (*Cornell Law School*, undated) <https://www.law.cornell.edu/wex/sovereignty> accessed 14 January 2020 ('Sovereignty is essentially the power to make laws . . .').

[5] N Bernasconi and others, 'Harnessing Investment for Sustainable Development: Inclusion of Investor Obligations and Corporate Accountability Provisions in Trade and Investment Agreements', Background document for the expert meeting co-hosted by the International Institute for Sustainable Development and Friedrich Ebert Stiftung (2018).

[6] *Metalclad Corpn v United Mexican States* (Award, 30 August 2000) 40 ILM 36.

NAFTA case, the first against Mexico. In a poorly reasoned decision, the tribunal took a strikingly pro-investor and anti-sovereign approach, especially in its view of what the concepts of 'fair and equitable treatment' and 'indirect' expropriation should mean.

The dispute itself was predictable, including for the investor. Metalclad Corporation, a US company, bought a Mexican company that had operated a hazardous waste facility in a rural area of Mexico but without having obtained a municipal permit to do so.[7] When it bought the Mexican company, Metalclad was aware of the issue of the missing permit, as its initial contract to buy the company made the purchase conditional on the Mexican company getting the permit or, alternatively, on a court decision excusing the Mexican company from having to obtain the permit.[8] The Mexican company received neither, but Metalclad bought the company anyway,[9] taking an obvious risk that its investment would fail.

Part of the challenge for the proposed waste facility was the spectre of past dumping at the site. Huge amounts of toxic waste, about fifty thousand barrels, had been buried there improperly a few years earlier, leading to understandably strong concern among residents and landowners. The company running the site at the time (which Metalclad later purchased) was 'disposing of untreated waste on the open land' instead of 'storing and transferring the waste as it was authorized to do'.[10] A local environmentalist described how '[t]he rains of 1991 carried toxic drums a great distance, most importantly into a reservoir that is used in the rainy season to water livestock, crops and people' such that '[s]everal animals died and the people stopped using the water'.[11] The local municipality commissioned a scientific study, which concluded that the regional geology was unsuitable for a hazardous waste facility because the site was crossed by seasonal streams and its soil was vulnerable to leakage.[12] A large coalition of groups—including the municipality, national and international environmental groups, and local environmentalists and landowners—opposed the facility for all of these legitimate reasons.[13] Public opinion in the state was also reportedly heavily opposed.[14] This opposition and the reluctance of municipality to grant a permit were therefore highly foreseeable for any diligent investor.

After buying the Mexican company, and lacking the municipal permit, Metalclad proceeded by meeting with Mexican federal officials to discuss approval

[7] *United Mexican States v Metalclad Corpn* (2001) 89 BCLR (3rd) 359, [8].
[8] ibid [8].
[9] ibid [8].
[10] SM Wilkinson, 'NAFTA, Mexico and Metalclad: Understanding the Normative Framework of International Trade Law' (LLM thesis, University of British Columbia 2002) 146.
[11] Cited in A Wheat, 'Toxic Shock in a Mexican Village' (1995) 16 Multinat'l Monitor 5, cited secondarily in Wilkinson (n 10) 147.
[12] Wilkinson (n 10) 148.
[13] ibid 144.
[14] ibid 144 (note 472).

of the facility. According to Metalclad, its representatives were assured verbally by federal officials that the facility could go ahead without a municipal permit.[15] Yet Metalclad did not get the purported assurances in writing and, when it later sued under NAFTA, Mexico responded with evidence that the assurances were not given at all.[16] (In the arbitration itself, witnesses called by Metalclad and Mexico gave different stories about the meeting between Metalclad and federal officials, the key witness for Metalclad's position being a former federal official who, directly or via his spouse, allegedly had financial ties to Metalclad itself.[17] With very little explanation why, the tribunal sided with Metalclad.[18])

After the Mexico City meeting, the municipality maintained throughout that Metalclad, like the Mexican company it had bought, needed a municipal permit to build the facility. However, Metalclad pushed ahead without a municipal permit and eventually in the face of a municipal stop-work order.[19] Metalclad held an opening day ceremony that was blockaded by protesters.[20] Eventually, the state governor ended the planned facility by creating a conservation area covering the site.[21] By that point, Metalclad had already invoked its NAFTA right to sue Mexico in ISDS.

In the NAFTA arbitration, Metalclad argued that the Mexican federal government in effect had approved the facility regardless of the municipality. It seems incredible that this argument went anywhere with the tribunal. Metalclad had known that the previous owner sought and failed to get municipal approval,[22] yet the tribunal avoided this weakness in Metalclad's case by neglecting even to mention the previous dumping at the site and by omitting from the tribunal's ruling on the facts of the dispute the reasons for public concern about the facility. Meanwhile, the tribunal condemned the protesters against the facility as having 'employed tactics of intimidation' and emphasized Metalclad's view—while ignoring Mexico's submissions to the contrary[23]—that the protests were staged.[24] This way of telling the story made it much easier for the tribunal to justify its award of USD 16.7 million to Metalclad. The omitted facts only became part of the ISDS record after Mexico sought to have the tribunal's ruling set aside in a court in British Columbia.[25]

15 *Metalclad* (n 6) [33]–[34].

16 *Metalclad Corpn v United Mexican States* (Respondent's post-hearing submission, undated) [73]–[79].

17 *United Mexican States* (n 7) [111]–[112]; *Metalclad* (Respondent's post-hearing submission) (n 16) [80]–[84].

18 *Metalclad* (n 6) [87]–[89].

19 *United Mexican States* (n 7) [10]–[11].

20 Wilkinson (n 10) 142–43.

21 *United Mexican States* (n 7) [17].

22 ibid [8].

23 *Metalclad* (Respondent's post-hearing submission) (n 16) [496]–[506].

24 *Metalclad* (n 6) [46].

25 *United Mexican States* (n 7) [18]. Pursuant to the UNCITRAL Rules under which Metalclad filed its claim, the tribunal had proposed (and the disputing parties accepted) British Columbia as the seat of the arbitration.

'Indirect' expropriation

More importantly for the inequality of ISDS, the *Metalclad* tribunal took highly expansive views of NAFTA's then-virgin investor protections. First, it interpreted the concept of 'indirect' expropriation[26] heavily in favour of investors and against states, by deciding:[27]

> ... expropriation under NAFTA includes not only open, deliberate and acknowledged takings of property ... but also *covert or incidental interference* with the use of property *which has the effect of depriving the owner, in whole or in significant part, of the use or reasonably-to-be-expected economic benefit of property* even if not necessarily to the obvious benefit of the host State.

This definition was extraordinarily broad, compared to definitions of indirect expropriation in domestic law, including that of the United States.[28] It created a huge overlap between the idea of general regulation—which does not come with public compensation for those who lose out economically, so as not to put legislatures and governments in a financial straitjacket—and that of indirect expropriation, which under NAFTA requires full compensation for the foreign investor, including, ominously, for future profits.[29] Thus, the tribunal greatly limited the budgetary space for good faith laws and regulations. To illustrate, it applied a threshold of 'significant' impact on the investor to describe an indirect expropriation, whereas in US law the comparable threshold would be 'near-complete' impact.[30] The tribunal also ruled out any requirement that a law must benefit the state in some way before it can be called an expropriation, and did not discuss at all how a duty to compensate investors for their lost profits may create a crippling burden for the state when trying to pass new laws and develop public policy. Applied broadly, the tribunal's approach would disrupt all sorts of fields of regulation: urban planning, pollution control, health protection, technology standards, infrastructure development, broadcasting policies, national security, and so on.

One would expect the tribunal to have justified this expansive interpretation with great care, as one expects lawyers and judges to rely on the law and its methods in the course of justifying their decisions. Yet the *Metalclad* tribunal offered no analysis, as it should have, of the text of the expropriation provision in NAFTA, of the context for that provision, or of its relationship to NAFTA's object and purpose. Each of these steps is stipulated in the rules of treaty interpretation applying to

26 NAFTA (n 2) Article 1110(1).
27 *Metalclad* (n 6) [103].
28 See eg MC Porterfield, 'International Expropriation Rules and Federalism' (2004) 23 Stan Envt'l LJ 3; *United Mexican States* (n 7) [99].
29 NAFTA (n 2) Article 1110(2).
30 Porterfield (n 28) 58–59.

international tribunals;[31] the *Metalclad* arbitrators basically skipped them in their ruling. Instead, they simply cut and pasted the relevant NAFTA provision and then declared their own bold view of what it should mean.[32] It was a remarkable example of inept legal reasoning.

Worse, the Canadian court that reviewed the decision was unable to repair the tribunal's dubious interpretation because, like in many jurisdictions, British Columbia's law on judicial enforcement of arbitration awards under the *New York Convention* mandates a high level of deference to international arbitrators.[33] The judge warned that the *Metalclad* tribunal 'gave an extremely broad definition of expropriation' but added that 'the definition of expropriation is a question of law with which this Court is not entitled to interfere'.[34] Thus, the tribunal's expansive approach was left in place, allowing many later ISDS tribunals to cite it as influential authority (unlike in legal systems based on the common law, there is no strict rule of precedent in international law) and making governments wary of it ever since.

'Fair and equitable treatment'

The *Metalclad* tribunal did not stop at indirect expropriation in its favouring of investors. Like most ISDS treaties, NAFTA also requires each country to ensure 'fair and equitable treatment' for foreign investors,[35] and the tribunal was one of the first to take an expansive approach to this much-abused concept.

As a source of wide-ranging power to discipline states, the 'fair and equitable treatment' protection has been especially useful to ISDS arbitrators because it is so vague. Obviously, fairness and equity can mean different things to different people. Yet, if one considers the range of other protections for foreign investors under the treaties, one might approach the standard of fair and equitable treatment—and its close counterpart, 'full protection and security'[36]—as back-ups for situations in which a country does not discriminate against or expropriate an investor, but still abuses the investor in some unexpected or roundabout way.[37] For this less

[31] Vienna Convention on the Law of Treaties, signed 22 May 1969, entered into force 27 January 1980 (1155 UNTS 331), Article 31(1).

[32] *Metalclad* (n 6) [102]–[103].

[33] *United Mexican States* (n 7) [50]–[51]. This high level of deference tracks back to lobbying in the 1980s by the Canadian arbitration industry to encourage legislatures to make Canada a haven for international arbitration: JEC Brierly, 'Canadian Acceptance of International Commercial Arbitration' (1988) 40 Maine L Rev 287, 295–96; S Kierstead, 'Referral to Arbitration under Article 8 of the UNCITRAL Model Law: The Canadian Approach' (1999) 31 Can Bus LJ 98, 99.

[34] *United Mexican States* (n 7) [99].

[35] NAFTA (n 2) Article 1105(1).

[36] ibid Article 1105(1).

[37] M Malik, 'The Full Protection and Security Standard Comes of Age: Yet Another Challenge for States in Investment Treaty Arbitration?', International Institute for Sustainable Development Best Practices Series (2011).

expansive approach, one would need to apply a fairly high threshold before finding that a country has breached the standard. That is indeed how the nearest comparator in international law, the customary 'minimum standard of treatment' (long championed by capital-exporting countries), typically worked. It is premised on a substantial degree of deference to sovereigns, as conveyed, for example, by the tribunal in the historical *Neer* arbitration and by the *ELSI* decision of a chamber of the International Court of Justice (ICJ):

> ... the treatment of an alien [ie foreign national], in order to constitute an international delinquency, should amount to an outrage, to bad faith, to wilful neglect of duty, or to an insufficiency of governmental action so far short of international standards that every reasonable and impartial man would readily recognize its insufficiency.[38]
>
> Arbitrariness is not so much something opposed to a rule of law, as something opposed to the rule of law ... It is a wilful disregard of due process of law, an act which shocks, or at least surprises, a sense of juridical propriety.[39]

Both of these decisions on the customary minimum standard came well before the boom in ISDS litigation. As such, they offered an obvious reference point for ISDS arbitrators who, out of respect for sovereignty, might have wished to exercise care when reviewing countries. Very few appear to have been interested in doing so.[40] The *Metalclad* tribunal thus helped to spark a major revision of international law by the arbitrators, who overwhelmingly have dismissed the more cautious approach in *Neer* and *ELSI* in order to constitute fair and equitable treatment as a far-reaching source of arbitrator power to review sovereigns. In its early reading of the concept, the *Metalclad* tribunal obligated the NAFTA countries to ensure that:[41]

> *all relevant legal requirements* for the purpose of initiating, completing and successfully operating investments made, or intended to be made, under [NAFTA] *should be capable of being readily known* to all affected investors.

Further, the tribunal said:[42]

> There should be *no room for doubt or uncertainty* on such matters. Once the authorities of the central government ... become aware of any scope for misunderstanding or confusion in this connection, it is their duty to ensure that

38 *Neer Claim (United States v Mexico)* (1926) 4 RIAA 60, 61–62.
39 *Elettronica Sicula SpA (ELSI) (United States v Italy)* [1989] ICJ Rep 15, [128].
40 G Van Harten, *Sovereign Choices and Sovereign Constraints: Judicial Restraint in Investment Treaty Arbitration* (OUP 2013) 101–02.
41 *Metalclad* (n 6) [76] (emphasis added).
42 ibid [76] (emphasis added).

> the correct position is promptly determined and clearly stated so that investors can proceed with all appropriate expedition in the confident belief that they are acting in accordance with all relevant law.

Frankly, this approach treated investors almost like children, by putting an unqualified onus on governments either to do the impossible—by avoiding *any* uncertainty in the laws applying to a business, no matter how recklessly or ignorantly the business owner proceeds—or to compensate the investor when legal uncertainty works to its disadvantage. Is there ever a law without some 'room for doubt or uncertainty'? The concept of fair and equitable treatment itself is a case in point. Holding countries to such an unforgiving requirement seems dismissive of the need to revise laws and regulations in response to changing circumstances and to plan for the cost of these decisions.

In *Metalclad*, the investor had been aware, even if the tribunal avoided the issue, that the company whose business Metalclad bought had failed to get the disputed permit. Presumably, Metalclad should also have been aware that it was important to obtain any federal assurances in writing before relying on them. These expectations seem run of the mill for any businessperson in a heavily regulated sector such as waste disposal.[43] Yet the tribunal entertained, on scant evidence, Metalclad's claim that it had received verbal guarantees,[44] thus creating generous protections for investors and unpredictable liabilities for regulators. Once exposed,[45] its ruling revealed from an early stage the lengths to which ISDS arbitrators could go to discipline countries in favour of investors.[46]

Metalclad set the stage for a long line of ISDS rulings—recently called 'a stunning example of expansive arbitral lawmaking' by Stone Sweet and Grisel—which have exploded fair and equitable treatment into a series of flexible and compensable entitlements from the state, including arbitrator-defined notions of regulatory consistency and transparency, good faith, adequate reasons, access to justice, due process, non-arbitrariness, non-discrimination, reasonableness, and proportionality on the part of state institutions.[47] None of these sub-standards are found

43 *Metalclad* (Respondent's post-hearing submission) (n 16) [25]–[29], [68], and [105].

44 *Metalclad* (n 6) [87]–[89].

45 The proceedings were initially kept confidential by the tribunal, but for specific disclosure obligations of the parties: *Metalclad Corpn v United Mexican States* (Procedural Order, 27 October 1997).

46 The NAFTA governments responded by making a joint statement in 2001 that attempted to limit the meaning of the NAFTA minimum standard of treatment, including its reference to 'fair and equitable treatment'. They also began putting similar limiting language in their new treaties. It did not work well. The challenge was that, whatever language governments used, it always retained some ambiguity that arbitrators could exploit to favour investors. Redrafting the treaties was a cat-and-mouse game with drafters usually too slow to catch the arbitrators. See eg E Boone Barrera, 'The Case for Removing the Fair and Equitable Treatment Standard from NAFTA', Centre for International Governance Innovation Paper No 128 (2017).

47 A Stone Sweet and F Grisel, *The Evolution of International Arbitration: Judicialization, Governance, Legitimacy* (OUP 2017) 191. For a pro-investor cataloguing of various arbitrator-invented protections, see A Diehl, *The Core Standard of International Investment Protection: Fair and Equitable Treatment* (Kluwer Law International 2012).

in the treaties' own definitions of fair and equitable treatment. They were invented by the arbitrators. Perhaps the most notorious are the wide-ranging requirements for states to meet an investor's 'legitimate expectations' and to ensure stability in the regulatory framework for the investor's business.[48] The crux of both of these is to help compensate the wealthy where they are disadvantaged by changes to laws or regulations. They make fair and equitable treatment into a shield against the economic costs of social change.

The exclusion of others

Metalclad helped to demonstrate the uneven playing field of ISDS in another important way, by allowing only the investor and Mexico's national government to participate as parties in the arbitration. All of the other Mexican actors whose interests were affected by the dispute—landowners, the municipality, the state government—were left out entirely. In a fair proceeding, it should be 'in the heart of every human judge' that all those with an affected interest have a right to be heard.[49] ISDS clearly should be fair in the same way.

When investors sue countries, they often raise issues that affect others. For example, as in *Metalclad*, the investor may make allegations about a subnational government whose interests diverge from those of the national government, and the tribunal may make findings against the subnational government without hearing from it.[50] Or, the investor may allege that a named person was involved in corrupt activities; in a fair proceeding, that person has a right of standing to reply to the accusation. To do so effectively, the person must be given access to all relevant evidence put before the tribunal, an opportunity to test that evidence, an opportunity to submit their own evidence, and so on. For a tribunal to make findings against a person without hearing from the person is obviously unfair.

Interests without representation

The case of *Von Pezold v Zimbabwe* underscores this procedural unfairness in ISDS.[51] The investor, Bernard Von Pezold, brought an ISDS claim relating to disputed lands in Zimbabwe. Four indigenous communities, joined by an organization called the European Center for Constitutional and Human Rights, claimed that some of the disputed lands belonged to them and that they should have a say

[48] Diehl (n 47) 366–87 and 441–42.

[49] JM Kelly, 'Audi Alteram Partem' (1964) 9 Nat'l L Forum 103, 110; SA de Smith, 'The Right to a Hearing in English Administrative Law' (1955) 68 Harv L Rev 569.

[50] See eg *AbitibiBowater v Canada* (Claimant's notice of intent, 23 April 2009) [8]–[9].

[51] *Von Pezold (Bernard) and Others v Republic of Zimbabwe* (Procedural order, 26 June 2012).

in the resolution of the 'dispute'.[52] In the ISDS proceeding, however, their only option to participate was by applying for 'amicus curiae' (friend of the court) status. This status, if granted, would allow the communities to access the proceedings and make short submissions, to the extent allowed by the tribunal. However, it would not give them full access to all the materials put to the tribunal by each party or a right to make submissions on all the issues affecting the communities' interests.

According to the tribunal, the indigenous communities had submitted to the tribunal that 'they each have a distinct cultural identity and social history which is inextricably linked to their ancestral lands', which were affected by the investor's claim.[53] They submitted further that the ISDS case went beyond the interests of the investor and government alone because it 'may also potentially impact on the indigenous communities' collective and individual rights'.[54] In response, the investor argued against giving the communities an opportunity to participate as amicus, even after acknowledging, as the tribunal put it, that the communities 'have some interest in the land over which the Claimants assert full legal title'.[55] Likewise, while the tribunal accepted that '[i]t may therefore well be that the determination of the Arbitral Tribunals in these proceedings will have an impact on the interests of the indigenous communities',[56] it refused to grant amicus status to the communities, due to the tribunal's 'reservations as to the independence and/or neutrality' of the communities.[57] On this point, the tribunal pointed to a requirement in the applicable arbitration rules that the communities should not only have an interest in the proceeding but also be 'independent' of the other parties.[58] Since the communities had links to the Zimbabwean state, the tribunal decided that giving them even the limited role of amicus would 'unfairly prejudice' the investor.[59]

This reasoning turned fairness upside down. Unfairness for the communities was justified as fairness for the investor. By the tribunal's reasoning, it was too much to ask the investor to make its claims in the presence of those with opposed interests. Even if the communities had some connection to the Zimbabwean government, a feature of the right to standing in a legal proceeding is the ability to decide on one's own position and not have it pre-determined by the judge. If the communities decided that their interests were best served by supporting Zimbabwe's position, they had the right to do so. The possibility that two parties might agree on aspects of the case should not disqualify either of those parties.

[52] ibid [1].
[53] ibid [21].
[54] ibid [21].
[55] ibid [62].
[56] ibid [62].
[57] ibid [62].
[58] ibid [62], citing International Centre for Settlement of Investment Disputes (ICSID), *Rules of Procedure for Arbitration Proceedings*, revised 26 September 1984 and 1 January 2003 (original rules 1968), reprinted in *Convention, Regulations and Rules* (ICSID 2003), Rule 37(2).
[59] *Von Pezold* (n 51) [62].

Thus, even the limited right to participate as amicus was denied to the indigenous communities in *Von Pezold*. Even where amicus status is granted, however, it does not address the much deeper unfairness of denying a party its fundamental right of standing. First, only some arbitration rules and treaties have been rewritten to clarify that tribunals have the power to grant amicus status.[60] Second, in ISDS, amicus status has been granted rarely and always with major restrictions.[61] Third, amicus status is clearly not a substitute for the right of standing itself. It does not give the affected party access to all documents before the tribunal, usually limiting the party instead to one or two short submissions, which must be written in the dark because the amicus cannot know all that the investor and government have put before the tribunal. Above all, tribunals are not required, as they would be in a fair process, to give full standing to any affected party that seeks it, to the extent of the party's interest.[62] The problem does not lie with the idea of amicus, but with the misuse of that idea in ISDS as a distraction from the real problem. For ISDS to be fair, it must safeguard the rights of all affected parties, including by ensuring they have standing to represent themselves.

Above all, *Von Pezold* shows how ISDS transforms complex disputes that affect many actors into an artificially narrow dispute between two parties. By this procedural design, only the foreign investor can challenge sovereign decisions and only the national government can defend them. Thus, ISDS treaties allow the wealthy to accuse others who have no right to reply or to expose the investor's own wrongs. No matter how profoundly the dispute affects them, they are always denied standing.

Nationality shopping

Lawyers regularly use holding companies to adjust the nationalities of their wealthy clients. Usually they do so to hide wealth and avoid tax.[63] This practice of nationality shopping allows those who can afford such services to exploit differences in

[60] See eg EU–Singapore Free Trade Agreement, signed 29 June 2015, Article 3 of Annex 9-G; Comprehensive and Progressive Agreement for Trans-Pacific Partnership (CPTPP) (released 21 February 2018) signed 8 March 2018 Article 9.23(3).

[61] P Wieland, 'Why the Amicus Curia Institution is Ill-Suited to Address Indigenous Peoples' Rights before Investor–State Arbitration Tribunals: *Glamis Gold* and the Right of Intervention' (2011) 3 Trade, Law & Dev't 334, 341–44.

[62] ibid 344–45 and 359–60; E Levine, '*Amicus Curiae* in International Investment Arbitration: The Implications of an Increase in Third-Party Participation' (2012) 29 Berkeley J Int'l L 200, 208–14; A Salazar, 'Defragmenting International Investment Law to Protect Citizen-Consumers: The Role of *Amici Curiae* and Public Interest Groups', Osgoode Hall Law School Comparative Research in Law & Political Economy Research Paper No 6/2013 (2013) 4–8.

[63] A Kellow, 'Multi-Level and Multi-Arena Governance: The Limits of Integration and the Possibilities of Forum Shopping' (2012) 12 Int'l Envt'l Agreements: Pol, L Econ 327; R Palan, 'Tax Havens and Commercialization of State Sovereignty' (2003) 56 Int'l Org 151.

regulation among countries.[64] Basically, it helps the wealthy to gain new rights and avoid responsibilities.

Nationality shopping is also important in ISDS. To qualify as a 'foreign' investor under an ISDS treaty, a company or individual must show that it has the nationality of the home country (ie not the sued country) under the treaty.[65] Many ISDS treaties allow investors to do so very easily, by setting up a holding company in the home country.[66] Others are somewhat more demanding, since they require an investor to show that it has a substantial business, or perhaps a head office, in the home country in order to qualify for protection under the treaty. Either way, the 'foreign' investor bringing the claim may be owned by a multinational or tycoon from elsewhere,[67] including from the sued country itself.[68]

In the case of *Tokios v Ukraine*, for example, the tribunal allowed an ISDS claim against Ukraine to go ahead, even though the claim was brought by a company that was 99 per cent owned by Ukrainians.[69] Thus, Ukrainians were able to use a Lithuanian company to bring a claim against their own country as 'foreign' investors. The tribunal also took the treaty's protections beyond the idea of actual flows of capital between Lithuania and Ukraine, declaring ambitiously that '[t]he origin of the capital is not relevant to the existence of an investment'.[70] In other cases, wealthy individuals have been allowed to use holding companies or other legal vehicles to acquire a nationality that gave them access to ISDS.[71] The most commonly used (or abused) platform for this manoeuvring appears to have been the Netherlands.[72]

[64] S Timberg, 'International Combines and National Sovereigns' (1947) 95 U Penn L Rev 575, 588; S Picciotto, *International Business Taxation* (Weidenfeld and Nicolson 1992) 94–96; WW Bratton and others, 'Introduction: Regulatory Competition and Institutional Evolution' in WW Bratton and others (eds), *International Regulatory Competition and Coordination* (Clarendon 1996) 9, 21 and 40–41. This is the flip side of inter-state competition to attract investment: nationality shopping by international capital: UNCTAD, *Taxation*, UNCTAD Series on Issues in International Investment Agreements (UN 2000) 62.

[65] R Donner, *The Regulation of Nationality in International Law* (2nd edn, Transnational Publishers 1994) 19 and 34–42.

[66] D Gaukrodger and K Gordon, 'Investor-State Dispute Settlement: A Scoping Paper for the Investment Policy Community', Organisation for Economic Co-operation and Development Working Paper on International Investment 2012/03 (OECD 2013) 55–56.

[67] See eg *Fireman's Fund Insurance Company v United Mexican States* (Award, 17 July 2003) 15(6) World Trade and Arb Mats 3, [5]; *Mondev International Ltd v United States of America* (Award, 11 October 2002) 42 ILM 85, [79].

[68] See eg *Wena Hotels Ltd v Egypt* (Award, 25 May 1999) 41 ILM 881, 888; *Tokios Tokelès v Ukraine* (Award, 29 April 2004) 20 ICSID Rev 2005, [21] and [38].

[69] *Tokios* (n 68) [21], [38], and [80].

[70] ibid [80].

[71] For some examples, see the table in G Van Harten and P Malysheuski, 'Who Has Benefited Financially from Investment Treaty Arbitration? An Evaluation of the Size and Wealth of Claimants', Osgoode Hall Law School Legal Studies Research Paper No 14 (2016) 3–5.

[72] R van Os and R Knottnerus, *Dutch Bilateral Investment Treaties—A Gateway to "Treaty Shopping" for Investment Protection by Multinational Companies* (SOMO 2011). In a study of which companies and individuals were ordered to receive compensation by ISDS tribunals up to the spring of 2014, Malysheuski and I found that, if one accounted for nationality shopping, 98 per cent of the

Nationality shopping in ISDS has led to infamous results. For example, in Ralph Lauder's dispute with the Czech Republic, which was mentioned in Chapter 1, the US billionaire used a Dutch company to bring parallel claims against the Czechs under separate treaties.[73] He won a massive award for one of the claims, while losing the other.[74] Another example is *Aguas del Tunari v Bolivia*, where the US multinational Bechtel 'migrated' (as its lawyers described the move) its ownership of a recently privatized water system in the city of Cochabamba, Bolivia, via a transfer of rights from holding companies in the Cayman Islands to holding companies in the Netherlands.[75] This legal switch was flipped as a major conflict over the privatization was unfolding in Bolivia. Many people in Cochabamba had rebelled against the privatization as a threat to their access to water; after first sending in the army to suppress the protests, the government pulled back to avoid further bloodshed.[76] By then, Bechtel, as a newly incorporated 'Dutch' investor, could file its claim under the Bolivia–Netherlands ISDS treaty, in the absence of an ISDS treaty between the United States and Bolivia or between the Cayman Islands and Bolivia. The tribunal let this manipulated claim go ahead.[77]

Most people do not have the means to acquire new nationalities in order to shift the rules in their favour. Most are rooted in a single country. In contrast, the wealthy can change their nationality as easily as others change their clothes. By doing so, they can gain access to ISDS platforms for attacking countries. In such cases, it is not their actual condition as 'foreigners', but rather their wealth that generates their access to ISDS.

A pioneering example

ISDS arbitrators first opened the door to nationality shopping—and to its close cousin, indirect ownership of 'investment'—in the early case of *Sedelmayer v Russia*.[78] The claim in *Sedelmayer* was the sixth under an ISDS treaty; the first five claims having been brought by companies that owned the disputed investment

compensation ordered for claimants from the Netherlands appeared to be attributable to a national of another country, usually the United States; Van Harten and Malysheuski (n 71) 7.

[73] *CME v Czech Republic* (Award, 14 March 2003); *Lauder v Czech Republic*, Award (3 September 2001).

[74] *CME* (n 73) part IX; *Lauder* (n 73) [235].

[75] *Aguas del Tunari SA v Republic of Bolivia* (Award, 21 October 2005) [69], [73], and [237].

[76] W Finnegan, 'Leasing the Rain' *The New Yorker* (New York, 31 March 2002); M de la Fuente, 'A Personal View: The Water War in Cochabamba, Bolivia: Privatization Triggers an Uprising' (2003) 23 Mountain Res Dev 98.

[77] *Aguas del Tunari* (n 75) [69], [73], and [237], and [4] and [10] (dissenting opinion of JL Alberto-Semerena). Netherlands-Bolivia investment treaty, signed 10 March 1992.

[78] *Sedelmayer (Franz) v Russian Federation* (Award, 7 July 1998).

directly. That is, their ownership was not owned via a chain of companies in multiple countries.

Before turning to the details of this case, it is important to highlight how the *Sedelmayer* arbitrators, in the course of asserting their power, had to cast aside an international legal principle that would otherwise have protected sovereignty from ISDS litigation. Two of the arbitrators, making up the tribunal's majority, agreed to put aside a rule that was established by the ICJ in its *Barcelona Traction* decision of 1970. Basically, the rule was that international claims could not be brought against a country if they were based on indirect ownership of assets.[79] Such claims had to be brought on behalf of the first-level 'foreign' owner of assets, not the second-, third-, or fourth-level ones. Thus, the ICJ limited the use of nationality shopping to sue countries, expressing concern that such practices could lead to an explosion of litigation.[80]

Not surprisingly, corporate lawyers had long derided *Barcelona Traction*,[81] which frustrated the ability of multinationals to connect and disconnect from countries as it suited them, and forced them to take care that the country from which they invested was reliable as a 'home' country. In turn, it was harder for the wealthy to avoid national regulation by obscuring what they owned and where. *Barcelona Traction* was therefore a predictable target for ISDS arbitrators, as confirmed by the *Sedelmayer* and virtually all subsequent tribunals.

Franz Sedelmayer was a German citizen who, in the early 1990s, went into the security business in post-Soviet Russia. The venture soon soured. However, Sedelmayer had channelled the ownership of his Russian business through a company in the United States (Missouri), apparently to avoid taxes in Germany,[82] meaning that his US company had no right to sue in ISDS because there was no ISDS treaty between the United States and Russia at the time. Instead, Sedelmayer tried suing under the Germany–Russia investment treaty of 1989, becoming the first 'indirect' foreign investor to attempt an ISDS treaty claim.[83]

Russia responded with the powerful argument, considering *Barcelona Traction*, that Sedelmayer's claim was outside the scope of the treaty, which allowed for claims

[79] *Barcelona Traction, Light and Power Co (Belgium v Spain)* [1970] ICJ Rep 3, 9 ILM 227. Belgium had tried to bring an international claim against Spain on behalf of the Belgian owners of a Canadian holding company that owned the disputed assets in Spain.

[80] ibid [96].

[81] See eg WP Rogers, 'The Rule of Law and the Settlement of International Disputes' (1970) 64 AJIL 285; FA Mann, 'The Protection of Shareholders' Interests in the Light of the Barcelona Traction Case' (1973) 67 AJIL 259; F Orrego Vicuña, 'Interim Report on the Changing Law of Nationality of Claims', International Law Association Committee on Diplomatic Protection of Persons and Property, London Conference (2000) 28; LJ Lee, 'Barcelona Traction in the Twenty-First Century: Revisiting Its Customary and Policy Underpinnings 35 Years Later' (2006) 42 Stanford J Int'l L 237.

[82] *Sedelmayer* (n 78) 21. Like most ISDS cases, only the tribunal's ruling is public.

[83] Germany–Russia investment treaty, signed 13 June 1989, UN Conference on Trade and Development (UNCTAD) International Investment Agreements Navigator: <https://investmentpolicy.unctad.org/international-investment-agreements> accessed 14 January 2020.

by German investors, not US ones. Here, the investor in Russia was the Missouri company by which Mr Sedelmayer owned his business interests in Russia, not Mr Sedelmayer himself.[84] As a result, the tribunal had no authority to decide the case. This position was rejected by the tribunal's presiding and investor-side arbitrators, and with it the ICJ's position in *Barcelona Traction*. It was an audacious step for two arbitrators to take, since the ICJ is the pre-eminent international court and its rulings are meant to be definitive of general matters of international law. One would expect the arbitrators to ensure they were on solid legal ground before taking such a step. To the contrary, the tribunal's majority pointed only to the opinions of several academics who had previously downplayed *Barcelona Traction* (in favour of another ICJ judgment in *ELSI v Italy*), even though none of the academics had discussed the Germany–Russia investment treaty or ISDS.[85] Notably, the ICJ's other judgment in *ELSI*, unlike *Barcelona Traction*, was not issued by the ICJ as a whole, but by a five-member chamber of the Court.[86] *ELSI* thus lacked the level of authority of *Barcelona Traction*.

One of the academics whose views the *Sedelmayer* arbitrators cited was Brigitte Stern, who later became a prominent ISDS arbitrator herself. In her academic work, Stern had expressed 'the *feeling* that the [*ELSI*] judgement ... implies a new direction' from the position in *Barcelona Traction*.[87] One should ask, do the views or feelings of a few academics offer a basis for overriding a rule of international law established by the ICJ? Clearly, they do not, making it extraordinary for the *Sedelmayer* arbitrators to use *ELSI* to lift the corporate veil between a German businessman and his Missouri company in order to allow his ISDS claim to go ahead. The arbitrators called Mr Sedelmayer a 'de facto' investor in Russia.[88] In other words, they recognized his ownership of assets in Russia, although that ownership did not exist in law.

National courts tend to lift the corporate veil between companies and their shareholders only in exceptional circumstances.[89] In *Sedelmayer*, the arbitrators lifted it on the basis that Mr Sedelmayer had been heavily involved in the business

[84] *Sedelmayer* (n 78) 36–37.

[85] The academic opinions cited by the tribunal were those of I Seidl-Hohenveldern, 'Die Entwicklung der kiplomatischen Protektion für juristische Personen', Lecture to the European Institute of the University of Saarland, Saarbrücken (27 June 1991) 28; B Stern, [title unknown] (1990) 117 J Droit Int'l 3; and H Nial, 'Selected Problems of Public International Law' (1968) 3 Acad Droit Int'l, Recueil de Cours 316.

[86] *ELSI* (n 39) 15. One member of the chamber was the future leading ISDS hawk, Stephen Schwebel, who dissented at length from the majority judgment in *ELSI*. Schwebel would have ruled in favour of the Italian company, Raytheon, that was said to be owned 100 per cent by US companies and on whose behalf the United States was allowed by the chamber to sue Italy in the state–state proceeding under the United States–Italy Treaty of Friendship, Commerce, and Navigation of 1948.

[87] *Sedelmayer* (n 78) 53 (emphasis added).

[88] ibid 57–59.

[89] See eg *Prest v Petrodel Resources Limited and Others* [2013] UKSC 34; SK Miller, 'Piercing the Corporate Veil among Affiliated Companies in the European Community and in the US: A Comparative Analysis of US, German, and UK Veil-Piercing Approaches' (1998) 36 Am Bus LJ 73, 79-84.

in Russia. They acknowledged that he 'channelled certain investments through [the Missouri company]', but nonetheless decided that 'any claim that the Claimant as an individual puts forth are admissible under and protected by the Treaty'.[90] They also noted that Mr Sedelmayer was 'in full control' of the Missouri company, having signed a 'control and profit sharing agreement' with it in 1991.[91] Applying this threshold for lifting the corporate veil, many holding companies would exist in law only to the extent that it suited their owner. In turn, the owner of any asset could make a holding company disappear in law if the owner was heavily involved in the underlying business (and agreed with the owner's own company, ridiculously, that the owner controlled it and should share its profits). Using this flexible threshold, the arbitrators were able to conclude that Mr Sedelmayer should be 'regarded' as an investor under the treaty 'even with respect to investments formally made by [the Missouri company]'.[92] Thus, he was allowed to have it both ways, operating by way of the Missouri company for tax reasons, while also owning the assets in Russia as if the Missouri company did not exist, when doing so offered a gateway to ISDS.

Russia's arbitrator vigorously objected to the majority's lifting of the corporate veil. He thought the description of Mr Sedelmayer as a 'de facto investor' was 'rather ambiguous in itself',[93] and expressed concern that this idea of a 'de facto investor' was not actually found in the treaty.[94] He also saw no evidence that the other arbitrators' so-called 'control theory', which they used to justify lifting the corporate veil, was accepted 'even implicitly' in the treaty.[95] He pointed out difficulties that could, and later did,[96] arise in terms of who should get priority when multiple companies sue in ISDS using different corporate chains of ownership.[97] He noted that '[t]he Claimant could have made investments personally or through a Germany company' but he 'preferred to act ... for tax reasons through a company of a third state'.[98] None of these concerns swayed the tribunal's other arbitrators, particularly the tribunal's presiding arbitrator, Staffan Magnusson. Incidentally, Magnusson had been chosen for this role by the Chair of the Arbitration Institute of the Stockholm Chamber of Commerce (SCC) (I discussed this ISDS arbitration house and others in Chapter 2, 'Origins of ISDS Treaties').[99]

In later ISDS cases, most arbitrators endorsed a similarly flexible approach to nationality shopping and indirect ownership. Doing so opened a world of possibilities

[90] *Sedelmayer* (n 78) 27 and 59.
[91] ibid 27 and 57.
[92] ibid 59.
[93] ibid (dissenting opinion of IS Zykin) 2.
[94] ibid 2.
[95] ibid 4.
[96] See eg *CME* and *Lauder* (both n 73).
[97] *Sedelmayer* (n 78) (dissenting opinion of IS Zykin) 3.
[98] ibid 4.
[99] This statement follows from the fact that Sedelmayer brought his claim under the SCC arbitration rules. Sedelmayer was represented in the case by Kaj Hobér, who was a partner with White and Case and has since worked in dozens of ISDS cases as a lawyer or arbitrator.

for lawyers, helping their clients to launch claims against countries from anywhere in a global network of companies. Where the ICJ had been cautious about an explosion of litigation, the ISDS arbitrators, by their rulings, facilitated it.

Avoiding the courts

Under ISDS treaties, foreign investors can avoid the institutions that govern others in a country by bringing claims against the country that sidestep its courts. Remarkably, the treaties give this power to investors regardless of whether the courts in question are fair and independent, whether they offer justice, and so on. By comparison, in customary international law, private actors have a duty to 'exhaust local remedies' before their grievances can lead to an international claim against a country.[100] This customary duty constitutes international tribunals as a supplement, instead of a substitute, for national courts. It also gives a country's institutions a chance to repair local injustice, and helps the international process by creating a judicial record and decision to inform the international tribunal. For foreign nationals, the duty to exhaust local remedies is a logical corollary to their choice to enter the country and respect its laws. It conveys therefore that no one is above the law. It also accounts for situations where a country's courts are unreliable, since the duty can be waived by the international tribunal if local remedies were not reasonably available or would obviously have been futile to pursue.

In ISDS, foreign investors have been excused completely from this duty.[101] The treaties typically do not remove it expressly; rather, arbitrators have interpreted them as having done so implicitly.[102] This expansive approach has in turn created myriad opportunities for creative lawyering by investors. Some go to national courts before bringing an ISDS claim. Others sidestep the courts entirely, while others go to both national courts and an ISDS tribunal.[103] This last manoeuvre allows the investor to claim compensation internationally (thus avoiding limits on state liability in national law), while pursuing non-monetary remedies, such as striking down the law, in the national context.[104] Investors can also play 'Gotcha'

[100] MD Brauch, 'Exhaustion of Local Remedies in International Investment Law', International Institute for Sustainable Development Best Practices Series (2017); S D'Ascoli and KM Scherr, 'The Rule of Prior Exhaustion of Local Remedies in the International Law Doctrine and Its Application in the Specific Context of Human Rights Protection', European University Institute Working Paper LAW No 2007/02 (2007); and PM Okowa, 'Admissibility and the Law on International Responsibility' in MD Evans (ed), *International Law* (2d edn, OUP 2006) 498.

[101] Or, the duty is removed subject to conditions, such as a six-month waiting period, which have themselves usually been discounted by ISDS tribunals using creative reasoning. For a discussion, see Van Harten, *Sovereign Choices* (n 40) 147–50.

[102] ibid 129 and 132–33 (note 84).

[103] See eg *GAMI Investments, Inc v United Mexican States* (Award, 15 November 2004) 44 ILM 545.

[104] For instance, the Comprehensive Economic and Trade Agreement (CETA) between Canada and the European Union, signed 30 October 2016 (not fully in force) tracks the old NAFTA approach, which merely requires foreign investors to pursue monetary remedies either in ISDS or domestic courts, but

by invoking ISDS for low-level decisions which could be fixed in the country's own courts. Relieved of the duty to exhaust local remedies, the wealthy win a unique freedom to shape their relationship with countries.

For example, national courts often show restraint when reviewing the decisions of an elected legislature or an expert agency.[105] They do so out of respect for the other's relative accountability or expertise. In international law, doctrines of judicial restraint are less developed, partly because, outside of ISDS, the duty to exhaust local remedies serves as a buffer between national institutions and international tribunals. By removing the duty, ISDS treaties enable investors to avoid judicial restraint, as ISDS tribunals overwhelmingly have not restrained themselves in a similar way, despite government requests that they should.[106] ISDS thus gives investors a more intrusive way to attack sovereign decisions, in this instance at the expense of public accountability and institutionalized expertise.

ISDS tribunals have also allowed investors to avoid their contractual obligations, particularly where the investor has agreed to resolve disputes about these obligations in national courts. Courts typically enforce such agreements out of respect for the sanctity of contracts, requiring all contracting parties to go to the contractually agreed forum before suing in court.[107] Ironically, ISDS arbitrators often invoke party autonomy and sanctity of contract to justify and define their own powers,[108] but they have, by a large majority, allowed ISDS treaty claims to go ahead, even though the investor previously agreed to use another forum.[109] This hospitality for ISDS claims has been very costly for states.[110] It also distorts markets by allowing foreign companies to negotiate state contracts without having to worry, as much as domestic companies, about the dispute settlement clause in the contract. In this way, arbitrators have intensified inequality even further by allowing multinationals and tycoons to avoid the courts after they have committed to use them.

ISDS promoters often argue that one should not subject foreign investors to weak courts in countries where they invest.[111] Their answer instead is to have ISDS

not both. This approach lets investors pursue compensation in ISDS, where it is the primary remedy, while pursuing non-monetary remedies in domestic courts where compensation is typically not the primary remedy: Van Harten, *Sovereign Choices* (n 40) 113–14.

105 Van Harten, *Sovereign Choices* (n 40) ch 2.

106 ibid 59–61.

107 MD Wasco, 'When Less is More: The International Split Over Expanded Judicial Review in Arbitration' (2010) 62 Rutgers L Rev 599, 610.

108 Van Harten, *Sovereign Choices* (n 40) 122–23 and 155.

109 ibid 135 (note 103), 136 (note 105), and 143.

110 Roughly half of ISDS cases appear to relate to a contract that likely has its own dispute settlement clause. Many of these cases would not exist had the tribunal required the investor to use the agreed forum: ibid 143–47.

111 See eg SW Schill, 'Reforming Investor–State Dispute Settlement (ISDS): Conceptual Framework and Options for the Way Forward', E15 Task Force on Investment Policy Think Piece (2015) 2; C Tietje, F Baetens, and Ecorys, 'The Impact of Investor–State Dispute Settlement (ISDS) in the Transatlantic Trade and Investment Partnership', Study prepared for the Minister for Foreign Trade and Development Cooperation and the Ministry of Foreign Affairs of the Netherlands (2014) 39 and 68.

treaties. That answer is flawed for at least four reasons. First, the treaties are too sweeping. They remove the duty to exhaust local remedies for all countries, not just those shown to have weak courts. Second, the customary duty always accounted for weaknesses of national courts by freeing foreign nationals from having to use the courts if they could demonstrate that the courts were not reasonably available. Why should an investor not also be asked to give evidence of problems with a country's courts before being allowed to bring an international claim against the country? Third, if foreign investors do not want to depend on a country's courts, they can choose to avoid the country altogether or to negotiate for an arbitration clause in their contracts with the state. ISDS treaties effectively override these market-based choices of investors about the degree of risk they find acceptable. Fourth, the treaties do not replace weak courts with strong ones; rather, they replace them with arbitrators who are not judicially independent and procedurally fair in the manner of a court.

ISDS treaties are fundamentally dismissive of all courts. By completely removing the duty to exhaust local remedies, they embody a presumption that courts everywhere are so inadequate that foreign investors should always be allowed to sidestep them, without ever having to explain why. In turn, they allow the wealthy to displace the courts as it suits them, in preference for an international tribunal that is lopsided in their favour. Moreover, for countries that do have weak institutions, the lopsidedness of ISDS helps investors to exploit these weaknesses when avoiding accountability at the national level and then, if the national institutions do not meet the investor's expectations, the investor can sue internationally. Thus, the wealthy can demand accountability for others, while avoiding it themselves.

Complex manoeuvres

The case of *Lanco v Argentina* is the first in which arbitrators allowed foreign investors to avoid courts, even after they had previously agreed to use them.[112] The case emerged from a dispute over the port of Buenos Aires, which had been privatized in 1994. At the time of the privatization, Argentina was headed by President Carlos Menem, whose government followed a shock programme of state asset sales, deregulation, and, it later emerged, widespread corruption.[113] The programme ended in the country's economic collapse in the early 2000s, and triggered a flood of ISDS claims against Argentina, most of them stemming from failed privatizations. *Lanco* itself came before this later wave of claims.

[112] *Lanco International Inc v Republic of Argentina* (Award, 8 December 1998), 40 ILM 457.

[113] D Azpiazu, EM Basualdo, and HJ Nochteff, 'Menem's Great Swindle: Convertibility, Inequality and the Neoliberal Shock', North American Congress on Latin America Report on the Americas (25 September 2007); J Bambaci, T Saront, and M Tommasi, 'The Political Economy of Economic Reforms in Argentina' (2002) 5 Policy Reform 75.

To privatize the Buenos Aires port, the Argentine government sold a concession to operate the port to an Argentine company which was partly owned by Lanco International, a US company.[114] That same year, 1994, the United States–Argentina bilateral investment treaty came into force.[115] Lanco then sued under the treaty, in a dispute about the port concession, in 1997. In a new twist for ISDS, Lanco sought to avoid the Argentine courts in its claim, even though the concession agreement said, '[f]or all purposes derived from the agreement . . . the parties agree to the jurisdiction of the Federal Contentious-Administrative Tribunals of the Federal Capital of the Argentine Republic'.[116] This contractual requirement to use Argentine courts appeared to apply clearly in *Lanco*, since the dispute arose directly from the concession agreement. However, Lanco claimed creatively—and the tribunal accepted—that Lanco's shares in the Argentine company (which owned the port concession) were an 'investment' under the treaty,[117] meaning that Lanco could sue in ISDS for something it did not own directly (the port concession) by calling a subsidiary company its 'investment', while also avoiding the subsidiary company's commitment to using the Argentine courts to resolve disputes.[118]

By their decision to allow Lanco's treaty claim to proceed in these circumstances,[119] the arbitrators blazed a trail for foreign investors to sidestep their contractual obligations. A large majority of later tribunals followed a similarly open-door approach to such 'parallel' treaty claims.[120] After *Lanco*, the leading example of this approach was the ICSID annulment committee decision in *Vivendi v Argentina* in 2002.[121] There, an ISDS tribunal had initially required the investor to use its contractually agreed forum before suing under the ISDS treaty. However, the ICSID annulment arbitrators—with a leading hawk, Yves Fortier,

[114] Besides Lanco, three other companies co-owned the Argentine company that in turn owned the port concession. Lanco's share of the Argentine company was reportedly 17.4 per cent or 18.3 per cent; *Lanco* (n 112) [5] and [10].

[115] United States–Argentina investment treaty, signed 14 November 1991, UNCTAD International Investment Agreements Navigator (n 83).

[116] *Lanco* (n 112) [7] and [32]. It is unclear whether the tribunal arrived at this observation of its own accord or based on a party's submission.

[117] ibid [9]. The US negotiating team included 'shares' of a company in the treaty's definition of 'investment': United States–Argentina investment treaty (n 115) Article I(1).

[118] In a further twist, the concession agreement was signed not only by the Argentine company but also by Lanco and the three other corporate owners of the Argentine company. In the contract, Lanco and the other co-owners were called 'awardees' and 'guarantors' of the Argentine company. This feature gave the tribunal an even stronger reason to require Lanco to sue in the Argentine courts before bringing an ISDS treaty claim. Instead, the tribunal pointed to a clause in the treaty that gave investors the option to sue under 'previously agreed' dispute-settlement procedures and decided Lanco's commitments in the concession agreement were a 'previously agreed' procedure such that Lanco could use the treaty to avoid that procedure in favour of ISDS. Was the treaty clear enough in endorsing this avoidance of the courts? Either way, the result is the same: Lanco could sign and benefit from a concession agreement while it committed, in the same agreement, to use the national courts: *Lanco* (n 112) [12]–[13], [21], [25], and [28].

[119] ibid [49].

[120] Van Harten, *Sovereign Choices* (n 40) 143–47.

[121] *Vivendi v Argentina (No 1)* (Annulment decision, 3 July 2002), 41 ILM 1135.

presiding—overrode that decision, calling it a 'manifest excess of power' for the original tribunal to have declined to hear the ISDS treaty claim.[122] The annulment arbitrators' dubious reasoning,[123] following from *Lanco*, contributed greatly to the expansion of ISDS.[124]

Chasing the assets

Another ISDS advantage for foreign investors is the exceptional enforceability of the compensation awards in their favour. For most people, a major drawback of international law, where it offers them any meaningful prospect of protection from state or corporate abuse, is the lack of enforcement.[125] Even at the national level, if the courts are accessible to victims of abuse who manage to finance a litigation, the courts' rulings would be very difficult to enforce abroad.[126] As a result, multinationals can avoid accountability in the courts simply by moving their assets from one country to another.

ISDS treaties fix this problem of enforcement, but only for investors. If a country does not pay an ISDS award, the investor can pursue enforcement with relative ease against the losing country's assets in other countries. Once the award clears annulment under the ICSID Convention (or set-aside proceedings in the case of the New York Convention), it becomes enforceable in all countries that are party to the relevant convention.[127] Either way, the losing country's assets are widely exposed to seizure. Such seizures are legitimized by the ostensibly fair process of ISDS arbitration. In addition, the country may face intense pressure to pay the award, whether from the investor's home country, the World Bank, or other financial institutions.[128]

[122] ibid [86]–[87] and [115].

[123] Van Harten, *Sovereign Choices* (n 40) 137–42.

[124] To illustrate, in cases where the tribunal was not found to have shown restraint (up to spring 2010), even though the investor's claim appeared to relate to a contract with a dispute settlement clause that had been agreed previously by the claimant or a related party, countries were ordered to pay total compensation of over USD 1.2 billion: Van Harten, *Sovereign Choices* (n 40) 156 (note 219).

[125] See n 1.

[126] Y Zeynalova, 'The Law on Recognition and Enforcement of Foreign Judgments: Is It Broken and How Do We Fix It?' (2013) 31 Berkeley J Int'l L 150; RA Brand 'Enforcement of Foreign Money Judgments in the United States: In Search of Uniformity and International Acceptance' (1991) 67 Notre Dame L Rev 253.

[127] Convention on the Settlement of Investment Disputes between States and Nationals of Other States (ICSID Convention) signed 18 March 1965, entered into force 14 October 1966, (4 ILM 524) Articles 53(1) and 54; United Nations Convention on the Recognition and Enforcement of Foreign Arbitral Awards (New York Convention) signed 10 June 1958, entered into force 7 June 1959 (330 UNTS 3) Articles 1, III, and V.

[128] JE Viñuales and D Bentolila, 'The Use of Alternative (Non-Judicial) Means to Enforce Investment Awards Against States' in L Boisson de Chazournes, M Kohen, and JE Viñuales (eds), *Diplomatic and Judicial Means of Dispute Settlement: Assessing their Interactions* (Brill 2012) 258–77; W Peter, *Arbitration and Renegotiation of International Investment Agreements* (Kluwer Law International 1995) 321.

Argentina offers an example of the exceptional sticking power of ISDS awards. After the country's economic crisis of 2001–02, it faced a wave of ISDS claims.[129] The government fought and lost many of them, and was ordered to pay a total of about one billion USD in compensation.[130] It resisted doing so for years.[131] Some of the investors pursued Argentine assets that were located abroad, or sold their award to vulture funds that specialize in chasing sovereign assets.[132] One managed to have an Argentine naval ship seized in Ghana, though the ship was later released.[133] In 2013, the government eventually agreed to pay five outstanding awards and, in 2015, a new conservative government—elected for the first time since the economic crisis that had triggered so many claims—quickly settled remaining cases, while putting in place other pro-arbitration reforms welcomed by ISDS lawyers.[134] Thus, ISDS makes sovereign assets vulnerable to seizure as a way to ensure the resilience of special protections for the wealthy.

Conclusion

In ISDS, foreign investors can force countries to answer to an international tribunal that has exceptionally strong powers of review. They can do so based on broadly worded protections that have been interpreted even more expansively by arbitrators. They can make allegations against others who have no right of standing to reply. Often, they can alter their nationality in order to access the treaties and avoid commitments to use national courts. By bringing an ISDS claim, the investor unlocks the power of arbitrators to rule on whether a law was discriminatory, whether a regulation was an expropriation, or whether a court decision was unfair.

As a legal weapon against countries, ISDS is most dangerous when employed by those most able to finance claims: multinationals and tycoons. For the great

[129] For an overview, see F Lavopa, 'Crisis, Emergency Measures and the Failure of the ISDS System: The Case of Argentina', South Centre Investment Policy Brief No 2 (2015).

[130] ibid.

[131] LE Peterson, 'Argentine Crisis Arbitration Aawards Pile Up, but Investors Still Wait for a Payout' *Law.com* (25 June 2009) https://bilaterals.org/?argentine-crisis-arbitration&lang=fr.

[132] D Dayen, 'A Monster Payday in Argentina Shows a Flaw in Trump's NAFTA Renegotiation' *The Intercept* (28 July 2017).

[133] R Merle, 'How One Hedge Fund Made $2 Billion from Argentina's Economic Collapse' *Washington Post* (Washington, DC, 29 March 2016); T Fernholz, 'First, a US Hedge Fund Tried to Seize Argentina's Boat, then Its Rockets—Now It's After a Person' *Quartz* (Uzabase, 5 November 2014).

[134] E Vetulli and EE Kaufman, 'Is Argentina Looking for Reconciliation with ISDS?' (*Kluwer Arbitration Blog*, 13 October 2016) <http://arbitrationblog.kluwerarbitration.com/2016/10/13/is-argentina-looking-for-reconciliation-with-isds/> accessed 14 January 2020.

majority of people, though, there is no prospect whatsoever of invoking ISDS because they do not own assets abroad or, if they do, their assets are not nearly valuable enough to justify an ISDS claim. For most people, their best hope for protection, even if it is a faint one, lies with the institutions of their own country, the very institutions that ISDS is used to intimidate and constrain.

5
Special Access to Public Funds

Investor–state dispute settlement (ISDS) treaties provide generous protections to foreign investors that would be impossibly expensive to provide to all. This more favourable treatment gives them special access to public compensation and bolsters the position of investors within the state apparatus by allowing them alone to make extraordinary legal threats against governments. Only foreign investors can force the state to submit to ISDS. Everyone else must rely on the usual institutions—legislatures, governments, courts—to protect their interests, now subject to review and condemnation in ISDS. Under many ISDS treaties, the investor can choose to use arbitration rules that allow for their claim to be kept secret or that remove judicial oversight of ISDS.[1] Thus, the ultra-wealthy can challenge a country's laws and win compensation, free from public or judicial scrutiny.

The treaties harness competitive pressure among arbitrators, lawyers, and arbitration houses to favour the ultra-wealthy.[2] Foreign investors decide when and where to bring claims against countries. The wealthiest among them are the most able to fund the litigation fueling the ISDS industry. The arbitrators who decide the investors' claims, and the lawyers who litigate them, all depend on such claims for future business.[3] Experts hired by investors and governments in ISDS proceedings, including many academics, can expect more income as more and more investors sue.[4] Likewise, the arbitration houses vie to attract ISDS claims, adopting investor-friendly rules or high levels of secrecy.[5] A central feature of the inequality of ISDS comes from its reliance on for-profit arbitration to make profoundly important decisions about the legal boundaries of sovereignty, the awarding of public funds, and the protection of some and not others.

[1] UN Conference on Trade and Development (UNCTAD), 'Investor–State Dispute Settlement: Review of Developments in 2017', IIA Issues Note (2018) 2; EM Hafner-Burton, S Puig, and DG Victor, 'Against Secrecy: The Social Cost of International Dispute Settlement' (2017) 42 Yale J Int'l L 279; G Van Harten, *Investment Treaty Arbitration and Public Law* (OUP 2007) 1543–64.

[2] E MacArthur, 'Regulatory Competition and the Growth of International Arbitration in Singapore' (2018) 23 Appeal 165; Y Dezalay and BG Garth, *Dealing in Virtue: International Commercial Arbitration and the Construction of a Transnational Legal Order* (University of Chicago Press 1996).

[3] G Van Harten, 'Investment Treaty Arbitration, Procedural Fairness, and the Rule of Law' in S Schill (ed), *International Investment Law and Comparative Public Law* (OUP 2010) 648–51.

[4] M Langford, D Behn, and RH Hilleren Lie, 'The Revolving Door in International Investment Arbitration' (2017) 20 JIEL 301, 316–17.

[5] D Gaukrodger, 'Appointing Authorities and the Selection of Arbitrators in Investor–State Dispute Settlement: An Overview', Organisation for Economic Co-operation and Development Consultation Paper (2018) 7, 51, and 59.

The promise of compensation

For the wealthy, a fortune can be lost from uncertainties of democracy, regulation, and courts. To protect their assets from this risk, multinationals hire lawyers and lobbyists who specialize in 'government relations',[6] a field in which politics and democracy are not values to be cherished but risks to be managed.[7] In this context, it is a boon to gain the power to sue a country before international tribunals if the country's institutions do not meet one's expectations. This power offers yet another tool to influence the state and to insulate revenues from regulation.

The essential reason for investors to use ISDS, and pay high fees to ISDS lawyers, is the prospect of receiving compensation from the state if the state does not otherwise accept the investor's will. Such compensation is usually generous because, in ISDS, it typically covers the investor's economic losses resulting from the law, regulation, or other decision that was found to have violated the foreign investor's broad protections under the treaty.[8] The covered losses usually include the investors' expected future profits in addition to its past costs. However, predicting future profits is a guessing game, and the experts hired by investors and countries to make these predictions in ISDS often produce wildly divergent estimates of future profitability for the arbitrators to consider.[9] From the outset, this arrangement is a dubious way to allocate public money.

ISDS promoters have long said that the treaties do not encroach on sovereignty because they only require countries to pay money if they have breached a treaty and do not require them to withdraw or modify their laws.[10] Any country can do what it wants, they argue, so long as it pays; thus, sovereignty is left intact. Even if it were factually accurate (it is not[11]), this argument for ISDS would still be weak

[6] See eg Crowell & Moring, 'Government Affairs' (*Crowell & Moring*, undated) <https://www.crowell.com/Practices/Government-Affairs> accessed 14 January 2020; Fasken, 'Government Relations and Strategy' (*Fasken*, undated) <https://www.fasken.com/en/solution/practice/government-relations-and-strategy/#sort=%40fclientworksortdate75392%20descending> accessed 14 January 2020.

[7] See egE Grishko, '4 Ways to Identify and Mitigate the Political Risks of Global Business' (*TradeReady Blog*, 17 May 2018) <http://www.tradeready.ca/2018/topics/international-trade-finance/4-ways-mitigate-political-risks/> accessed 14 January 2020 ('Create an inventory of political risk types, ranging from capital controls to increased taxation, labor strikes and protests, which could impact your company').

[8] S Ripinsky and D Williams, *Damages in International Investment Law* (British Institute of International and Comparative Law 2015) ch 7; I Marboe, *Calculation of Compensation and Damages in International Investment Law* (OUP 2009) 85–90.

[9] G Kahale III, 'ISDS: The Wild, Wild West of International Law and Arbitration', Brooklyn Lecture on International Business Law, Brooklyn Law School (3 April 2018) 13–17.

[10] See eg S Miller and GN Hicks, 'Investor–State Dispute Settlement: A Reality Check', Report of the CSIS Scholl Chair in International Business (Center for Strategic and International Studies) (2015) v.

[11] ISDS tribunals also make other kinds of orders, requiring countries to stop criminal investigations, for example, or stay enforcement of court judgments. Typically, they base these rulings on their obscure power to make interim orders or emergency awards: G Zarra, 'The Interference of ICSID Provisional Measures with National Criminal Proceedings' (2017) 26 Italian YB Int'l L 83; HG Burnett and J Beess und Chrostin, 'Interim Measures in Response to the Criminal Prosecution of Corporations and their Employees by Host States in Parallel with Investment Arbitration Proceedings' (2015) 30 Md J Int'l L 31; C Mouawed and E Silbert, 'A Guide to Interim Measures in Investor–State Arbitration' (2013) 29

because the cost of compensating a multinational or billionaire may have huge impacts on a country's ability to regulate and to fund its programmes. Any compensation for an investor obviously denies public funds for other purposes. The risk of it also frustrates the country's ability to plan for the costs of its decisions.[12] In some cases, the amounts at stake are in the millions or tens of millions of dollars. Many other awards have been for much larger amounts—hundreds of millions and even billions of dollars—that would devastate any budget and can be outright catastrophic for countries struggling to recover from war, dictatorship, or economic crisis. Even in wealthy countries, the risk of 'small' awards of millions of dollars can have a chilling effect on regulation.[13] Indeed, the risk of arbitrators ordering uncapped compensation would be a concern for any responsible and informed official when contemplating a law or regulation that an investor might oppose, a concern that has been strong enough to stay the hand of national legislators and cause regulators to act less assertively.

Critically, in ISDS, the orders to pay compensation are retrospective, and unforgivingly so. They combine high levels of ambiguity with potentially huge financial penalties, where a country is found not to have met its obligations to protect investors.[14] Years after the country makes a decision, an ISDS tribunal may condemn it with no opportunity for the country to avoid having to pay compensation. When a new law or regulation is proposed, it is impossible for the government to be sure whether it has complied with all areas of existing law that are relevant to investors. Yet the financial risks of ISDS make it far more hazardous than other areas of law. ISDS treaties are vague in their descriptions of foreign investor protections and arbitrators have relied on this vagueness to make decisions that expand the prospects for compensation.[15]

What if everyone could obtain compensation for government decisions that were later declared unlawful by a court or tribunal? The state would soon go bankrupt. It could not finance itself if every loss that flowed from the act of law making and regulating (or from official mistakes) had to be covered by the public purse. To fulfil its functions, the state needs some leeway in the face of uncertainty.[16] Otherwise, the unpredictability of litigation over public money makes it perilous

Arb Int'l 381; MA Gómez, 'The Global Chase: Seeking the Recognition and Enforcement of the Lago Agrio Judgment Outside of Ecuador' (2013) 1 Stan J Complex Litig 429, 445–48; S Joseph, 'Protracted Lawfare: The Tale of Chevron Texaco in the Amazon' (2012) 3 J Human Rights and Env't 70.

[12] E Biber, 'The Importance of Resource Allocation in Administrative Law' (2008) 60 Admin L Rev 1, 16–18, and 23–25; JA King, 'The Justiciability of Resource Allocation' (2007) 70 MLR 197.

[13] Confidential interviewees cited in G Van Harten and DN Scott, 'Investment Treaties and the Internal Vetting of Regulatory Proposals: Further Findings from a Case Study from Canada' in LE Sachs and L Johnson (eds), *Yearbook on International Investment Law and Policy 2015–2016* (OUP 2018) 427–29.

[14] ibid 101–09.

[15] Van Harten, *Investment Treaty Arbitration and Public Law* (n 1) 80–93.

[16] See n 11.

for governments to act in any area that has significant economic consequences for anyone.

National and international courts have developed a variety of doctrines to manage this challenge.[17] Typically, they lead to courts showing caution when ordering compensation for sovereign acts. These doctrines make it less likely that a government will face a damages award, especially if it regulates in good faith. Courts usually prioritize other remedies, such as an order to reconsider a decision or revise a law.[18] Where compensation is allowed, courts tend to limit the types and amounts that can be recovered.[19] These practices guard against a system of judge-run public insurance and against putting the state in a fiscal prison. In contrast, ISDS treaties favour the public insurance and the fiscal prison, but only where it benefits foreign investors. Thus, they compensate the wealthy where, if everyone had the same protection, the state could not afford to regulate.

Dependent tribunals

Ordinarily, one who sues the state does not also choose the judge. Rather, one appears before a judge who has been appointed or elected on behalf of the public. Judges have secure tenure and guaranteed salaries to make them financially independent of the state and other powerful actors. These are important guarantors of equal access to justice and the rule of law.[20]

Remarkably, ISDS treaties do not incorporate these safeguards. A foreign investor picks one arbitrator directly and another—the presiding arbitrator—jointly with the sued country.[21] If the investor and the country do not agree on a presiding arbitrator, the investor can refer the matter to an appointing body with the power to impose one. Thus, the treaties effectively allow foreign investors to decide who should hold half the power to arbitrate the dispute, with a key back-up role for the appointing bodies. This feature of ISDS is profoundly important. By sharing

17 G Van Harten, *Sovereign Choices and Sovereign Constraints: Judicial Restraint in Investment Treaty Arbitration* (OUP 2013) 24–47.

18 ibid 46–47.

19 S Lavrijssen, A Gerbrandy, and O Essens, 'European and National Standards of Review: Differentiation or Convergence' in O Essens, A Gerbrandy, and S Lavrijssen (eds), *National Courts and the Standard of Review in Competition Law and Economic Regulation* (Europa 2009) 87; B Foley, *Deference and the Presumption of Constitutionality* (Institute of Public Administration 2008) 79 (note 25), 90, and 123; I Marboe, 'State Responsibility and Comparative State Liability for Administration and Legislative Harm to Economic Interests' in Schill, *International Investment Law* (n 3) 408–09; A Biondi and M Farley, *The Right to Damages in European Law* (Wolters Kluwer 2009) 107.

20 Van Harten, 'Investment Treaty Arbitration' (n 3) 167–68.

21 C Giorgetti, 'The Arbitral Tribunal: Selection and Replacement of Arbitrators' in C Giorgetti (ed), *Litigating Investment Disputes: A Practitioner's Guide* (Brill 2014) 143–48; S Puig, 'Social Capital in the Arbitration Market' (2014) 25 EJIL 387, 397–99; Gaukrodger (n 5) 17–19; J Paulsson, 'Moral Hazard in International Dispute Resolution', Inaugural Lecture as Holder of the Michael R Klein Distinguished Scholar Chair, University of Miami School of Law (29 April 2010) 8–11.

appointment power with a sovereign, the investor in principle shares it with all those represented by, and all the institutions of, the sued country. A vast combination of interests is thus reduced to representation by a national government, while investors are elevated to the level of the sovereign.

Only investors can bring claims under the treaties. As a result, all those making money from ISDS litigation depend on investors, especially deep-pocketed ones, for their income. The dependents include arbitrators, lawyers, paid experts, and staff of arbitration houses. Most importantly, a powerful core of arbitrators has been appointed repeatedly and, as result, has been able to shape ISDS in ways that have transformed international law by expanding and intensifying the constraints it puts on democracy and regulation.[22] In their interpretations of the treaties, repeat arbitrators appear to have favoured foreign investors by a large margin, at the expense of the many other constituencies represented by states.[23]

The role of the presiding arbitrator on an ISDS tribunal is obviously critical. He or she breaks deadlocks between the investor's and the country's arbitrators. In principle, presiding arbitrators are selected by an agreement of the investor and the country or, under some arbitration rules, by an agreement of the two side arbitrators.[24] This process may sound balanced, but it is not. Negotiations between the investor and the country over who to appoint take place in the shadow of whichever outside organization can impose an arbitrator upon them. In weighing its position in these negotiations, each side must consider what the outside organization would likely do if the parties were to disagree. As it stands, the outside organizations named in the treaties tend to be skewed in favour of multinationals or major Western countries, or both.[25] Usually they have a record of frequently appointing arbitrators from the 'club' of repeat players.[26] It is therefore risky for a country to hold out for a presiding arbitrator, or appoint its own arbitrator, from outside the club. With such high stakes, the chance to sway the presiding arbitrator is usually much more important than a strong dissent. By appointing arbitrators from within the club, then, the appointing organizations indirectly influence the make-up of the whole tribunal.

While foreign investors have the power to trigger ISDS review of a country, arbitrators have the power to condemn it. The latter power, where the stakes run into billions of dollars, is among the greatest powers of any adjudicator in the world. It

[22] JA Fontoura Costa, 'Comparing WTO Panelists and ICSID Arbitrators: The Creation of International Legal Fields' (2011) 1 Oñati Socio-Legal Ser 1, 11; J Pauwelyn, 'The Rule of Law without the Rule of Lawyers? Why Investment Arbitrators Are from Mars, Trade Adjudicators Are from Venus' (2015) 109 AJIL 761, 774–75; P Eberhardt and C Olivet, *Profiting from Injustice* (CEO and Transnational Institute 2012) 38; Puig (n 21); Langford, Behn, and Hilleren Lie (n 4).

[23] G Van Harten, 'Leaders in the Expansive and Restrictive Interpretation of Investment Treaties: A Descriptive Study of ISDS Awards to 2010' (2018) 29 EJIL 507, 525–30.

[24] Giorgetti (n 21) 145.

[25] Van Harten, 'Investment Treaty Arbitration' (n 3) 170–71.

[26] Van Harten, 'Leaders' (n 23) 521–25; Puig (n 21) 417–18; Langford, Behn, and Hilleren Lie (n 4) 309–10.

is at least well beyond the powers of compensation that usually emerge from national courts. Moreover, at the national level the apex of the adjudicative system is a supreme or constitutional court, not an arbitration tribunal. Who sits on that top court is a major political question, with some appointments so momentous that they become a daily part of the news cycle for weeks. National elections can turn on the issue.[27] The political attention is understandable, since those who are chosen will have immense clout over other state institutions, especially in constitutional matters. In most countries, such immense power is assigned to individuals via publicly accountable processes.[28] These processes vary from country to country and are presumably never ideal, yet rarely, if ever, are they so debased as to give a direct role in judicial appointments to companies or tycoons who have a direct financial interest in how the judges will decide an upcoming case. The wealthy may be able to influence judicial appointments in all sorts of ways at the national level, but only in ISDS can they directly choose an arbitrator who, at their request, will review and potentially condemn the sovereign.

The arbitrators' accordion

ISDS tribunals have adopted many contortive interpretations which facilitate investor access to compensation. An excellent example is the byzantine standard of 'most-favoured-nation' (MFN) treatment for investors.[29] The ruling in *Maffezini v Spain* focused on this concept, which has since emerged as the most curious protection in the treaties. MFN treatment basically requires a country to give no less favourable treatment to foreign investors from one country than it gives to foreign investors from any other country. One could call it a 'me too' clause, entitling one group of investors to whatever privileges are enjoyed by another group. MFN treatment was originally developed in trade agreements to ensure that importers from all countries received the same tariff treatment.[30] It is questionable whether the protection belongs in investment treaties at all, considering the differences between tariffs in trade and the general regulation of asset owners.[31] Even so, virtually all investment treaties include it alongside many other protections for investors.

[27] E Bradner and J Biskupic, 'How the Supreme Court Could Shape the 2020 Presidential Race' (*CNN*, 23 January 2019).

[28] K Malleson and PH Russell (eds), *Appointing Judges in an Age of Judicial Power: Critical Perspectives from Around the World* (University of Toronto Press 2006); L Epstein, J Knight, and O Shvetsova, 'Comparing Judicial Selection Systems' (2001) 10 Wm & Mary Bill Rts J 7.

[29] SH Nikièma, 'The Most-Favoured-Nation Clause in Investment Treaties', International Institute for Sustainable Development Best Practices Series (2017); M-F Houde, 'Most-Favoured-Nation Treatment in International Investment Law', Organisation for Economic Co-operation and Development Working Paper on International Investment No 2004/2 (OECD 2004).

[30] Nikièma (n 29) 2; Houde (n 29) 3.

[31] Van Harten, *Investment Treaty Arbitration and Public Law* (n 1) 73–80.

MFN treatment is wondrously complicated and very much open to divergent interpretations.[32] Should a country's treatment of different investors be compared only in the context of the country's own laws so that, for example, they receive the same tax rate for the same business activities? Or should it be compared at the international level too, such that a country's commitments to protect investors from one country are automatically extended to all foreign investors? In that case, should the treatment be limited to substantive protections for the investors, or should it also cover institutional and procedural rights? If it covers institutional and procedural rights, should it go so far as to include the ultimate power to bring ISDS claims where one treaty bestows that power on investors but another does not?

For governments, the most manageable of these various interpretations would be that MFN treatment protects foreign investors from having to pay higher taxes or satisfy more onerous regulations than other foreign investors.[33] This view would create a level playing field in a country, without extending MFN treatment to the country's treaties with other countries. Where MFN treatment is extended to the latter, however, it can quickly get out of control by allowing investors to pick and choose clauses from the country's treaties in order to make a bespoke treaty for themselves.[34] That result would nullify differences among treaties and ultimately make aspects of the negotiation of them redundant. It erects as many privileges as possible for all foreign investors who can point to an MFN treatment clause in a treaty covering their assets.[35]

In *Maffezini v Spain*, these complexities of MFN treatment were resolved overwhelmingly in favour of foreign investors.[36] Mr Maffezini, an Argentine businessman, had sued Spain after his planned chemicals plant in Galicia failed. He claimed that a regional development agency had given him bad advice about the project.[37] In particular, he had not expected to have to do an environmental assessment (for a chemicals plant) and ended up having to commit more money than he originally anticipated. The arbitrators decided that Spain owed him compensation, but only after a convoluted detour into the role of the Spanish courts and, most importantly for our purposes, MFN treatment.

[32] Nikièma (n 29) 10–20; UNCTAD, 'Most-Favoured-Nation Treatment', UNCTAD Series on Issues in International Investment Agreements II (United Nations 2010) 2.

[33] Nikièma (n 29) 21.

[34] S Batifort and J Benton Heath, 'The New Debate on the Interpretation of MFN Clauses in Investment Treaties: Putting the Brakes on Multilateralization' (2017) 111 AJIL 873, 909–10; S Menon, 'The Transnational Protection of Private Rights: Issues, Challenges, and Possible Solutions' (2015) 108 ASIL Proc 219, 232–33; T Cole, *The Structure of Investment Arbitration* (Routledge 2013) 81–82 and 89–90.

[35] ISDS promoters have pushed this prospect of ad hoc expansion of bilateral investment treaties: eg SW Schill, *The Multilateralization of International Investment Law* (CUP 2009) 139–42, 146–50, and 173–96.

[36] *Maffezini (Emilio Agustín) v Kingdom of Spain* (Award, 25 January 2000) 16 ICSID Rev 212; *Maffezini (Emilio Agustín) v Kingdom of Spain* (Award, 13 November 2000) ICSID Case No ARB/97/7.

[37] *Maffezini* (13 November 2000) (n 36) [44].

On the first issue, the role of the Spanish courts, the Spain–Argentina investment treaty seemed to be clear. It required investors, before suing under the treaty, to bring their dispute to the national courts and wait for a resolution for at least eighteen months.[38] Mr Maffezini had not gone to the courts and waited the eighteen months. Therefore, Spain argued,[39] the tribunal could not hear the case due to the 'Claimant's failure to give Spanish courts the opportunity to resolve the issues in dispute'.[40] Judging this clear requirement in the treaty, it looked like an easy case.

The tribunal handled things differently, reasoning creatively that Mr Maffezini could in fact avoid the eighteen-month waiting period. The tribunal pointed to the International Centre for Settlement of Investment Disputes (ICSID) Convention, which says that the states parties to the Convention can require foreign investors to use domestic courts when they consent to ICSID arbitration.[41] This statement in the ICSID Convention is perilous for countries because it opens the door for arbitrators to create a reverse presumption; that is, all countries that sign an ISDS treaty allowing for ICSID claims can be assumed *not* to have required investors to use the courts, despite the customary duty of foreign nationals to do so, unless the country has explicitly re-asserted the customary duty in the relevant treaty.[42] In *Maffezini*, the tribunal decided that the Spain–Argentina treaty did not sufficiently reassert the duty, making the Spanish courts optional for Mr Maffezini.[43] Thus, the customary presumption that local courts must be used, out of respect for sovereignty, was put aside.

The tribunal was especially dismissive of Spain's further and eminently sensible view that the treaty required investors to try and resolve their disputes in the national courts and then, if they brought an ISDS claim, to prove that the courts had denied justice to the investor.[44] From this perspective, the treaty—like customary international law—would give the courts a primary role in shaping the dispute and mediating between national institutions and the international tribunal. The arbitrators seemed horrified by Spain's 'proposition', as they called it, and declined to limit their power accordingly. Doing so, they said, would deny the investor its

38 Spain–Argentina investment treaty, signed 3 October 1991, Articles X(2) and X(3)(a), UNCTAD International Investment Agreements Navigator: <https://investmentpolicy.unctad.org/international-investment-agreements> accessed 14 January 2020.

39 Again, the parties' submissions are not public, so we rely on the tribunal's presentation of what the parties argued.

40 *Maffezini* (25 January 2000) (n 36) [25].

41 ibid [27].

42 Convention on the Settlement of Investment Disputes between States and Nationals of Other States (ICSID Convention), signed 18 March 1965, entered into force 14 October 1966 (4 ILM 524) Article 26; IFI Shihata, 'The Settlement of Disputes regarding Foreign Investment: The Role of the World Bank, with Particular Reference to ICSID and MIGA' (1986) 1 Am U Int'l L Rev 97, 105.

43 *Maffezini* (25 January 2000) (n 36) [28] (relying for this narrow interpretation of the duty to exhaust local remedies on ISDS expert and arbitrator Christoph Schreuer's 'Commentary on the ICSID Convention. Article 25' (1997) 12 ICSID Rev—FILJ 59, 201.

44 *Maffezini* (25 January 2000) (n 36) [31].

'right to challenge the domestic court's interpretation of the [bilateral investment treaty]'.[45] With very little analysis of the treaty itself, they opined that Spain's argument 'can be reconciled neither with the language nor object and purpose of the dispute resolution provisions' of the treaty and of 'bilateral investment treaties in general',[46] declaring that 'these [ISDS] clauses are designed to give foreign investors the right to have their disputes under a [bilateral investment treaty] decided either exclusively or ultimately by international arbitration'.[47]

To support this sweeping assessment of all bilateral investment treaties, the arbitrators cited Christoph Schreuer, the investment law academic and ISDS arbitrator whose writings on the point had been published in ICSID's official journal (with Schreuer having expressed his thanks to ICSID staff).[48] Incidentally, the presiding arbitrator in *Maffezini* was leading ISDS hawk Francisco Orrego Vicuña who, before *Maffezini*, was the presiding arbitrator in *Fedax v Venezuela*, where Schreuer was also cited to support the tribunal's expansive orientation to 'investment'. Orrego Vicuña had been chosen for the *Maffezini* tribunal about a year after the *Fedax* ruling emerged, having been picked for the role by World Bank officials, who appear also to have picked him for the *Fedax* tribunal.[49]

The *Maffezini* tribunal's discounting of the role of the Spanish courts was especially questionable because of the treaty's eighteen-month waiting period. If, as the arbitrators decided, the treaty did not require investors to use the courts, why did it have a waiting period at all? The arbitrators acknowledged that the waiting period clause 'suggests' that Argentina and Spain 'wanted to give their courts the opportunity' (over the eighteen months) 'to resolve the dispute before it could be taken to international arbitration'.[50] It followed that Mr Maffezini's claim should be dismissed since he had not waited the eighteen months and, by implication, that there was no consent by Spain to the arbitration.

Facing this challenge to their reasoning, the tribunal turned to the treaty's MFN treatment clause. It observed that Spain had other investment treaties, besides the one with Argentina, and that some of these other treaties did not have the eighteen-month waiting period. Some had a shorter period, some had no waiting period at all.[51] Then the tribunal stretched the MFN accordion—beyond the notion of treatment of foreign investors in national law alone—to include the treatment of foreign investors under all of Spain's investment treaties. In response to this stretch of MFN treatment, Spain argued that MFN treatment should at least be limited to 'substantive matters or material aspects' of the treaties and should not extend

45 ibid [31].
46 ibid [31].
47 ibid [31].
48 ibid [31], citing Schreuer (n 43) 59, 199–202.
49 *Maffezini* (25 January 2000) (n 36) [8]; *Fedax NV v Republic of Venezuela* (Award, 11 July 1997) 37 ILM 1378 [7].
50 *Maffezini* (25 January 2000) (n 36) [35].
51 ibid [58]–[59].

to 'procedural or jurisdictional questions'.[52] Again, the tribunal pressed forward. It pointed to a historical arbitration ruling called *Ambatielos*, which offered some support for the view that MFN treatment covers dispute resolution procedures in different treaties.[53] However, *Ambatielos* dealt with a dispute between states, not an investor and a state, and the tribunal did not mention other rulings by international tribunals which favoured sovereignty in the face of an ambiguous consent by a country to be sued internationally.[54] Beyond this selective reliance on *Ambatielos*, the tribunal also stressed that the Spain–Argentina treaty said that MFN treatment applied to 'all matters' that were 'subject to' the treaty.[55] Did such 'matters' include other dispute resolution provisions? Could a waiting period be 'subject to' the treaty? I suppose reasonable people may give different answers to these questions. More fundamentally, the ambiguity in the treaty's language here points to the importance of the tribunal's presumptions.

In *Maffezini*, the arbitrators presumed that the door should be open to ISDS claims instead of safeguarding the principle of clear sovereign consent. Even if the treaty 'does not refer expressly to dispute settlement being covered by the MFN clause', they said, nevertheless 'the Tribunal considers that *there are good reasons* to conclude that today's dispute settlement arrangements are inextricably related to the protection of foreign investors'.[56] What were these 'good reasons' to allow ISDS claims? According to the tribunal, 'investors ... have traditionally *felt* that their rights and interests are better protected by recourse to international arbitration than by submission of disputes to domestic courts'.[57] The feelings of investors, as opposed to the intentions of the states that concluded the treaty, thus served to justify the tribunal's ousting of national courts.

At this point, the tribunal's reasoning seems to have gone haywire. Perhaps the arbitrators felt they had stretched the MFN accordion so far that they had to stop it breaking. Out of nowhere, the tribunal listed four exceptions to their conclusion that MFN treatment should cover dispute settlement provisions, such that an investor can avoid a waiting period in a treaty. First, the arbitrators declared that, if countries incorporate a duty to exhaust local remedies into a treaty, then MFN treatment would not extend to that duty.[58] They gave no reasons at all for this conclusion. Second, the arbitrators said that MFN treatment could not be used to bypass another limitation on the sovereign consent to be sued—so-called 'forks

[52] ibid [41].
[53] ibid [48]–[53], citing *Ambatielos Claim (Greece v United Kingdom)* (1956) 12 RIAA 83.
[54] See eg *The Lotus Case*, PCIJ, Ser A, No 10 (1927) 18; *Interpretation of Article 3, Paragraph 2, of the Treaty of Lausanne (Frontier between Turkey and Iraq)*, PCIJ, Ser B, No 12, (1925) 25; World Trade Organization (Appellate Body), *EC Measures Concerning Meat and Meat Products (Hormones)* (Decision, 16 January 1998) [165 (note 154)].
[55] *Maffezini* (25 January 2000) (n 36) [49].
[56] ibid [54] (emphasis added).
[57] ibid [55] (emphasis added).
[58] ibid [63].

in the road', which oblige investors to choose between courts and ISDS—since allowing that bypass 'would upset the finality of arrangements that many countries deem important . . . '.[59] Absurdly, the arbitrators did not extend this concern for the 'finality of arrangements' to the waiting period they had just avoided in relation to Mr Maffezini's claim. Third, the arbitrators declared that, if a treaty designates 'a particular arbitration forum, such as ICSID', then MFN treatment cannot be used to substitute an alternative forum from a different treaty.[60] Again, they gave no reasons at all for this conclusion. Fourth, the arbitrators said that MFN treatment could not be used to change the dispute settlement provisions in some ISDS treaties because the provisions would be too specific; in such treaties, 'these very specific [dispute settlement] provisions reflect the precise will' of the countries that signed the treaty.[61] Yet an eighteen-month waiting period also seems 'very specific' in expressing Argentina and Spain's 'precise will' to require investors to wait eighteen months before bringing an ISDS claim, and the arbitrators did not explain how they would distinguish such a provision from others in the treaties.

Based on this reasoning, the tribunal awarded compensation to the investor. The amount awarded was piddling compared to later ISDS rulings (just USD 490,000), but the ruling was vitally important for the coming ISDS litigation boom. It led the way for dozens of later claims that adopted a similarly flexible view of MFN treatment. At my last count, up to 2010, ISDS tribunals had split evenly on whether MFN treatment should extend to dispute resolution processes in other treaties or whether it should be limited to substantive protections only.[62] Some even extended the *Maffezini* approach to treaties that did not have the Spain–Argentina treaty's language saying that 'all matters' were 'subject to' MFN treatment.[63] In contrast, it seems that no ISDS tribunal limited MFN treatment, as at least one treaty negotiator says was expected,[64] to investors' treatment in national law. As a result, governments must now assume that any privileges they give to foreign investors in a single treaty will be extended to foreign investors under all of their treaties. Starting with *Maffezini*, MFN has become a wand for arbitrators to wave when converting ISDS treaties—each supposedly between two countries—into a functionally multilateral deal that maximizes special protections for foreign investors in general.[65]

[59] ibid [63].

[60] ibid [63].

[61] ibid [63].

[62] G Van Harten, 'Arbitrator Behaviour in Asymmetrical Adjudication: An Empirical Study of Investment Treaty Arbitration' (2012) 50 Osgoode Hall LJ 211, 238, and 267–68.

[63] *Siemens AG v Argentine Republic* (Award, 3 August 2004) [103] (where the tribunal included leading hawks Andrés Rigo Sureda and Charles Brower as, respectively, the presiding arbitrator and investor's arbitrator).

[64] A Faya Rodriguez, 'The Most-Favored-Nation Clause in International Investment Agreements—A Tool for Treaty Shopping?' (2008) 25 J Int'l Arb 89.

[65] Schill, *Multilateralization* (n 35) 173–96.

Competition to satisfy investors

By allowing only foreign investors to bring ISDS claims, the treaties create intense competitive pressures within the ISDS industry.[66] ISDS arbitrators, lawyers, and arbitration houses all do business only if more claims come. In turn, those who make decisions in ISDS—where they want more work in the field—have an apparent financial interest in the outcome of their decisions. They judge, argue, or manage cases while depending financially, some more than others, on foreign investors to invoke the treaties. The more narrowly the treaties are applied (to the general benefit of countries), the less it makes sense for investors to fund ISDS litigation. Does this temptation affect the lawyers or arbitrators in fact? No one can know, except the potentially tempted individual,[67] but the fact that it is reasonably possible creates a sound basis to doubt the legitimacy of the whole system.

Until the early 1990s, hardly anyone earned income from litigating under ISDS treaties. There were no claims. Today, the treaties are a huge business. Law firms can bill tens of millions of dollars in a single case; some lawyers charge USD 800 an hour or more.[68] The firms promote ISDS by educating their clients on how to use it. Many lawyers and arbitrators defend the treaties publicly, at times in ways that are deceptive or misleading.[69] Their advocacy makes it difficult, when the treaties do get public attention, to discuss them from an accurate baseline of information. However honourable the individual, all those who have staked a career in ISDS have a corollary interest in the expansion and activation of the treaties, and thus in supporting the treaties' inequality.

The competitive pressures also implicate the arbitration houses that oversee ISDS litigation. In Chapter 2, 'Origins of ISDS Treaties', I discussed how the treaties allow foreign investors to choose the rules under which a claim is filed. The investor thus decides which arbitration house will have the default power to appoint arbitrators in that investor's case. Some of the houses are public bodies, such as ICSID (which is the house if the investor files under the ICSID Rules or the ICSID Additional Facility Rules) and the Permanent 'Court' of Arbitration (PCA) (under

66 MacArthur (n 2); Dezalay and Garth (n 2); Gaukrodger (n 5) 14–15.

67 *Locabail v Bayfield Properties* [2000] QB 451, 471–72.

68 D Gaukrodger and K Gordon, 'Investor–State Dispute Settlement: A Scoping Paper for the Investment Policy Community', Organisation for Economic Co-operation and Development Working Paper on International Investment 2012/03 (OECD 2013) 20; D Rosert, 'The Stakes Are High: A Review of the Financial Costs of Investment Treaty Arbitration', International Institute for Sustainable Development Research Report (2014) 9.

69 For a few examples, see G Van Harten, *Sold Down the Yangtze: Canada's Lopsided Investment Deal with China* (Lorimer 2015) chs 31 and 32; Corporate Europe Observatory and Friends of the Earth Europe, 'Lawyers Subverting the Public Interest: Lobby Group EFILA's Stake in Investment Arbitration', Briefing report (2015); D Schneiderman, K Tienhaara, and G Van Harten, 'Reply to EFILA' (*Investor–State Dispute Settlement*, 6 July 2015) <https://gusvanharten.wordpress.com> accessed 14 January 2020; G Van Harten '"International Law Experts" Release Misleading Promo of ISDS' (*Investor–State Dispute Settlement*, 3 May 2015) <https://gusvanharten.wordpress.com> accessed 14 January 2020.

the United Nations Commission on International Trade Law [UNCITRAL] Rules). Others are part of a business organization, such as the International Chamber of Commerce's (ICC's) International 'Court' of Arbitration (under the ICC Rules) and the Stockholm Chamber of Commerce's (SCC's) Arbitration Institute (under the SCC Rules). None of these houses are courts in the common sense of the word. Their main role in ISDS is to administer the arbitrations, appoint the arbitrators, and decide conflict-of-interest challenges against the arbitrators. All of them have a stake in ISDS; some—especially ICSID, the PCA, and the SCC[70]—depend heavily on ISDS treaties for their arbitration business.

As an example of how the houses compete for claims, the SCC's Arbitration Institute recently amended its arbitration rules to allow for 'emergency' claims by foreign investors.[71] The word 'emergency' here might as well mean deeply unfair to everyone else. The amended rules give the SCC's house the power to select an arbitrator within twenty-four hours of the filing of a claim, without consultation with the disputing parties as a whole.[72] The arbitrator is then directed to issue an award within five days of the claim and can grant in the award any interim measures the arbitrator thinks appropriate.[73] It is hard to understand how any lawyer would think such a high-stakes process of adjudication against a country could be fair in such an abrupt time frame. Justifiably, a sued country might ignore such a process entirely, but the arbitrators could then issue their order without hearing from the country at all and the award would become internationally enforceable against the country's assets. This example shows the carelessness of governments that signed onto treaties that allow claims under the SCC rules, thus allowing a business organization to rewrite the rules for ISDS claims in favour of investors, including the organization's own members, without state oversight or approval.

In the case of the arbitrators, ISDS lacks essential controls against conflicts of interest. For example, the arbitrators are allowed to—and often do—work as lawyers, whether for the investor or the government, in other ISDS cases. This dual role creates situations of 'issue conflict', where arbitrators may interpret the law liberally

[70] For its part, the ICC 'Court' mostly handles commercial arbitrations, including many arising from contractual claims against states. It was described by Dezalay and Garth (n 2) 45, based on interviews with arbitration lawyers, as 'really an oversight committee that reviews arbitration appointments and decisions [and] appears to be particularly sensitive to the business clientele . . .'. In 2008, the chair of the ICC Court, Pierre Tercier, resigned, reportedly because of his objections that the body was not sufficiently independent of the ICC secretariat; 'ICC Left Reeling as Arbitration Court Chairman Tercier Resigns' *The Lawyer* (31 March 2008).

[71] Gaukrodger (n 5) 7–8 and 51–53.

[72] Stockholm Chamber of Commerce Arbitration Institute, Arbitration Rules 2017 (SCC Rules), Article 4(1) of Appendix II.

[73] ibid Articles 1(2), 8(1), and 37(1) and (3) of Appendix II.

in one case to help a client in another.[74] If a disputing party suspects a conflict, it can bring a challenge against the individual arbitrator, but many ISDS treaties allow for completely secret litigation, making it impossible for the disputing parties to verify whether any of the arbitrators has a conflict due to another appointment elsewhere. Thus, in ISDS, no one can comprehensively check an arbitrators' disclosure of potential conflicts.

If a disputing party does find evidence of apparent conflict, the challenge is often heard, problematically, by the other arbitrators on the tribunal, and then by the relevant arbitration house.[75] Yet the house may have its own interest in the matter. Its power to decide conflicts challenges, and above all to appoint arbitrators, gives officials at the house the ability to keep sensitive cases in safe hands, after learning who has sued whom and why. Borrowing from Lord Denning, ISDS treaties in this way make the judicial power 'simply a part of the executive machine'.[76]

Investors or governments have brought conflicts challenges in various cases, but they have rarely succeeded, especially at ICSID.[77] Whatever the outcome of a particular challenge, it should not distract from the fundamental flaw: all ISDS treaty arbitrations are beset by issues of arbitrator dependence and unfairness. The treaties may say that arbitrators must be impartial, but statements on paper are not a substitute for well-established institutional safeguards of judicial independence, including secure tenure, a set salary, an objective means of case assignment, and judicially governed rules against conflicts. These institutional safeguards define all courts worthy of the name in litigation over the permissible role and boundaries of sovereignty; they were dropped from ISDS treaties in favour of for-profit arbitration.[78] Now the 'judge' is appointed case by case and gets paid by the claim. Executive officials have a central role in assigning cases to arbitrators and navigating apparent conflicts. All outcomes in ISDS are unfortunately open to doubt, regardless of who wins or how well the arbitrators make and justify their decisions. Unless the actual aim is to have a skewed process, there is no sensible justification for removing the judicial safeguards.

[74] See eg S Luttrell, *Bias Challenges in International Commercial Arbitration: The Need for a 'Real Danger' Test* (Wolters Kluwer 2009) 93; LE Peterson, 'Challenge to Arbitrator Schwebel Rejected by Belgian Court, Poland Seeks Appeal' *Investment Treaty News* (17 January 2007).

[75] K Daele, *Challenge and Disqualification of Arbitrators in International Arbitration* (Kluwer Law International 2012) ch 4; S Grimmer, 'The Determination of Arbitrator Challenges by the Secretary-General of the Permanent Court of Arbitration' in C Giorgetti (ed), *Challenges and Recusals of Judges and Arbitrators in International Courts and Tribunals* (Brill 2015); WM Tupman, 'Challenge and Disqualification of Arbitrators in International Commercial Arbitration' (1989) 38 ICLQ 26, 31.

[76] Lord Denning, 'The Independence of the Judges', Presidential Address to the Holdsworth Club of the University of Birmingham (1949–50) 1.

[77] BS Vasani and SA Palmer, 'Challenge and Disqualification of Arbitrators at ICSID: A New Dawn?' (2015) 30 ICSID Review—FILJ 194, 195; Grimmer (n 75) 83.

[78] Pending modifications in treaties of the European Union would improve this situation.

Limited judicial oversight

As mentioned, most ISDS treaties allow a foreign investor to choose the arbitration rules under which to sue a country. This choice allows the investor to select among different arbitration houses, different processes for appointing arbitrators and deciding conflicts challenges, and different levels of secrecy in the proceedings. The choice also allows the investor to affect how much judicial oversight will apply to the arbitrators' decisions. For example, if an investor sues under the ICSID rules, the claim will proceed entirely outside of the courts. It will be heard first by a tribunal of three arbitrators (or occasionally a single arbitrator), whose decisions can be challenged only on limited grounds at an ad hoc ICSIC annulment committee.[79] The annulment committee itself has three arbitrators, all of whom are chosen by the World Bank President on the advice of ICSID. If the original ruling clears annulment, it becomes final and enforceable under the ICSID Convention, meaning that the states parties to that Convention have agreed to treat the ruling as if it were a final decision of the country's own courts. As former ICSID Secretary General Ibrahim Shihata put it, 'ICSID proceedings are insulated in all Contracting States from any form of judicial intervention or control'.[80] An ICSID award is like a supreme court judgment, but without the judges and without an actual court.

Investors usually can bring claims under other arbitration rules too: the ICSID additional facility rules, the UNCITRAL rules, the SCC rules, the ICC rules. Each of these allows for only limited judicial oversight. The arbitrators' original ruling can be set aside by the courts in the 'seat' of the arbitration, such as England or Washington, DC, but this seat is often picked by the original arbitrators themselves, even though it is their decisions that are subject to review.[81] Moreover, since the 1980s, many countries have passed laws that limit judicial oversight of international arbitration (often at the urging of the local arbitration industry).[82] At the time, there were relatively few ISDS treaties and no known claims. Now, the resulting laxity in national laws makes it easier for ISDS arbitrators to avoid judicial oversight.

Thus, the courts are limited in their ability to review ISDS rulings, as are annulment committees at ICSID.[83] A court can usually set aside a ruling only if it decides

[79] ICSID Convention (n 42) Articles 53–55.

[80] Shihata (n 42) 105.

[81] Some investment treaties limit which jurisdictions can serve as a seat in ISDS under the treaty.

[82] Y Dezalay, 'Between the State, Law, and the Market: The Social and Professional Stakes in the Construction and Definition of a Regulatory Arena' in WW Bratton and others (eds), *International Regulatory Competition and Coordination* (Clarendon 1996) 84–86; Van Harten, *Investment Treaty Arbitration and Public Law* (n 1) 155 (note 9).

[83] United Nations Convention on the Recognition and Enforcement of Foreign Arbitral Awards (New York Convention), signed 10 June 1958, entered into force 7 June 1959 (330 UNTS 3) Article V; Inter-American Convention on International Commercial Arbitration (Panama Convention), signed 30 January 1975 (14 ILM 336) Articles 4–5. See also UN Commission on International Trade Law (UNCITRAL), Model Law on International Commercial Arbitration, 21 June 1985, UNCITRAL UN Doc A/40/17, Annex I, 24 ILM 1302, Articles 34–35; United Nations (UN), *Report of the*

that there was a jurisdictional error, procedural abuse, or a serious violation of public policy. Very few rulings have been set aside on any grounds. Critically, a court cannot correct legal errors by the arbitrators in their interpretations of the treaties,[84] leaving arbitrators to decide what the treaties' vague language means and to expand ISDS through investor-friendly approaches.

This structure for domestic enforcement of arbitration rulings rests mainly on the New York Convention and the ICSID Convention, both of which pre-date today's ISDS treaties. Both conventions were originally tools to support the international arbitration of contractual disputes. The aim was to give options for companies from different countries to settle disputes outside of each other's court systems. Limits on judicial oversight made sense in this context because they enabled companies to resolve their discrete disputes as they preferred. Such limits are another matter entirely in ISDS, however, since the disputes raise profound questions of policy and sovereignty. It is a giant leap to go from resolving commercial disputes between companies to reviewing national laws and, as one ISDS practitioner put it, 'to tell a government what tobacco regulations go too far, how much taxation is too much taxation, how to exercise its police powers or what measures are appropriate for its national security' and 'to decide fundamental issues of international law and policy that affect an entire society, not to mention the international community in general'.[85] Since ISDS was activated in the 1990s, sovereigns have been subject to this extra-judicial structure of scrutiny and discipline, mostly at the behest of the ultra-wealthy.

Options for secrecy

By choosing the arbitration rules, an investor also decides the level of secrecy that will apply for its case. Some rules require the whole case to be kept secret; others publicize the fact of the claim, but hide the documents and the arbitrators. The most transparent rules require information to be made public about the arbitrators and their rulings, while keeping other materials secret, including the parties'

Secretary-General: Analytical Commentary on Draft Text of a Model Law on International Commercial Arbitration, UN Doc A/Cn.9/264 (25 March 1985) 16 YB UNCITRAL 104, [44].

[84] *United Mexican States v Metalclad Corporation* (2001) 89 BCLR (3rd) 359, 38 CELR 284, [50]–[56] ('The Tribunal gave an extremely broad definition of expropriation for the purposes of Article 1110 ... However, the definition of expropriation is a question of law with which this Court is not entitled to interfere under the *International Commercial Arbitration Act* [of British Columbia]'); *United Mexican States v Marvin Roy Feldman Karpa* (2003) 16(2) World Trade and Arb Mat 167, [77]–[86] (Ont SCJ); *United Mexican States v Marvin Roy Feldman Karpa* (2005) aff'd 193 OAC 216, 248 DLR (4th) 443, [34]–[43] (Ont CA); *Attorney General of Canada v SD Myers, Inc* [2004] 3 FCR 368, 5 CELR (3rd) 166 (Fed Ct TD) paras 42–44; *Ecuador v Occidental Petroleum & Production Co* [2006] 1 Lloyd's Rep 773 (QB), [124]–[125].

[85] Kahale III (n 9) 7.

submissions. None of the rules allow for the standard openness that is present in courts. That is, none presumptively require all documents and hearings to be publicly accessible. In courts, there can be closed proceedings, but only based on specific rationales approved by the court. This presumption of openness allows for public accountability on the part of the disputing parties and the judge. It supports public confidence by alleviating concerns that the judge, the state, or a powerful litigant has something to hide.

Presumed confidentiality is acceptable in some forms of arbitration, where the disputing parties have agreed to it and the dispute does not affect others or the public. Yet in ISDS arbitrators regularly review legislatures, governments, and courts in their sovereign role and they can order vast amounts of public compensation for private parties. These are among the most significant powers that any adjudicator can wield.[86] The proclivity for secrecy in this context has been criticized from early days.[87] In 2001, the New York Times reported on ISDS tribunals under the North American Free Trade Agreement (NAFTA):[88]

> Their meetings are secret. Their members are generally unknown. The decisions they reach need not be fully disclosed. Yet the way a small group of international tribunals handles disputes between investors and foreign governments has led to national laws being revoked, justice systems questioned, and environmental regulations challenged.

If anything, this description of ISDS secrecy understates the point, since some treaties allow for the claims themselves to be kept confidential. Meanwhile, members of the ISDS industry have worked to preserve this secrecy. For example, in 2010, when the UN Commission on International Trade Law (UNCITRAL) developed new transparency rules for ISDS cases under the UNCITRAL rules, ISDS lawyers lobbied successfully to gut much of the reform. In the result, the new rules were limited to future treaties only, thus maintaining existing levels of secrecy for all arbitrations under the hundreds of existing treaties that already allow for UNCITRAL claims.[89]

The most open arbitration house is ICSID. It requires the existence of a claim, the name of the investor and the sued country, the names of the arbitrators, the outcome of the arbitration, and usually the text of rulings to be made public. This relative openness has been exploited by other houses, seeking to compete with ICSID

[86] Van Harten, *Investment Treaty Arbitration and Public Law* (n 1) ch 3.
[87] Van Harten, *Sold Down the Yangtze* (n 69) chs 11 and 21.
[88] A DePalma, 'Nafta's Powerful Little Secret; Obscure Tribunals Settle Disputes, but Go Too Far, Critics Say' *New York Times* (New York, 11 March 2001).
[89] UNCITRAL, *Rules on Transparency in Treaty-Based Investor–State Arbitration* (United Nations 2014). Other arbitration reforms, in contrast, have been applied to new arbitrations under existing treaties; eg the SCC's creation of 'emergency' ISDS procedures; Gaukrodger (n 5) 7–8 and 51–53.

by offering more secrecy. As staff at the Singapore International Arbitration Centre (SIAC)—an ambitious newcomer among the arbitration houses—have put it, their centre's rules 'allow for the option that [ISDS] proceedings remain confidential unlike the ICSID system where the Secretary-General of ICSID is under an obligation to publish information about the existence and progress of pending disputes'.[90] Similarly, at the PCA, the secretariat often keeps secret who it has chosen as the default appointing authority (in cases under the UNCITRAL rules). In some cases where its choice was revealed, the PCA had picked a business organization to act as the appointing authority and, in one case, it picked the ISDS academic and arbitrator Christoph Schreuer, who in turn appointed his colleague at the University of Vienna, August Reinisch, to be the presiding arbitrator.[91]

Some governments—and more recently the European Union—have taken important steps to try and make ISDS more public. For example, they have supported ISDS openness at UNCITRAL and in new treaties. Even so, secrecy is still widespread in ISDS, such that policy makers, journalists, and citizens are precluded from reviewing important decisions affecting the public. How can a decision-maker be held accountable when the fact of the decision is kept secret? Worse, here the choice of whether to keep this fact secret originates with an investor that is seeking an award of compensation from the state. Secrecy is another example of how the wealthy receive special treatment in ISDS: they can hide the cost of their protections and privileges from the public.

Conclusion

ISDS treaties are an affront to the idea that the law should protect the weak. They authorize public compensation for foreign investors alone, where it could never be funded for all. They make such compensation the primary remedy for sovereign violations of vague provisions, often based on little more than guesswork about an investor's future profits. The arbitrators who decide whether to award compensation have an apparent financial interest to do so, since they depend on claimants for future appointments. This incentive extends also to lawyers, experts, and arbitration houses that play important roles in the litigation of investor claims. Judicial oversight of ISDS is limited or, under the ICSID Convention, non-existent. Court decisions themselves can be condemned by the arbitrators, and compensation ordered, without further review in a court. Under many ISDS treaties, compensation can be ordered in secrecy, thus hiding the implications of the treaties' inequality.

[90] Gaukrodger (n 5) 15, citing N Vivekananda and JJ Menezes, 'Singapore as a Seat for Investor–State Disputes' (*SIAC*, nd) <https://www.siac.org.sg/newsite/index.php/70-articles/169-singapore-as-a-seat-for-investor-state-disputes> accessed 14 January 2020.

[91] *Mytilineos Holdings v Serbia* (Award, 8 September 2006) [9] and [11].

It seems that the highest priority of governments in international law has not been climate change, employment, public health, arms control, or other pressing concerns. Judging from ISDS treaties, it has been to fortify inequality. Where there are prospects for reducing inequality, they usually emerge from national institutions or from the hope, at least, that such institutions can be strengthened. Yet ISDS treaties diminish these prospects in an exceptionally powerful way.

6
Intimidating Sovereigns

The power of investor–state dispute settlement (ISDS) rests ultimately in fear. It rests in the fear of officials, governments, countries, and their people. The more far-reaching the treaties, and the more expansively their protections are interpreted, the more they create apprehension for the sovereign. As knowledge of the risks of ISDS litigation and the costs of awards grows within state institutions, the more those institutions confront pressures to avoid offending those who are most able to finance claims. ISDS thus supplements other political, economic, and media strategies that empower the wealthy in their relations with the state.

This elevation of investors comes at the expense of all those who would benefit from whatever an investor opposes. It comes at the expense of those who lose their homes or drinking water to make way for a mine that was approved under ISDS pressure, who breathe dirtier air because legislators withdrew a ban on a pollutant as part of an ISDS settlement, who vote for a government that later retreats from its electoral platform to avoid claims. It also comes at the expense of those who lose access to services which can no longer be funded due to ISDS costs. It may come at a terrible cost to those who try to defend their land and communities against the destructive actions of an investor and are hurt or killed by security officials charged with protecting the investor's assets.[1]

These are some ways in which ISDS jeopardizes others by undermining regulation, democracy, or security. I examine these implications of ISDS in this chapter, focusing on the 'regulatory chill'[2]—or, more comprehensively, the reconfiguration of the state's governing apparatus—that ISDS generates.

[1] I allude here to the incentive created by the treaties for states to suppress protests in order to ensure 'full protection and security', especially for resource companies: M Malik, 'The Full Protection and Security Standard Comes of Age: Yet Another Challenge for States in Investment Treaty Arbitration?', International Institute for Sustainable Development Best Practices Series (2011) 6.

[2] K Tienhaara, 'Regulatory Chill in a Warming World: The Threat to Climate Policy Posed by Investor–State Dispute Settlement' (2018) 7 Transnat'l Env L 229, 233–39; JG Brown, 'International Investment Agreements: Regulatory Chill in the Face of Litigious Heat' (2013) 3 Western J Legal Stud (Article 3) 18.

The legal infrastructure for regulatory chill

The pressures that ISDS puts on states are one of many forms of litigation risk that can change organizational conduct.[3] Yet the stakes in ISDS are higher than other forms of such risk because the organization is the state itself and all of its institutions, and because the relevant conduct is the regulatory enterprise as a whole.[4] The most salient elements of ISDS treaties, taken together, create an exceptionally powerful tool for changing sovereign minds.[5] These elements are:

- exclusive access by foreign investors to ISDS, which allows them to challenge sovereign decisions in a process not available to others;
- the ability of investors to win uncapped amounts of compensation, which creates a potentially huge fiscal risk for the state if it is found to have breached the treaty;
- the breadth and ambiguity of the protections, which go far beyond clear situations of direct expropriation or discrimination, and thus make it hard for a government to predict, when contemplating a decision, if it will later be condemned;
- the vagueness of treaty safeguards for the state's regulatory role, which leaves the state exposed to potential liability whenever it makes a decision that carries significant economic consequences for private actors;
- the international enforceability of ISDS rulings, which frustrates the state's ability to refuse to pay a ridiculous award;
- the use of for-profit arbitration to decide claims, with little or no access to judicial review, which requires governments to submit to a forum where the 'judges'—if they are interested in future ISDS work—have a financial incentive to encourage more claims by investors;
- the inability of the state to bring a claim against the investor, which removes a possible counterbalance to the investor's special protections.

This combination of features is unique in ISDS as a source of litigation risk. It allows the owners of high-value assets to put immense pressure on a country, even without an actual claim. ISDS can be invoked, not only by lawyers representing multinationals, but also by officials in either the host or the home country who back the investor's position.[6] It is not that ISDS makes companies too big to fail;

[3] DB Hertz and H Thomas, *Risk Analysis and Its Applications* (John Wiley & Sons 1983); DL Olson and D Wu, *New Frontiers in Enterprise Risk Management* (Springer-Verlag 2008).

[4] T Prosser, *The Regulatory Enterprise* (OUP 2003); J Braithwaite and P Drahos, *Global Business Regulation* (CUP 2000).

[5] G Van Harten, *Investment Treaty Arbitration and Public Law* (OUP 2007) chs 5 and 7.

[6] J Kelsey, 'Regulatory Chill: Learning from New Zealand's Plain Packaging Tobacco Law' (2017) 17 QUT L Rev 21, 25 ('the calculus is not simply actuarial or legal. It is heavily influenced by the disposition, competing priorities and relative power of different politicians, official agencies, policy advisers and government lawyers, and the access and effectiveness of the various lobbying interests').

rather, it makes them too risky to regulate. ISDS treaties lead to an unparalleled set of legal, financial, and reputational rationales for countries to favour investors at the expense of those with a conflicting interest and no access to ISDS.

One can divide the risks of ISDS for countries into four categories: (i) the money cost of compensation orders; (ii) the money cost of the litigation; (iii) the cost in staff time and other resources to manage the litigation and vet internal proposals to avoid the litigation risk; and (iv) unquantifiable but still tangible costs such as political and reputational harm.[7]

The first category, the money cost, is often very high for the state, averaging around USD 500 million per investor 'win'.[8] Obviously, it always carries an opportunity cost for the use of public money.[9] Its retrospective nature, usually including some speculative tally of the investor's lost future profits, can greatly disrupt government planning. In public law generally, it is rare to use retrospective compensation as a remedy against the sovereign in its role as legislator and regulator, at least without significant limitations well beyond those in ISDS.[10] Even when government lawyers assess that a potential ISDS claim is weak on its merits, the risk of losing can still be a powerful deterrent, most glaringly in the case of billion-dollar assets.

The second category is the cost of fees for lawyers, arbitrators, arbitration houses, and experts in ISDS litigation. These costs have averaged about USD 5 million per case for the sued country, sometimes reaching tens of millions of dollars.[11] The fees appear to be so astronomical partly because ISDS operates on a for-profit model of adjudication and lacks important cost controls that courts have.[12] The sued country must also usually cover its own legal costs, even if it successfully avoids losing the claim[13] and, when the country does receive a costs order against an investor, it is unlikely to recover all its costs and the investor may simply refuse to pay, with limited options to chase the investor for enforcement.[14] Thus, even when countries 'win' in ISDS, they still must pay.

[7] K Tienhaara, *The Expropriation of Environmental Governance: Protecting Foreign Investors at the Expense of Public Policy* (CUP 2009) 262–64.

[8] UN Conference on Trade and Development (UNCTAD), 'Special Update on Investor–State Dispute Settlement: Facts and Figures', IIA Issues Note (2017) 3; TR Samples, 'Winning and Losing in Investor–State Dispute Settlement' (2019) 56 Am Bus LJ 115, 150.

[9] Samples (n 8) 149–50; D Rosert, 'The Stakes Are High: A Review of the Financial Costs of Investment Treaty Arbitration', International Institute for Sustainable Development Research Report (2014) 3–4.

[10] A van Aaken, 'Primary and Secondary Remedies in International Investment Law and National State Liability: A Functional and Comparative View' in SW Schill (ed), *International Investment Law and Comparative Public Law* (OUP 2010) 723 and 725–30.

[11] Samples (n 8) 151–52.

[12] D Gaukrodger and K Gordon, 'Investor–State Dispute Settlement: A Scoping Paper for the Investment Policy Community', Organisation for Economic Co-operation and Development Working Paper on International Investment 2012/03 (2013) 20–21.

[13] ibid 22–23.

[14] S Brewin, 'Security for Costs', International Institute for Sustainable Development Best Practices Series (2018) 1–2 and 5.

The third category is the cost of managing ISDS litigation and vetting internal decisions to mitigate the corresponding risk. Since an ISDS claim can target almost any action (or inaction) of the state, this demand on public officials can devour huge amounts of time.[15] To avoid it, officials may choose to appease investors in order to free up time for other priorities. According to an official in Canada's provincial government of Ontario, '[t]he last thing any government person ever wants to be is an expert in NAFTA [North American Free Trade Agreement] litigation' since 'it's a waste of time' in that '[y]ou could be changing policies for the benefit of Ontario or you could be defending a decision that was taken a long time ago and getting dragged through the courts'.[16] Yet it is virtually impossible to track this cost and measure its impact on all the others who would have benefited from proposals that were diluted or dropped due to ISDS.

In the fourth category are other costs, such as political and reputational consequences for a government and career risks for officials. These are far-reaching but also hard to measure. An ISDS claim may affect a government's relations with other countries, with international organizations, or with creditors.[17] As two ISDS lawyers explained, '[f]rom a claimant's perspective, the publicity surrounding ICSID [International Centre for Settlement of Investment Disputes] claims can provide useful leverage' as 'there is a perception that where a country faces a number of investor protection claims this acts as a disincentive to investment'.[18] Claims may also fuel political controversy for a government at home.[19] At the individual level, officials would typically have a career incentive to avoid decisions that risk dragging their country into a costly international litigation.[20]

These costs reflect how ISDS helps foreign investors, especially deep-pocketed ones. ISDS is always just one factor a government may have to consider, but the design of ISDS makes it particularly potent. A government may change a decision after a claim is threatened, or such changes may come systematically in the state's own vetting of its laws and policies.[21] As knowledge of the risk of ISDS grows within

[15] G Van Harten and DN Scott, 'Investment Treaties and the Internal Vetting of Regulatory Proposals: Further Findings From a Case Study from Canada' in LE Sachs and L Johnson (eds), *Yearbook on International Investment Law and Policy 2015–2016* (OUP 2018) 421–23.

[16] ibid 423.

[17] CM Ryan, 'Discerning the Compliance Calculus: Why States Comply with International Investment Law' (2009) 38 Ga J Int'l & Comp L 63, 93–94; T Allee and C Peinhardt, 'Contingent Credibility: The Impact of Investment Treaty Violations on Foreign Direct Investment' (2011) 65 Int'l Org 401, 412.

[18] I Meredith and C Tanner, 'Investment Treaties: Taking Advantage of the Protections on Offer' *Practical Law* (15 September 2006).

[19] JW Yackee, 'Do Investment Treaties Work—In the Land of Smiles?' in J Chaisse and L Nottage (eds), *International Investment Treaties and Arbitration across Asia* (Brill/Nijhoff 2017) 83.

[20] Van Harten and Scott, 'Investment Treaties: Further Findings' (n 15) 421–22.

[21] G Van Harten and DN Scott, 'Investment Treaties and the Internal Vetting of Regulatory Proposals: A Case Study from Canada' (2016) 7 J Int'l Disp Settlement 92; Van Harten and Scott, 'Investment Treaties: Further Findings' (n 15).

the state, the treaties help to institutionalize a pro-foreign investor presumption as part of the state's regulatory role.[22]

Undoubtedly, ISDS has costs and risks for investors too, but these are more limited than the risks for states. Fundamentally, investors face no risk in ISDS of having to pay compensation for having harmed anyone. Investor costs arise mostly in the category of ISDS litigation fees.[23] For a billionaire, the cost of litigating an ISDS claim is piddling compared to the costs of ISDS for all but the wealthiest countries when trying to regulate a wealthy investor.[24] Finally, it is the investor that has the power to sue, not the state, meaning that the investor alone can do a cost-risk analysis before entering into an ISDS litigation, after having been able to shape the record in anticipation of the claim.

Confidentiality and chill

ISDS promoters often say there is little evidence of ISDS-induced regulatory chill, and then reject its existence in sweeping terms.[25] In doing so, they fail to account for the obstacles to investigation of chill, typically not having taken serious steps themselves to look for evidence. Such evidence is difficult to uncover for straightforward reasons. The specifics of chill are usually documented in internal legal opinions or confidential settlements.[26] To investigate these sources thoroughly requires the authority to compel officials to testify and produce documents. Only the state can authorize such an inquiry. As a result, it is ultimately the state's responsibility to investigate and report on ISDS-induced chill. Yet governments that are chilled may have an interest to withhold information about such impacts in order to avoid embarrassment. Officials who lead the internal chilling of decisions often work in a trade ministry which negotiated and promotes the treaties. ISDS is sometimes even promoted on the basis that it delivers secrecy,[27] thus helping governments and companies to make controversial deals without informing the public, as if undermining accountability in this way were a good thing.

[22] Van Harten and Scott, 'Investment Treaties: A Case Study' (n 21) 96–100 and 109–16; Kelsey (n 6) 25.

[23] R Wellhausen, 'Recent Trends in Investor–State Dispute Settlement' (2016) 7 J Int'l Disp Settlement 117, 122.

[24] MD Goldhaber, 'Arbitration Scorecard 2011: The Biggest Cases You Never Heard Of' *American Lawyer* (New York, 6 July 2011).

[25] See eg N Lavranos, 'After Philip Morris II: The "Regulatory Chill" Argument Failed—Yet Again' (*Kluwer Arbitration Blog*, 18 August 2016) <http://arbitrationblog.kluwerarbitration.com/2016/08/18/after-philipp-morris-ii-the-regulatory-chill-argument-failed-yet-again/> accessed 14 January 2020; C Hamby, 'The Secret Threat that Makes Corporations More Powerful than Countries' *BuzzFeed News* (30 August 2016) (quoting ISDS arbitrator Jan Paulsson).

[26] Van Harten and Scott, 'Investment Treaties: A Case Study' (n 21) 113–14.

[27] SE Blythe, 'The Advantages of Investor–State Arbitration as a Dispute Resolution Mechanism in Bilateral Investment Treaties' (2013) 47 Int'l Lawyer 273, 289.

Some commentators assume that evidence of ISDS-induced chill would be so explosive that it is bound to leak over time.[28] This assumption was not supported by the results of interviews I co-conducted with officials in Canada, where it was clearly unrealistic to expect to be given information about how specific decisions were chilled by ISDS, even when the interviewee was assured of stringent confidentiality.[29] Asked about the impacts of ISDS under NAFTA, one official said that '[ISDS] definitely has an impact on our thinking' but would not discuss the specifics, saying the government 'is a very risk averse organization' and that senior officials 'don't even like it when we talk about stuff'.[30] Trade officials working in three different provincial governments also declined to speak about specific files,[31] and an Ontario environmental official noted the importance of confidentiality as a safeguard against ISDS claims, saying '[y]ou don't want to talk about things that maybe didn't turn into something'.[32] Thus, ISDS itself can deter disclosure about chill. It was especially hard to speak with government lawyers, who play a key role in assessing ISDS risks and implementing chill. The legal director of one provincial ministry refused to allow access to any of the ministry's lawyers, even on the condition that any privileged issues would not be discussed.[33] An ISDS specialist with a background in government reported: '[t]he problem is you have a paper trail [that] is limited with this stuff. It's all conversations at meetings or stuff that might have come in a memo, but you can never get it because it would be considered legal advice to government'.[34] This sensitive context precludes thorough study of chill by outsiders, and of the resulting changes to decisions. From the outside, one can at best make educated guesses about how states have been affected by ISDS by studying the claims, rulings, and settlements, by tracking media reports or government statements, by reviewing reports by companies and ISDS lawyers, by interviewing insiders, or by pursuing official access to information from the state.[35]

[28] C Kirkpatrick and others, *A Trade SIA Relating to the Negotiation of a Comprehensive Economic and Trade Agreement (CETA) between the EU and Canada*, Final Report (2011) 375, commissioned by European Commission:

> while it will never be known if certain measures in Canada were not enacted in the past because of a chilling effect, it seems reasonable that if the chilling effect was significant enough, given Canada's solid institutions and communications mechanisms, as well as an informed population, then government, academics, or other stakeholders would have pointed to the most significant and solid examples of regulatory chill.

[29] Van Harten and Scott, 'Investment Treaties: A Case Study' (n 21) 113–14.

[30] ibid: interview with BJ (28 March 2014). Another Ontario government official, when asked if a decision challenged in an ISDS case was previously vetted for trade issues, told us, 'I know the exact answer to that but I don't know if I'm allowed to say under the confidentiality agreement'; interview with AF (15 April 2011).

[31] ibid: interview with AX (22 November 2013); interview with BK, BL, and BM (23 June 2014); interview with BN (11 July 2014).

[32] ibid: interview with AH (25 March 2013).

[33] ibid.

[34] ibid: interview with AG (14 April 2011).

[35] The examples of chill discussed in this section emerge from investigative work by myself and others, including several research assistants, using ISDS case documents, media reports, official documents on government regulatory impact assessment processes, statements by government insiders,

Each of these investigative techniques is useful; each is also limited in its potential to uncover all of the relevant information. Keeping in mind these limitations, I offer below some illustrations of how ISDS has induced changes in state decision making.

Examples of chill

From the examples highlighted in this section, ISDS has clearly contributed to changes in state decisions and, in some cases, has led governments even to reconfigure their institutional processes. The latter step seems especially important because it shows how ISDS pressure—and the elevation of investor interests—is systematized within the state, from the early brainstorming of ideas to the implementation of laws and policies. Either way, ISDS has contributed to chill by causing the state to alter its conduct in ways that benefit investors at the expense of others.

Canada concedes to Ethyl Corporation

In *Ethyl v Canada*, a foreign investor used ISDS to stymie the Canadian government's efforts to check pollution by banning trade in a gasoline additive called MMT (for methylcyclopentadienyl manganese tricarbonyl), primarily due to concerns that it harmed new emissions control technology in automobiles. MMT was manufactured by US-based Ethyl Corporation, whose lawyers creatively invoked ISDS as part of a larger strategy against the ban. Ethyl was supported by Canadian oil refineries, which balked at the cost of re-tooling refineries for MMT substitutes,[36] and by the government of oil-dependent Alberta, which launched a lobbying campaign to defend MMT. In contrast, the automobile industry, environmental groups, and health researchers supported the ban, the latter due to concerns that inhalation of MMT gasoline fumes contributed to neurological diseases in children.

statements by private companies and ISDS law firms, leaked documents, and the texts of ISDS treaties. See Van Harten and Scott, 'Investment Treaties: A Case Study' (n 21).

[36] The cost of retooling the refineries was reportedly about USD 85 million. North American automobile companies pointed to their own investment of several billion dollars to develop the new emissions control systems. This and other factual information about the case is drawn from contemporary media coverage, including R Palmer, 'Coalition Calls for Ban on Additive MMT' *Calgary Herald* (Calgary, AL, 19 September 1996); S Feschuk, 'Marchi Advocates Ban on MMT' *Globe and Mail* (26 September 1996); G Keenan, 'Car Dealers Join Fight to Ban Gas Additive MMT' *Globe and Mail* (27 September 1996); B Avery, 'MMT Not an Issue in US' *Edmonton Journal* (Edmonton, AL, 22 November 1996); A Boras, 'Ethyl Fights Ban on MMT' *Calgary Herald* (Calgary, AL, 22 January 1997).

The pro-MMT coalition was helped by two trade agreements of the mid-1990s: NAFTA and an internal Canadian deal called the Agreement on Internal Trade (AIT), which was itself modelled on NAFTA.[37] Each of these agreements offered new ways for Ethyl or (under the AIT) a provincial government to oppose the federal government's ban. Ethyl used the NAFTA ISDS chapter to sue Canada, arguing that its status as a foreign investor, based on its manufacture and sale of MMT, entitled it to compensation for expected losses from the proposed ban, including even for harm to its reputation outside Canada.[38] The ISDS tribunal, whose members included now-leading hawks Charles Brower and Marc Lalonde, allowed the claim to go ahead, reportedly shocking Canadian officials.[39]

Meanwhile, Alberta challenged the proposed ban under the AIT, and won. This pro-MMT victory came after the NAFTA tribunal issued its ruling on its jurisdiction to hear Ethyl's ISDS claim, but before any ruling on the merits. At the AIT tribunal, two of its three members condemned the federal government's use of MMT trade restrictions to achieve health and environmental goals,[40] while the dissenting member thought that a direct ban on MMT would have been unfeasible under federal environmental law since 'on the evidence MMT, while noxious in large amounts, did not appear to be dangerous in small quantities' and its environmental effects 'are cumulative and indirect'.[41] The dissenting member would therefore have dismissed Alberta's claim, saying that the federal government's action 'was necessary for air quality and the improvement of the environment' and that the AIT's purpose 'was not to dilute the ability of responsible governments to improve the environment of Canadians'.[42] Overall, the AIT panel's decision highlighted limitations of environmental regulation in Canada, while also showing how the AIT could be used to frustrate the use of trade measures to address health or environmental risks.

Having lost under the AIT, the federal government decided to drop its MMT ban and, partly on that basis, to settle Ethyl's ISDS claim under NAFTA. As part of the settlement, the government also gave an apologetic statement to Ethyl, declaring that MMT was not a health or environmental threat, and paid Ethyl about USD 15 million in compensation (an amount that reportedly exceeded the annual budget of the federal environment ministry's enforcement and compliance programs at the time).[43] In exchange, Ethyl withdrew its NAFTA claim, thus

[37] Agreement on Internal Trade (Canada), Consolidated Version, 2015 (entered into force 1 July 2005).

[38] *Ethyl Corpn v Canada* (Statement of claim, 2 October 1997) [51].

[39] *Ethyl Corpn v Canada* (Award, 24 June 1998) 38 ILM 708; Van Harten and Scott, 'Investment Treaties: A Case Study' (n 21) 110–11.

[40] Agreement on Internal Trade (Canada), *Report of the Article 1704 Panel concerning the Dispute between Alberta and Canada Regarding the Manganese-Based Fuel Additives Act* (*Report of the Article 1704 Panel*) (2 June 1998).

[41] ibid 14.

[42] ibid 14.

[43] A Duffy, 'Canada Drops Ban on Gas Additive: MMT Now Permitted' *Ottawa Citizen* (Ottawa, ON, 21 July 1998); K Traynor, 'How Canada Became a Shill for Ethyl Corporation' (1998) 23 *Intervenor*

winning a major victory against the MMT ban by invoking ISDS in conjunction with Alberta's use of the AIT. Both agreements were effective tools to elevate oil industry priorities where doing so conflicted with the interests of others.[44]

Yet ISDS promoters have often downplayed or denied *Ethyl* as an example of chill. Usually they do so by misrepresenting the case, by adopting an outlandishly high threshold for establishing a link between ISDS and the *Ethyl* settlement, or by deflecting to a debate about the merits of the MMT ban itself.[45] Yet the *Ethyl* settlement was clearly a response to ISDS; in particular, Canada's statement of apology and payment of compensation were only necessary to settle with Ethyl under NAFTA. It is also hard to attribute the withdrawal of the MMT ban to the AIT case only, since the AIT panel only made a non-binding recommendation to remove the ban and this recommendation applied only to MMT's inter-provincial trade, not its international trade.[46] *Ethyl* is therefore a compelling example of ISDS-induced chill because Canada's acceptance of ISDS in NAFTA contributed to the government's decision to expose people to the health and environmental risks associated with MMT in gasoline, helping Ethyl Corporation to maintain its MMT profit stream at others' risk and expense.

MMT was never used widely in the United States, and it was eventually phased out of Canadian gasoline in 2004, about six years after the government's ban was abandoned.[47] By that point, ISDS had contributed to the exposure of many in Canada to MMT by their inhalation of gasoline fumes. It had also contributed to their exposure to air pollution, assuming that automobile emissions control systems sometimes failed due to MMT, and to their costs for trips to the repair shop when a car's engine light came on. It would take substantial resources to research and assess the extent of these impacts; for present purposes, the key is simply that they were harmful to others and arose from ISDS.

Indonesia appeases mining companies

Foreign investors in Indonesia have used ISDS to frustrate government efforts to unwind deals that dated from the corrupt era of General Suharto. In the early

(Canadian Environmental Law Association) 3; G Fletcher, 'US Bans It; Canada Burns It' *National Post* (6 September 2002).

[44] In contrast, Ethyl had lobbied unsuccessfully to keep leaded additives in gasoline in the 1970s, despite scientific uncertainty about the risks. JO Nriagu, 'The Rise and Fall of Leaded Gasoline' (1990) 92 Sci Total Environ 13; JL Kitman, 'The Secret History of Lead' *The Nation* (2 March 2000).

[45] See eg C Tietje, F Baetens, and Ecorys, 'The Impact of Investor–State Dispute Settlement (ISDS) in the Transatlantic Trade and Investment Partnership', Study prepared for the Minister for Foreign Trade and Development Cooperation and the Ministry of Foreign Affairs of the Netherlands (2014) 43–44.

[46] *Report of the Article 1704 Panel* (n 40) 13.

[47] K Blumberg and MP Walsh, *Status Report concerning the Use of MMT in Gasoline* (International Council on Clean Transportation 2004) 8.

2000s, a first wave of ISDS threats helped investors to carry on destructive open-pit mining in the country's rainforests and, more recently, the mining giant Newmont used ISDS to obstruct a regulatory requirement to process raw materials domestically before exporting them.

The threats started in the early 2000s, when foreign investors targeted a forestry law that would have prohibited open-pit mining in protected forests.[48] Mining companies had opposed the forestry law from its introduction in 1999 and, in 2002, it was revealed publicly that they had threatened to sue in ISDS and seek tens of billions in compensation.[49] In June 2002, Indonesia's environment minister announced that '[t]here were investment activities before the Forest Act was effective' and that, if they were shut down, 'investors demand compensation and Indonesia cannot pay'.[50] He said the country had to choose between authorizing the mining or paying a fine.[51] At a special hearing of the country's parliament the following month, the forestry minister alone defended the forestry law, while four other ministers wanted the mining to go ahead, amidst fears of arbitration claims.[52] A few months later, the House of Representatives and forestry ministry announced that they would exempt companies linked to ISDS threats from the law (and review other companies' situation) by changing the companies' approvals or clarifying that their operations were not in a protected forest.[53] Ultimately, thirteen companies with operations covering about 11 million hectares of forest were given exemptions in 2004[54] and, in 2009, the government clarified that underground mining in protected forests also complied with the forestry law.[55]

Thus, foreign investors used ISDS to frustrate protection of the rainforest after the overthrow of the Suharto dictatorship in 1999.[56] ISDS worked to elevate their position relative to others who suffered from harms caused by logging and mining. Under Suharto, the mining industry had long profited from 'close relationships with central power brokers who prioritized the development of the Indonesian mining industry over all other concerns and who often had a personal stake in its success'.[57] The companies exploited a system 'rife with official corruption, rule breaking, and illegality which benefited a tiny minority of well-connected elite

[48] SG Gross, 'Inordinate Chill: BITs, Non-NAFTA MITS, and Host-State Regulatory Freedom—An Indonesian Case Study' (2003) Mich J Int'l L 894, 894–5 (citing various local media reports).
[49] ibid 895.
[50] ibid 895.
[51] ibid 895.
[52] ibid 894.
[53] ibid 894.
[54] F Wulandari, 'Indonesia to Allow Underground Mining in Forests' *Reuters* (21 April 2009); 'Mining Bane: Stir over Fresh Threat to Indonesian Forests' *DowntoEarth News* (4 July 2015); Hamby (n 25); P Jacobson, 'Revealed: Australian Miner Used Arbitration Threat to Upend Indonesian Environmental Law' *Mongabay* (15 September 2016).
[55] Wulandari (n 54).
[56] Tienhaara, *The Expropriation of Environmental Governance* (n 7) 217–27; Hamby (n 25).
[57] Gross (n 48) 903.

while causing enormous ecological and social disruption in resource rich areas'.[58] A mining ban would have ameliorated this harm at a time when Indonesia's forests were the third most expansive in the world, supporting incredible biodiversity and up to 65 million people.[59] Allowing the open-pit mining to go ahead led to widespread land clearings and long-term pollution, erosion, and acid rock drainage,[60] bringing untold misery to many people and communities.

This climb-down by Indonesia was the country's first setback in ISDS. Another came in 2014 when the national parliament reformed the country's mining law to require companies to process minerals domestically before exporting them.[61] Some semi-finished mineral exports would be allowed to continue for several years, with progressive export taxes of up to 60 per cent. The law also aimed to reduce foreign ownership in the sector by requiring foreign investors to become minority shareholders over the course of a decade. One of the world's largest mining multinationals, Newmont, brought an ISDS claim against the reforms.[62] Ironically, it did so under Indonesia's tainted bilateral investment treaty (BIT) with the Netherlands.[63] The company stated that its goal was to win an order from the arbitrators that would allow the company to resume exports of copper concentrate.[64] A few weeks later, Newmont discontinued the claim based on what it called 'encouraging recent developments', including a government commitment to negotiate an agreement leading to 'the safe ramp-up of copper concentrate production and export'.[65] Newmont's lawyers announced that the ISDS settlement showed

[58] ibid 902, referencing World Bank, *Indonesia: Environment and Natural Resource Management in a Time of Transition* (2001) ii, 1 and 24; International Crisis Group, *Indonesian Natural Resources and Law Enforcement*, Asia Report No 29 (2000) i–3 and 22; and Forest Watch Indonesia, World Resources Institute, and Global Forest Watch, *The State of the Forest: Indonesia* (2002) 23.

[59] Gross (n 48) 903, citing *State of the Forest: Indonesia* (n 58).

[60] Gross (n 48) 894; J Atkinson, 'Case 3: Barisan Gold Mine', Oxfam National Policy Coordinator and Mining Ombudsman for Community Aid Abroad (2000); Center for International Environmental Law and others, *Whose Resources? Whose Common Good? Towards a New Paradigm of Environmental Justice and the National Interest in Indonesia* (Center for International Environmental Law 2002) 40.

[61] PwC, *Mining in Indonesia—Investment and Taxation Guide* (7th edn, PwC 2015) 2; H van der Pas and R Damanik, *Netherlands–Indonesia Bilateral Investment Treaty Rolls Back Implementation of New Indonesian Mining Law: The Case of Newmont Mining vs Indonesia*, Briefing report (Indonesia for Global Justice, Transnational Institute, and EU–ASEAN FTA Network 2014).

[62] *Nusa Tenggara Partnership BV and PT Newmont Nusa Tenggara v Republic of Indonesia* (Order of the Secretary General, 29 August 2014) ICSID Case No ARB/14/15.

[63] Netherlands–Indonesia investment treaty, signed 6 April 1994, UNCTAD International Investment Agreements Navigator: <https://investmentpolicy.unctad.org/international-investment-agreements> accessed 14 January 2020.

[64] PT Nusa Tenggara, 'PTNNT to Resume Operations and Copper Concentrate Exports' (*Newmont*, 4 September 2014) <https://www.newmont.com/document/ptnnt-to-resume-operations-and-copper-concentrate-exports/> accessed 14 January 2020.

[65] PT Newmont Nusa Tenggara, 'PTNNT Discontinues and Withdraws Arbitration Claim in Anticipation of Formal MoU Negotiations with Indonesia' (*Newmont*, 26 August 2014) <https://s2.q4cdn.com/575378270/files/doc_news/archive/Final-NNT-News-Release-26-August-2014-PTNNT-Discontinues-and-Withdraws-Arb_v001_w0g1d7.pdf> accessed 14 January 2020; *Nusa* (n 62); M Taylor and Y Supriatna, 'Newmont Withdraws Mining Arbitration Case against Indonesia' *Reuters* (26 August 2014).

'the effectiveness of treaty protections in negotiating with host states', 'how foreign investors can take action to protect their investments', and that 'ICSID arbitration provides a good background within which negotiations with the Indonesian Government can be conducted'.[66]

It seems the Indonesian government had a different view of Newmont's success. It had announced earlier that year that it would not renew its treaty with the Netherlands and, later, that it would exit all of its BITs, most of which had been negotiated under Suharto.[67] The foreign affairs minister stated that '[o]ur perspective on BITs has changed', that '[i]t seems very much in favor of the investor', and that '[o]ur number one problem is ISDS'.[68] Withdrawal from the treaties was a long-awaited step towards restoring Indonesia post-colonial sovereignty even if, as the ISDS lawyers noted, most of the treaties had provisions purporting to maintain foreign investor protections in Indonesia for at least another decade.[69]

Colombia privileges a private health insurer

Colombia's health care system is largely privatized. To protect the poor, Colombian courts sometimes order health companies to provide medicines and other care at a reduced rate or for free.[70] From 2008 to 2010, a Spanish company in the sector, Sanitas, challenged this limitation on its for-profit 'care' by quietly threatening an ISDS claim.[71] The government responded by setting up a special inter-institutional process to consult with the company, thus giving the company access to officials at the highest level. This process was managed by the President's office and included representatives of the national trade ministry (which had negotiated the treaties), the national ministry of social protection, and a national health funding agency.[72] According to a letter from the Colombian trade ministry (responding to questions

[66] M Bonnell and others, 'Strike 1: Rights of Investors against Indonesian Mining Laws' (King & Wood Mallesons, 28 August 2014).

[67] B Bland and S Donnan, 'Indonesia to Terminate More than 60 Bilateral Investment Treaties' *Financial Times* (London, 26 March 2014); van der Pas and Damanik (n 61).

[68] E Schram, 'Newmont Escaped Indonesian Law via Investment Treaty' *Mines and Communities* (28 December 2015).

[69] See eg Baker McKenzie, 'Withdrawal from Investment Treaties: An Omen for Waning Investor Protection in AP?' *Lexology* (12 May 2017).

[70] The orders were authorized by Decision No T-760 (31 July 2008) (Colombian Constitutional Court); AE Yamin and O Parra-Vera, 'How Do Courts Set Health Policy? The Case of the Colombian Constitutional Court' (2009) 6(2) PLoS Med.

[71] The investor's claim under the Spain–Colombia ISDS treaty (signed 31 March 2005) was filed in December 2008 but only officially confirmed in 2014 in a nine-page letter of 4 December 2014 from Cecilia Álvarez-Correa Glen, Minister of Commerce, Industry, and Tourism, responding to questions from Jorge Enrique Robledo, a Colombian Senator (on file with author; author's translation). I also rely on information from an insider, BC, who was interviewed on 30 January 2014 as part of the project reported in Van Harten and Scott, 'Investment Treaties: A Case Study' (n 21).

[72] Álvarez-Correa Glen (n 71) 3. The funding agency was the Fondo de Solidaridad y Garantía (Fosyga).

from a national senator), one or more of these agencies met to discuss the investor's complaints at least nine times over an eleven-month period, from late 2008 to late 2009, eventually bringing in at least six other agencies beyond the original four.[73] Fourteen times over the same period, officials from the President's office or one of the other agencies met the investor.[74]

I first learned of this example of chill from a confidential source who had direct knowledge of the government's response to Sanitas's ISDS threat in 2008.[75] According to the source, Colombian officials were surprised by the threat, and even trade officials 'saw it as impossible', asking, 'Why would Sanitas sue for something that is rightful here in Colombia?'[76] The officials did not seem to have detailed knowledge of ISDS treaties, the source said, believing that they were meant to attract investment without realizing that Colombia could be sued. By creating the special process to consult with Sanitas, trade officials were seeking 'to make an arrangement in order not to get sued' but 'that arrangement ... has never been public'.[77] Instead, the case 'became very private' a few months after the original threat was made.[78]

If trade officials were surprised by the Sanitas threat, it is reasonable to expect that other agencies had very little, if any, awareness of ISDS, up to the President's office itself. In turn, the government would have been vulnerable to manipulation by others with more specialized expertise in ISDS. How then did the trade ministry respond to the situation? It hired a private law firm called Gómez-Pinzón Zuleta to participate in the special process with Sanitas and to assess the ISDS threat.[79] This firm is at the heart of the ISDS industry in Colombia, advertising that its arbitration team 'clearly leads this field, handling national and international commercial and investment arbitrations'.[80] The firm's named partners—Enrique Gómez-Pinzón and Eduardo Zuleta Jaramillo—are prominent arbitrators with significant positions in international business and ISDS. Eduardo Zuleta, in particular, has been vice president of the International Chamber of Commerce's (ICC's) 'Court' of International Arbitration and a nominee of Colombia to the ICSID roster of arbitrators.[81]

The firm also has close ties to Colombia's trade ministry. One of the few officials at the ministry who understood ISDS treaties at the time reportedly used to work at the firm and was said to be 'very close' to people there.[82] Eduardo Zuleta himself

73 Álvarez-Correa Glen (n 71) 3–6.
74 ibid 3–6.
75 Interview with BC (n 71).
76 ibid.
77 ibid.
78 ibid.
79 Álvarez-Correa Glen (n 71) 3.
80 Gómez-Pinzón, 'Firm Profile' (*Chambers and Partners*, undated) <https://chambers.com/profile/organisation/3304?publicationTypeId=2> accessed 14 January 2020.
81 ICSID, 'Panels of Arbitrators and of Conciliators' (*ICSID*, 27 June 2019) <https://icsid.worldbank.org/en/Pages/about/Panels-of-Arbitrators-and-Conciliators.aspx> accessed 14 January 2020.
82 Interview with BC (n 71)T.

was known to be personally 'close to the people at the trade ministry', such that 'every time there is any question they have about investment law, they will contact this firm'.[83] Thus, a private firm of specialist ISDS lawyers and arbitrators helped Colombia to implement its special protections for foreign investors.

The actual outcomes of the Sanitas process are murky. The trade minister reported in her letter that the government had designed, reviewed, and put forward a resolution 'to correct the problems of the general system of social security in health for Sanitas'.[84] The government also put forward a 'procedure for payments' to private health companies from the national funding agency 'to solve the problems arising for private health companies in the payments process'.[85] It took measures 'to correct the problem that gave rise to the present claim [by Sanitas]', pointing to a resolution, two circulars, and three decrees to that effect, all passed in 2010.[86] Thus, it appears that extensive steps were taken to appease Sanitas and other private health insurers, but the details are unclear. No specific agreement was reached with Sanitas, according to the trade ministry, and there is no record of a formal ISDS claim.[87] Yet the government clearly gave Sanitas privileged access to decision makers, excluding from the process, for example, those who were denied access to medicine and sought protection in the courts. These others could not join or know about the ISDS-induced consultations until years later when a senator investigated it. For Colombia, this change in the government's processes was a precursor of things to come, as I discuss in section 'Reconfiguration of the governing apparatus' in this chapter .

Germany compromises marine habitat and the climate

The Swedish company Vattenfall used ISDS to pressure for approval of a coal-fired power plant in Hamburg, Germany. It did so by disputing a permit for the power plant, issued in 2008, which put strict limits on the plant's releases of hot water into the Elbe River. The releases posed a threat to migration routes for marine life, such as sea lamprey and salmon, between the mouth of the Elbe and upstream habitat, which formed part of the European Natura 2000 network of protected areas.[88] The

83 ibid.
84 Álvarez-Correa Glen (n 71) 6.
85 ibid 7.
86 ibid 7.
87 ibid 8.
88 Case C-142/16, *European Commission v Federal Republic of Germany* (Second Chamber) (26 April 2017) (European Court of Justice) [6]; R Verheyen, 'The Coal-Fired Power Plant Hamburg–Moorburg, ICSID Proceedings by Vattenfall under the Energy Charter Treaty and the Result for Environmental Standards' (*Greenpeace*, 11 April 2012) <https://www.greenpeace.de/sites/www.greenpeace.de/files/publications/icsid_case_regarding_the_vattenfall_coal-fired_power_plant_hamburg-moorburg.pdf> accessed 14 January 2020.

purpose of the Natura 2000 network is to provide 'a haven to Europe's most valuable and threatened species and habitats'.[89]

The power plant was also deeply controversial because of public concern about the climate crisis. It was forecast to emit about 9.9 million tons of CO_2 annually until after 2050 and was one of several coal-fired plants put into service in Germany between 2013 and 2015, undermining Germany's climate action planning.[90] Proponents of the plant complained that the permit was made overly stringent by a newly elected government in Hamburg that had campaigned against the power plant for, among other reasons, its carbon emissions.[91] Either way, the permit was meant to protect the environment.

While Vattenfall complained that the permit was overly stringent, in fact the permit still raised significant doubts about the plant's impact on habitat protection, prompting the European Commission to launch enforcement proceedings against Germany under the European Union Habitats Directive, as I discuss below. For its part, however, Vattenfall objected to the permit's conditions on water releases and sued both Germany (in ISDS under the Energy Charter Treaty [ECT] and the ICSID rules) and the Hamburg government (in German courts).[92] The Hamburg government defended the permit's conditions as justified and required under national and EU environmental law. In the ISDS claim, Vattenfall argued that the permit and approvals process violated its foreign investor protections under the ECT. The claim reportedly amazed German officials; according to Germany's deputy environmental minister, '[i]t's really unprecedented how we are being pilloried just for implementing German and EU laws'.[93]

The story became even more confused as Vattenfall's claims proceeded, roughly in parallel, in ISDS and the German courts. It is also opaque as a result of the high level of secrecy surrounding the settlement discussions among Vattenfall, Hamburg, and the German trade ministry (the latter being able to insert itself into the dispute because of the ISDS claim; it also negotiates Germany's ISDS treaties.[94] By 2010, however, both the ISDS claim and the domestic German lawsuit were resolved in a settlement premised on Vattenfall receiving a permit that was even more lenient than the one originally issued.[95] The specific terms of the settlement

[89] European Commission, 'Natura 2000' (*European Commission Environment*, undated) <http://ec.europa.eu/environment/nature/natura2000/index_en.htm> accessed 14 January 2020.

[90] Verheyen (n 88); L Wicke, 'Either with CCS or Not at All' (2008) 58(11) Energiewirthschaftliche Tagesfragen 8.

[91] *Vattenfall AB and Others v Federal Republic of Germany* (Claimant request for arbitration, 30 March 2009) ICSID Case No ARB/09/6, [27]–[40]; S Knauer, 'Vattenfall vs Germany: Power Plant Battle Goes to International Arbitration' *Spiegel Online* (15 July 2009) <http://> accessed 14 January 2020.

[92] *Vattenfall AB* (Claimant request) (n 91).

[93] Quoted in Knauer (n 91).

[94] Knauer (n 91); N Bernasconi, 'Vattenfall v Germany Arbitration', International Institute for Sustainable Development background paper (2009) 2.

[95] Verheyen (n 88) 6. The ISDS settlement was finalized in 2011 after both parties declared all conditions met, leading to a formal settlement award by the ISDS tribunal: *Vattenfall AB and Others v Federal Republic of Germany* (Award, 11 March 2011) ICSID Case No ARB/09/6.

were kept confidential but, in 2012, a German law firm obtained enough documentation to review the revised permit and assess whether it diluted the original permit of 2008 by allowing the power plant to emit more heat into the river (thus weakening fish protection) and to emit more greenhouse gases.[96] The lawyer who did the review found that the revised permit 'considerably lowered the environmental standards' compared to the original permit.[97]

The power plant ultimately went into operation in 2015.[98] That year, the European Commission also began its case against Germany for allegedly failing to comply with the EU Habitats Directive when the power plant was authorized in 2008.[99] According to the Commission's submissions to the European Court of Justice (ECJ) in the matter, the power plant 'risks having a negative impact on a number of protected fish species' and '[w]hen authorising the plant, Germany failed to carry out an appropriate assessment as required by the Directive, and to assess alternative cooling processes which could avoid the killing of the protected species'.[100] The ECJ agreed with the Commission in 2017, finding that Germany had breached its obligations under the Habitats Directive 'by authorising the construction of the coal-fired power plant ... without conducting an appropriate and comprehensive assessment of its implications'.[101] German authorities should not have approved the plant, the ECJ decided, until after investigating its impact on the Natura 2000 network of protected areas.[102]

Importantly, this decision dealt with the original permit of 2008, not the watered-down permit that was later issued to settle Vattenfall's ISDS claim and domestic lawsuit. While Germany should have been intensifying its controls on the plant to comply with EU law, therefore, it was instead appeasing Vattenfall under ISDS pressure. According to the law firm's review of the watered-down permit, '[t]here is no question that the ICSID case has, throughout, much increased the pressure on the City of Hamburg' to settle both in ISDS and in the German court case.[103] The ISDS claim raised the spectre of a 1.4 billion Euro damages claim and brought the German trade ministry into the discussions, which 'would otherwise have no power over the authority in Hamburg granting a water use permit'.[104] The

[96] Verheyen (n 88) 8–10.
[97] ibid 8 (emphasis in original).
[98] D Williams, 'Vattenfall's Hamburg Coal-Fired Power Unit Finally Set to Activate' *Power Engineering International* (25 February 2015).
[99] European Commission, 'Environment: Commission Refers Germany to Court over Coal Power Plant in Moorburg', Press release (*European Commission Press corner*, 25 March 2015) <http://europa.eu/rapid/press-release_IP-15-4669_en.htm> accessed 14 January 2020; EU Council, Directive 92/43/EEC of 21 May 1992 on the conservation of natural habitats and of wild fauna and flora, Official Journal of the European Communities No L 206/7 (22 July 1992).
[100] European Commission, 'Environment' (n 99).
[101] *European Commission v Federal Republic of Germany* (n 88) [74].
[102] ibid [22].
[103] Verheyen (n 88) 10.
[104] ibid 11.

review noted that the ISDS claim 'generally increased public fear and aversion within authorities' for decisions 'that are progressive with respect to environmental standards'.[105] A senior environmental official in the Hamburg government at the relevant time reportedly said that the ISDS claim pressurized Hamburg to settle, and Hamburg's environment minister likewise reportedly stated, 'I suspect that the goal [of the international tribunal] was to build pressure, instead of accepting that there is a system of law within Europe where one can resolve this.'[106] Ultimately, ISDS helped an investor to increase pollution at the expense of biodiversity and the climate.

Countries delay anti-tobacco measures

At the expense of public health, the tobacco multinational Philip Morris used ISDS to delay anti-tobacco regulations. It did so in various countries, but the clearest case is in New Zealand. There, the government delayed a law on plain packaging of cigarettes while awaiting the outcome of Philip Morris's ISDS claim against Australia for that country's ground-breaking plain packaging law. Among the other targeted countries, several, at least, appear to have buckled under the pressure. This obstruction of regulation presumably contributed to more people taking up smoking, more costs to society, and more illness and death.

The anti-tobacco measures targeted by Philip Morris were inspired by the Framework Convention on Tobacco Control of 2005, led by the World Health Organization (WHO).[107] According to a WHO expert committee in 2000, tobacco companies operated for many years 'with the deliberate purpose of subverting the efforts of the WHO to address tobacco issues'.[108] The attempted subversion was reportedly 'elaborate, well financed, sophisticated and usually invisible'.[109] ISDS emerged as a tool for the tobacco companies around 2010, although an earlier ISDS threat under NAFTA may have delayed similar proposals in Canada in the mid-1990s.[110] The ISDS option supplemented an array of other aggressive tactics by the

105 ibid 12.

106 J Vasagar and C Oliver, 'German Fear of Tribunals Threatens EU–US Trade Deal' *Financial Times* (London, 28 January 2015).

107 World Health Organization (WHO) Framework Convention on Tobacco Control, adopted 21 May 2003, entered into force 27 February 2005.

108 T Zeltner and others, *Tobacco Company Strategies to Undermine Tobacco Control Activities at the World Health Organization*, Report of the Committee of Experts on Tobacco Industry Documents (WHO 2000) 18.

109 ibid 228.

110 In 1993, tobacco companies threatened to sue Canada under NAFTA if its federal government adopted proposed plain packaging rules for cigarettes; the proposed rules were dropped but it is unclear the degree to which the NAFTA threat contributed to the government's decision not to proceed with them. D Schneiderman, *Constitutionalizing Economic Globalization: Investment Rules and Democracy's Promise* (CUP 2008) 120–29.

tobacco lobby, including the manipulation of science, discrediting of health advocates, use of front groups, advancement of pro-industry versions of laws, efforts to delay the regulatory process, and evasion of laws and regulations.[111] Among these tactics, the best fit for ISDS appears to be as part of a global 'intimidation by litigation campaign' by which tobacco companies 'sue governments ... that are enacting bold health measures'.[112]

Here, the tobacco companies' 'investments' are in fact a horrible scourge to human health. Should one even use the word investment to describe the production, sale, and promotion of an addictive poison, 'the only legal consumer product that kills up to half of its users when used exactly as intended by its manufacturer'?[113] Such investments underwrite 'the leading global cause of preventable death'[114] which, in the twentieth century, caused about a hundred million deaths.[115] Tobacco use continues to cause more than 7 million deaths annually, including 884,000 from second-hand smoke, and the toll is forecast to reach 8 million deaths annually by 2030.[116] More than 80 per cent of these tobacco-related deaths are in low- and middle-income countries.[117] Further, the economic cost of tobacco use exceeds USD 1.4 trillion annually, about 1.8 per cent of global economic output.[118] This figure does not include the costs of second-hand smoke or of environmental and health impacts of tobacco farming.[119]

The aim of plain packaging requirements for tobacco products is to reduce smoking, especially among young people. Australia proposed relatively stringent packaging requirements in 2011, despite lobbying pressure—including ISDS threats—from tobacco companies and the US Chamber of Commerce.[120] Having failed to block enactment of the requirements by other means, Philip Morris ultimately sued Australia both in ISDS and in the Australian courts.[121] Philip Morris was

[111] Corporate Accountability International, Southeast Asia Tobacco Control Alliance (SEATCA), and Global Center for Good Governance in Tobacco Control, *Anti-Corruption and Tobacco Control* (SEATCA 2017) 4.

[112] ibid 4.

[113] Pan American Health Organization (PAHO), 'Tobacco Facts', Press release (*PAHO*, undated) <https://www.paho.org/hq/index.php?option=com_content&view=article&id=1318:about-tobacco-control-program&Itemid=1187&lang=en> accessed 14 January 2020.

[114] WHO, *Report on the Global Tobacco Epidemic, 2011: Warning about the Dangers of Tobacco* (WHO 2011) 8.

[115] Corporate Accountability International and others (n 111) 3, citing WHO (Western Pacific Region), 'Tobacco Factsheet' (21 June 2016).

[116] J Drope and AW Schluger (eds), *Tobacco Atlas* (6th edn, American Cancer Society and Vital Strategies 2018) 28; WHO, *Report on the Global Tobacco Epidemic* (n 114).

[117] WHO, 'Tobacco and the WHO Framework Convention on Tobacco Control: Online Q&A' (*WHO*, May 2017) <https://www.who.int/features/qa/tobacco/en/> accessed 14 January 2020.

[118] Drope and Schluger (n 116) 30.

[119] ibid 30.

[120] J Zarocostas, 'Australia's Proposals on Plain Packaging Set New Global Benchmark in Anti-Smoking Efforts' (2011) BMJ 342; Campaign for Tobacco-Free Kids, *US Chamber of Commerce: Blowing Smoke for Big Tobacco* (July 2015) 11.

[121] *Philip Morris Asia Limited v Commonwealth of Australia* (Notice of Arbitration, 21 November 2011); *JT International SA v Commonwealth of Australia* [2012] HCA 43.

also helped by World Trade Organization (WTO) claims brought against Australia by Cuba, the Dominican Republic, Honduras, and Indonesia.[122] Australia defeated Philip Morris in the national courts in 2012 and in ISDS in 2015.[123] The latter victory turned on the issue of nationality shopping as the ISDS tribunal, in an exceptionally state-friendly ruling, refused to hear Philip Morris's claim where it had been brought by a Hong Kong subsidiary of the US-based company.[124] In 2018, a WTO panel also ruled in Australia's favour.[125]

For Australia, then, ISDS did not induce regulatory chill; the government maintained its plain packaging law. Yet the government had to commit a huge amount of resources to the litigation, recouping from Philip Morris only half of its litigation costs of AUS 24 million.[126] Further, any tobacco company, including Philip Morris itself, can still bring more ISDS claims over the same type of regulations in other countries, or even in Australia itself, thus making the Australian case a continuing deterrent for all.

In the shadow of the Australian case, other countries delayed their own plain packaging laws. Most clearly, New Zealand introduced a proposed law in December 2013,[127] but then declined to enact it until September 2016.[128] The delay included a two-year period when the proposed law was considered at a Cabinet subcommittee, which had received advice from the civil service that was heavily redacted in its public version but implied that delaying the proposed law was warranted by litigation risk.[129] In appearances at the subcommittee and more widely, the

[122] World Trade Organization (WTO) Dispute Settlement Body, *Australia—Certain Measures concerning Trademarks, Geographical Indications and Other Plain Packaging Requirements Applicable to Tobacco Products and Packaging*, Reports of the Panels, WT/DS435/R, WT/DS441/R, WT/DS458/R, WT/DS467/R (28 June 2018). WTO dispute resolution takes place between states and does not allow for ISDS.

[123] *JT International SA* (n 121); *Philip Morris Asia Limited v Commonwealth of Australia* (Award, 17 December 2015).

[124] *Philip Morris Asia Limited* (Award, 17 December 2015) (n 123) [1], [5]–[6], and [585]–[588].

[125] R Ireland, 'The Tobacco Plain Packaging Wars Continue Following Appeal of WTO Ruling' (*Regulating for Globalization*, 12 September 2018) <http://regulatingforglobalization.com/2018/09/12/tobacco-plain-packaging-wars-continue-following-appeal-wto-ruling/> accessed 14 January 2020.

[126] J Hepburn, 'Final Costs Details are Released in Philip Morris v Australia Following Request by IAReporter' *IAReporter* (California, IL, 21 March 2019).

[127] New Zealand Parliament, 'Smoke-Free Environments (Tobacco Standardised Packaging Amendment Bill) Progress of the Bill' (*New Zealand Parliament*, undated) <https://www.parliament.nz/en/pb/bills-and-laws/bills-proposed-laws/document/00DBHOH_BILL12969_1/smoke-free-environments-tobacco-standardised-packaging> accessed 14 January 2020 (indicating the Bill was introduced in December 2013, received first reading in February 2014, received second reading in June 2016, and received third reading and was enacted in September 2016). The Bill was introduced after being recommended by a parliamentary committee in 2010; New Zealand House of Representatives (Māori Affairs Committee), *Inquiry into the Tobacco Industry in Aotearoa and the Consequences of Tobacco Use for Māori*, Report 1.10A (2010).

[128] By comparison, a proposed law to ban public displays of tobacco products in stores in 2010 was enacted after less than nine months: New Zealand Parliament, 'Smoke-Free Environments (Controls and Enforcement) Amendment Bill, Progress of the Bill' (*New Zealand Parliament*, undated) < https://www.parliament.nz/en/pb/bills-and-laws/bills-proposed-laws/document/00DBHOH_BILL10487_1/smoke-free-environments-controls-and-enforcement-amendment> accessed 14 January 2020.

[129] Kelsey (n 6) 34.

tobacco industry itself stressed the ISDS threat against the proposed law.[130] Based on a close review of the law, Kelsey concluded that its delayed enactment arose from ISDS and WTO litigation risk, political considerations, and the government's onerous risk assessment process for new regulations.[131] Concerning the ISDS and WTO risk, she said the government 'was concerned about the *potential* for litigation and its effects, not just the legality of its actions'.[132] Various other sources have reported that the government delayed the law to await the outcome of the litigation against Australia.[133] New Zealand finally enacted its law after the ISDS claim against Australia was resolved and while the WTO litigation against Australia was ongoing. According to Kelsey, trade and investment agreements also reinforced the government's internal risk assessments of the law and gave the trade ministry an in-built role in assessing the ISDS risk.[134]

Philip Morris similarly targeted other countries. It sued Uruguay in ISDS, when the country's government introduced tobacco packaging restrictions in 2009.[135] The Uruguayan government had to rely on outside donations to finance its defence of the long and costly ISDS case,[136] which ended in a split decision favouring Uruguay.[137] The majority of the tribunal endorsed the law as a legitimate public health measure and deferred to the regulators' and the WHO assessments of the effectiveness of plain packaging in addressing the health risks of smoking.[138] In an astonishing dissent, Philip Morris's arbitrator (Gary Born) engaged in a highly critical assessment of the scientific evidence of the effectiveness of plain packaging in the course of defending his view that Uruguay had violated the ISDS treaty.[139] Thus, Uruguay narrowly avoided a devastating loss, finally going ahead with its plain packaging regulation in 2018.[140]

Big Tobacco has also threatened other countries with ISDS or other forms of trade litigation. Between 2011 and 2017, according to a *Guardian* report, tobacco companies 'threatened governments in at least eight countries in Africa', including

[130] ibid 32.

[131] ibid 44–45.

[132] ibid 35.

[133] E Crosbie and G Thomson, 'Why Did It Take 53 Months for NZ to Introduce Plain Cigarette Packs?' *Noted* (14 June 2018); M Heron, 'Government Confident It Can Send Tobacco Companies Packing' *RadioNZ* (9 September 2016); R Edwards and J Hoek, 'Protect our Children: Standardise Tobacco Packaging Now', *Aspire2025* (7 October 2017).

[134] Kelsey (n 6) 22.

[135] *Philip Morris Brands SÀRL and Others v Uruguay* (Award, 8 July 2016).

[136] D Wilson, 'Bloomberg Backs Uruguay's Anti-Smoking Laws' *New York Times* (New York, 15 November 2010).

[137] *Philip Morris Brands SÀRL* (n 135).

[138] ibid [295], [306]–[307], [399], [409], and [432]–[434].

[139] *Philip Morris Brands SÀRL* (n 135) (Separate Opinion of Gary Born) [87], [126]–[128], [157]–[159], [163]–[165], [172]–[173], and [176].

[140] International Union against Tuberculosis and Lung Disease, 'Uruguay Becomes the First Country to Require Plain Packaging of Tobacco Products in Latin America' (*The Union*, 9 August 2018) <https://www.theunion.org/news-centre/news/uruguay-becomes-the-first-country-to-require-plain-packaging-of-tobacco-products-in-latin-america> accessed 14 January 2020.

Burkina Faso, the Democratic Republic of Congo, Ethiopia, Gabon, Namibia, Togo, and Uganda.[141] They demanded that governments 'axe or dilute the kind of protections that have saved millions of lives in the west' and accused governments 'of breaching their own laws and international trade agreements'.[142] The Tobacco Atlas project likewise reported in 2018 that the tobacco industry 'has been actively litigating tobacco control regulations in dozens of countries' and that 'litigation threats "chill" similar measures in other countries'.[143] According to a report by the Campaign for Tobacco-Free Kids in 2014, the US Chamber of Commerce warned Burkina Faso's prime minister that the country's proposed labels for tobacco packages violated its trade agreements, 'implying that the tobacco industry might use international trade agreements to entangle the Burkina Faso proposal in costly trade litigation, which as a low-income country it cannot afford'.[144] According to the same report, the US Chamber of Commerce and its European affiliate also intervened in European Union (EU) processes to revise the EU Tobacco Products Directive, which establishes a framework for member states to regulate packaging for the reduction of tobacco use. Tobacco lobbyists argued that proposed measures like plain packaging and warning labels 'would violate EU law, EU and international intellectual property law and EU member states' international trade obligations', and the Directive 'was significantly delayed for five years due in large part to interference by the tobacco industry and its allies'.[145] This lobby effort 'served the tobacco industry's objectives of significantly weakening the [Directive]—including the removal of standardized packaging and a ban on point-of-sale displays—and delaying its adoption' until 2014.[146] The report found that similar lobbying tactics were used against Jamaica, Nepal, the United Kingdom, and other countries.[147]

In reaction to the litigation threats, some countries went ahead with plain packaging requirements, albeit often with lengthy delays, while others watered them down.[148] In each case, it is virtually impossible to isolate ISDS as the sole or leading cause of chill because the ISDS threats were part of a larger campaign to frustrate health regulations. It is also impossible to know whether ISDS claims were filed against other countries, especially in Africa, where many countries have treaties that allow for secret ISDS claims (especially under the ICC arbitration rules).[149]

141 S Boseley, 'Threats, Bullying, Lawsuits: Tobacco Industry's Dirty War for the African Market' *The Guardian* (London, 12 July 2017).

142 ibid.

143 Drope and Schluger (n 116) 49.

144 Campaign for Tobacco-Free Kids, *US Chamber of Commerce* (n 120) 8. Burkina Faso's proposals were introduced in 2011 but regulations were not passed until 2015.

145 ibid 8–9.

146 ibid 8–10.

147 ibid.

148 ibid.

149 O Akinremi, 'An Empirical Analysis of the Bilateral Investment Treaties of the Top Ten GDP Producing African States', JD Student Paper for International Investment Law course, Osgoode Hall Law School (2014) (reviewing English-language investment treaties of ten African countries and

A lawyer with the US International Trade Commission, Robert Ireland, commented in a personal capacity that '[a]lthough multiple legal actions never stopped plain packaging in Australia, it is likely that many countries delayed their own plain packaging laws for fear of huge litigation costs'.[150] Thus, it appears the impact of ISDS extended well beyond the delays in New Zealand and Uruguay.

All delays to anti-tobacco measures benefit tobacco companies at the expense of others. Research indicates that plain packaging contributes to lower smoking rates and fewer premature deaths.[151] In Australia, it was estimated that plain packaging led to 108,228 fewer smokers over a thirty-four-month period between 2012 and 2015.[152] According to the New Zealand Cancer Society, 'tobacco companies use cigarette packets as a powerful marketing tool to attract young people'.[153] By mid-2016 in New Zealand, shortly before implementation of the plain packaging law, tobacco use had not fallen significantly among the New Zealanders who smoke the most: Maori, Pacific, those on low incomes, and those with mental illness. These people would have been safer had plain packaging been implemented sooner, at the expense of the tobacco industry. In 2015, the combined profits of the largest tobacco companies exceeded USD 60 billion;[154] each new smoker represents an average of USD 9,730 in profit.[155] The fact that Philip Morris could sue at all as an 'investor' reveals the deeply skewed design of international law.

Romania pulls back from heritage protection

In 2018, the Romanian government dropped a bid to have the Roşia Montană Mining Landscape in central Romania recognized as a United Nations Educational, Scientific and Cultural Organization (UNESCO) World Heritage Site.[156] The bid was submitted in early 2016 but, shortly before UNESCO met to decide it,

finding seventeen treaties (of Angola, Egypt, Ethiopia, South Africa, and Sudan) where the African country consented to ISDS under the ICC rules).

[150] Ireland (n 125).

[151] For an overview, see Campaign for Tobacco-Free Kids, 'Research Evidence' in *Plain Packaging of Tobacco Products Toolkit* (2016).

[152] T Chipty, 'Addendum to Study of the Impact of the Tobacco Plain Packaging Measure on Smoking Prevalence in Australia' (*Australian Government Department of Health*, 19 May 2016) <https://www1.health.gov.au/internet/main/publishing.nsf/content/study-pp-measure> accessed 14 January 2020.

[153] New Zealand Cancer Society, 'What are the Smokefree Laws in New Zealand?' (*Cancer Society*, undated) <https://auckland-northland.cancernz.org.nz/reducing-cancer-risk/what-you-can-do/smoking-and-cancer/tobacco-control-nz/what-are-the-smokefree-laws-in-new-zealand/?divisionId=17&centreId=1> accessed 14 January 2020.

[154] American Cancer Society, 'Report: Big Tobacco is Targeting the World's Most Vulnerable to Increase Profits' (2018).

[155] ibid.

[156] D Main, 'In Transylvania, A Fierce Battle over Gold and Roman History' *National Geographic* (12 July 2018).

Romania's culture minister announced that the government had to delay the bid because of an ISDS claim by a Canadian mining company, Gabriel Resources.[157] The company was seeking USD 4.4 billion in damages for Romania's non-approval of a proposed mine,[158] which, if approved, would be the largest industrial gold mine in Europe and destroy much of Roşia Montană.[159] The culture minister reportedly called the arbitration 'a national security priority'.[160]

Local communities had opposed the proposed mine for years, but it became especially controversial in 2013 when the government introduced a draft law to approve the mine.[161] The draft law led to widespread public opposition in Romania, and was ultimately rejected by a parliamentary committee and by the national senate.[162] This opposition victory is described by a Romanian academic as 'an example of what can be achieved through peaceful and resilient citizen pressure upon state institutions'.[163] Gabriel Resources responded by declaring that the company would 'assess all possible actions open to it, including the formal notification of its intentions to commence litigation for multiple breaches of international investment treaties'.[164] Its CEO reportedly said '[o]ur case is very strong and we will make it very public that Romania's effort to attract foreign investment will suffer greatly',[165] describing the company's 'overriding wish' as being 'to achieve an amicable resolution that allows for the construction and operation of a world-class gold mine at Rosia Montana'.[166] Thus, the company employed ISDS to pressurize the government over the mine.

157 O Posirca, 'It's Official: Romania's Government Backs Move to Delay Rosia Montana Inclusion in UNESCO World Heritage Network' *Business Review* (28 June 2018).

158 The amount claimed appears extraordinary compared to the size of the company, indicating an effort by the company to use ISDS as an intimidation tool. At the end of 2015, the company reportedly held USD 18.6 million in cash or cash equivalents and intended, according to its Chief Executive Officer (CEO), to raise 'up to $20 million by way of a non-brokered private placement to finance, amongst other things, the ICSID arbitration': 'Gabriel Resources Pushes Arbitration Case over Gold Mine Rosia Montana Romania' *Mining See* (12 April 2016).

159 Posirca (n 157); C Jamasmie, 'Romania Wants City of Rosia Montana Application to be Pulled from UNESCO List' *Mining.com* (30 August 2017); Chipty (n 152); I Marica, 'UNESCO Postpones Evaluation of Rosia Montana Nomination for World Heritage List' *Romania Insider* (2 July 2018).

160 Posirca (n 157).

161 C Ciobanu, 'Romania to Withdraw Rosia Montana UNESCO Application' (*BlogActiv*, 31 August 2017) <https://guests.blogactiv.eu/2017/08/31/romania-to-withdraw-rosia-montana-unesco-application/> accessed 14 January 2020.

162 S Manea, 'The Dispute over the Rosia Montana Mining Project Represents an Opportunity to Reshape Romania's Sustainable Development Policy' (*LSE European Institute European Politics and Policy*, 28 November 2013) <http://blogs.lse.ac.uk/europpblog/2013/11/28/the-dispute-over-the-rosia-montana-mining-project-represents-an-opportunity-to-reshape-romanias-sustainable-development-policy-2/> accessed 14 January 2020.

163 ibid.

164 E Reguly, 'Gabriel Threatens Romania with Billion-Dollar Lawsuit' *Globe and Mail* (11 September 2013).

165 ibid.

166 'Gabriel Resources' (n 158).

If the mine was approved, it would reportedly do immense harm to others. According to the Save Roşia Montană campaign:[167]

- It would be the biggest open-pit mine in Europe and destroy four mountains, creating craters with a diameter of over 8 km.
- It would require the relocation of over 2,000 private properties and 11 cemeteries and the destruction of 975 houses and 7 churches.
- It would use 12,000 tons of cyanide annually and 240,000 tons in total, thirteen times more than currently used in Europe as a whole.
- It would create a 300-hectare tailings 'pond' of heavy metals and cyanide that would cover the village of Corna entirely.
- The rock-fill dam to contain the tailings 'pond' would be 185 m high and over 1 km long, located 2 km upstream from the town of Abrud, with 6,000 residents.
- The project would create only 634 direct or indirect jobs over a 17-year period.

Besides its wide-ranging impacts on the environment and local communities, the mine would mostly destroy the cultural heritage of Roşia Montană, which Romania's UNESCO bid had sought to protect. According to an expert report for UNESCO in 2017, the Roşia Montană site was recognized as having 'the most significant, extensive and technically diverse underground Roman gold mining complex currently known in the world'.[168] Further:[169]

> Roman archaeology at surface is prolific and pervasive, comprising ore-processing areas, living quarters, administrative buildings, sacred areas and necropolises, some with funerary buildings with complex architecture, all set in relation to over 7 km of ancient underground workings that have been discovered to date.

The report stressed the vulnerability of the site due to the proposed mine:[170]

> A resumption of mining at the scale that has been proposed would transform the region, creating four new open cast mines, and a tailings pond that would drown the Corna valley. Only a small portion of the Roman mining galleries would be

[167] Save Roşia Montană, 'All about Rosia Montana Mining Project' (*Salvaţi Roşia Montană*, undated) <https://www.rosiamontana.org/node/1825?language=en> accessed 14 January 2020. Note that, as of 28 May 2020, this website seems to have disappeared.

[168] International Council on Monuments and Sites (ICOMOS), *Evaluations of Nominations of Cultural and Mixed Properties*, Report for the World Heritage Committee (ICOMOS 2018) 245.

[169] ibid 250.

[170] ibid 245.

> preserved in the immediate area of the town of Roşia Montană. The majority of the Roman remains described in the nomination dossier would be destroyed.

It was noted that, in pursuing the project, the Roşia Montană Gold Corporation (owned by Gabriel Resource) 'has been systematically buying houses and encouraging residents to move away [from the municipality] with the result that the population of the municipality has fallen from 3,800 in 2002 to under 1,000 today'.[171] The company also 'attempted to obtain an archaeological discharge to allow mining in some of the areas with historic underground works, but it has been blocked by the Romanian courts'.[172] The company's push for the mine had left the site 'highly vulnerable', with the main threat being 'potential resumption of large scale gold mining' as a 'specific and proven imminent danger [that] could lead to significant loss of historical authenticity and of cultural significance'.[173] In the report, it was recommended that the site should be recognized as a UNESCO world heritage site and simultaneously listed as being 'in danger', as a way 'to ensure that the attributes are not impacted by the resumption of mining, that resources are mobilized to address the conservation problems, and that the protection, management and monitoring regimes for the property are completed and implemented', but noted further that the ISDS claim 'limits the actions of the State Party'.[174] Considering this recommendation, the government's withdrawal of its bid for UNESCO recognition has itself compromised the conservation and protection of Roşia Montană.[175]

ISDS claims take years to litigate. During this time, the Roşia Montană site faces further deterioration and Gabriel Resources can continue to push the government for approval of the mine. It may be that the government's withdrawal of its UNESCO bid was part of a strategy to help its position in the ISDS proceeding, rather than a pathway to a planned settlement premised on approval of the mine. Regardless, ISDS has strengthened Gabriel Resources' bargaining position relative to all others whose property and way of life are threatened by the mine, and heightened the risk to Romania's world-class cultural heritage.

Reconfiguration of the governing apparatus

As governments learn about their ISDS liabilities, unsurprisingly they try to manage them. An obvious way to do so is to avoid the liabilities completely by withdrawing from the treaties and using other means, accessible to all, to protect investors. A more common and insidious way of managing the liabilities, however,

171 ibid 247.
172 ibid 247.
173 ibid 250.
174 ibid 250.
175 ibid 250.

is to implement 'systemic' chill, meaning the wide-ranging internalization of foreign investor protections within the state.[176] By this form of chill, ISDS provokes a reconfiguration of the country's governing apparatus to appease the ultra-wealthy as the deepest-pocketed and most dangerous investors.

To institutionalize chill, governments establish processes to vet their proposed laws, policies, regulations, and so on.[177] By definition, these processes elevate the interests of foreign investors in decision making. Often the process is run by trade officials; for example, in Colombia and Germany, the filing of an ISDS claim spurred each country's trade ministry to intervene in decisions by other agencies or another level of government.[178] In both instances, the trade ministry was advised by lawyers from the ISDS industry.[179] The Colombian case shows further how ISDS can provoke a transformation of the governing apparatus.

In 2010, after the Sanitas threat, four Colombian ministries (foreign affairs, justice, finance, and trade) developed a national plan to manage the country's ISDS risks.[180] Colombia had assumed these risks in the mid-2000s, much later than most countries, and after the ISDS litigation boom had begun.[181] The national plan it later developed to manage the risks reads like a celebration of ISDS treaties, which are said 'to attract foreign investment' by creating a 'predictable framework of rules to reduce non-commercial risks of foreign investors'.[182] Like the rosy portrayals

[176] Kelsey (n 6) 25.

[177] UNCTAD has a history of promoting this form of institutionalization of regulatory chill: UNCTAD, *Investor–State Disputes: Prevention and Alternatives to Arbitration* (United Nations 2010) 65–98; UNCTAD, *Best Practices in Investment for Development: How to Prevent and Manage Investor–State Disputes: Lessons from Peru* (United Nations 2011).

[178] See also Van Harten and Scott, 'Investment Treaties: Further Findings' (n 15).

[179] The Colombian example was discussed above. In the German example, the trade ministry—called the Federal Ministry of Economy and Technology—was represented by Sabine Konrad of the law firm K&L Gates: *Vattenfall AB* (Award) (n 95). Konrad now works with another law firm whose website describes her as one who 'advises investors and governments in matters of investment protection' and who 'acts as arbitrator in investment treaty arbitration and international commercial arbitration cases': McDermott Will & Emery, 'Dr Sabine Konrad' (*McDermott Will & Emery*, undated) < https://www.morganlewis.com/bios/sabinekonrad> .

[180] Colombia (Consejo Nacional de Política Económica y Social República), *Fortalecimiento de la Estrategia del Estado Para Prevención y Atención de Controversias Internacionales de Inversión*, Conpes Doc 3684 (author's translation) (19 October 2010).

[181] Colombia concluded its first ISDS treaties in the mid-2000s, led by a trade deal with the United States in 2006. In the mid-1990s, the country's constitutional court had declared the treaties unconstitutional due to their interference with public purpose regulation and the inequality they created between citizens and foreign investors: Decisions C-358/1996; C-379/1996; C-008/1997; and C-494/1998 (Colombian Constitutional Court): Schneiderman (n 110) 177–79. The Colombian government then intervened to safeguard its ISDS treaty policy by amending the constitution: MA Velásquez Ruiz, 'The Colliding Vernaculars of Foreign Investment Protection and Transitional Justice in Colombia: A Challenge for the Law in a Global Context' (PhD thesis, Osgoode Hall Law School of York University, 2016) 61–85. In a more recent decision, the constitutional court has added conditions to its determination that Colombia's ISDS treaty with France is constitutional: G Prieto, 'The Colombian Constitutional Court Judgment C-252/19: A New Frontier for Reform in International Investment Law' (*EJIL Talk! Blog*, 29 July 2019). <https://www.ejiltalk.org/the-colombian-constitutional-court-judgment-c-252-19-a-new-frontier-for-reform-in-international-investment-law/> accessed 14 January 2020.

[182] Conpes (n 180) 4.

of ISDS by other trade ministries,[183] the plan neatly avoids discussing the risk of ISDS claims against general laws and regulation[184] and relies on the pretence that the 'rules' of foreign investor protection are clear and that arbitrator power is predictable. According to the plan, the government should facilitate 'the best use' of the treaties by trying 'to reduce the risks of non-compliance with the international obligations'.[185] It warns that '[t]he country is not prepared to prevent and solve' controversies that may arise and that its 'actual institutional scheme is not able to prevent and attend effectively to this type of controversy'.[186] There is a sense of alarm that 'the novelty and complexity' of the treaties 'makes urgent the implementation of the required adjustments' to the governing apparatus, that this risk is exacerbated by a 'lack of knowledge of officials at all levels', that 'it is probable that the state's defence [to ISDS attacks] will be ineffective', and that there will be inadequate resources 'to bear the costs of the process and the possible condemnations' by arbitrators.[187] The plan then warns that ISDS disputes 'can affect the international image and credibility of the state' and might end up discouraging foreign investment, which would achieve 'the opposite effect to that pursued' by signing the treaties.[188] In other words, by a curious logic, Colombia ill-advisedly exposed itself to ISDS risk in the treaties and now must appease investors in order to avoid that risk. Fundamentally, the plan does not question the treaties. It is more an oath of fealty to them.

The Colombian plan institutionalizes foreign investor protections at the national level by directing them into a 'high-level agency' process, where the trade ministry plays the lead role and the targeted regulators are required to answer for any ISDS risks they unwittingly created.[189] The trade ministry's Directorate of Foreign Investment and Services—which negotiated the treaties, and later hired Gómez-Pinzón Zuleta, the private ISDS law firm, to help manage the Sanitas case—is named to lead 'all matters related to promotion' of foreign investment, identify 'obstacles' to investment, and act as the 'facilitator of friendly settlements

[183] For instance, a Canadian federal policy document, in the course of describing how proposed regulations should be vetted for compliance with international trade obligations, struggles to explain the meaning of 'indirect' expropriation in NAFTA and resorts to a statement of the federal government's view of its meaning, without mentioning the more expansive interpretations of ISDS tribunals. The bugbear standards of 'fair and equitable treatment' and 'full protection and security' are not mentioned at all in the Canadian or the Colombian document. Treasury Board of Canada Secretariat, *Guidelines on International Regulatory Obligations and Cooperation* (Treasury Board of Canada 2007) 9; Conpes (n 180).

[184] Conpes (n 180) 4.

[185] ibid 4. The document also notes (at 9) in passing, and without flagging the point, the absurdity that 'a measure adopted by a municipal public company can lead to a condemnation that the state is required to pay [compensation], independent of the capacity of the company to respond to its commitments'.

[186] ibid 13.

[187] ibid 13.

[188] ibid 15.

[189] ibid 24–25.

of differences' arising from the treaties.[190] Long-term 'decisions on the strategy for prevention and defence' in ISDS 'will be centralized' and all officials 'who may affect the obligations' of Colombia under the treaties 'shall understand the consequences of their actions'.[191] The trade ministry thus wields the ISDS whip internally[192] and its crack is meant to be heard all down the line.

Ultimately, in the 2013 law enacting the plan, final authority over the ISDS process was given to the national agency that otherwise represents Colombia in international litigation.[193] Beyond that concession, the trade ministry maintained its dominance of all aspects of the country's new structure for ISDS-induced chill. The trade ministry defends ISDS claims and its Directorate of Foreign Investment serves as the technical secretariat for the national agency. The Directorate has the power to set the agenda for the high-level meetings, to 'receive information from investors and other interested parties on foreign investment disputes' that come before the high-level agency process, and to request 'documents and other evidence' from any state entity that is 'possibly involved in an international investment dispute', backed by a power to '[f]ollow up on the commitments' made and agreed within the high-level agency process.[194] The Directorate also has a wider power to '[d]esign, coordinate and execute outreach and training programs' on the treaties for state entities that are 'strategic in the prevention of international investment disputes'.[195] Further, the trade ministry serves as 'the sole spokesperson in relation to the investor who is a party to the controversy' and as the facilitator of 'friendly agreements aimed at solving international investment disputes extrajudicially'.[196] Meanwhile, the 'lower entity whose role generated the presented dispute' in ISDS—in other words, the targeted regulators—'will have a voice but not a vote' in the high-level agency process.[197] For actual ISDS claims, the trade ministry leads the defence and decision making on the state's arguments.[198] It also recommends to the high-level agency process the individuals who Colombia can appoint to the ICSID list of arbitrators.[199]

In this elaborate process for ISDS-induced chill, there is also a subsidiary body—below the high-level agency process—called the 'Inter-institutional

[190] ibid 16. Another body, the Office of International Legal Affairs, represents the state in international disputes with a commercial character.
[191] ibid 21.
[192] The document notes that the trade ministry was given this role, by law, in 2003, suggesting that a plan to internalize chill was in the works at early stages of Colombia's treaty programme and of the ISDS litigation explosion: ibid 15–16.
[193] Colombian Decree No 1939 (9 September 2013) Article 7.
[194] ibid Articles 6(1), 6(5), and 6(8).
[195] ibid Article 6(9).
[196] ibid Article 8.
[197] ibid Article 7(1).
[198] ibid Article 9(4).
[199] ibid Article 9(5).

Support Group' for international investment disputes. Its main role is to make recommendations about ISDS disputes that are taken to the high-level agency process.[200] The Support Group is coordinated by the trade ministry, but may allow attendance by officials of other state entities, 'including the officials of the entity whose action or omission allegedly generated the international investment controversy'.[201] These investor-offending officials are listed in the national plan of 2010 as potentially including a wide range of actors, including other ministers, the executive manager of the central bank, governors, mayors, or legal representatives of decentralized entities.[202] Any of these 'may be invited' to attend the Support Group, presumably to discuss what they did and how it could be changed to limit ISDS risk.[203] If there is 'a discrepancy regarding the development or execution of a strategy for the solution of a controversy', it is to be resolved through consultations among the higher-level agency process, the investor-offending officials, and the trade ministry.[204] The latter is again 'the leading entity responsible for coordinating and guiding aspects related to international disputes', with the authority 'to access all documents relevant to the dispute, in order to ensure a possible negotiation or an effective defence'.[205] In essence, the Support Group appears to be a permanent forum to interrogate and re-educate other decision makers, both proactively and in response to specific ISDS threats.

Beyond the high-level agency process and its Support Group, the national plan also envisions a mass education programme across the Colombian bureaucracy. It will be necessary 'to train . . . public officials who could affect the interests of foreign investors on the state's obligations and on prevention of, and attention to, investment controversies'.[206] The trade ministry will provide such training to spread knowledge of ISDS across government and thus 'reduce the risk of eventual breaches'.[207] Its officials have carried out training sessions at all levels of government 'to explain to state employees and agents what [bilateral investment treaties] or [free trade agreements] are, and what are the obligations acquired by the State' and to '[g]ive conscience to all possible actors involved with an investor that their actions can have a vast impact'.[208] In one presentation, the trade ministry informed officials from other agencies that it will use a system of 'Identification,

[200] ibid Article 9.
[201] ibid Article 9.
[202] Conpes (n 180) 25.
[203] ibid 25.
[204] ibid 25.
[205] ibid 26–27.
[206] ibid 23.
[207] ibid 29.
[208] Colombia (Ministry of Commerce, Industry, and Tourism), 'Managing Investment Disputes in Colombia', Power Point presentation (on file with author) (14 March 2012). The presentation notes that over 400 state employees were registered for the trade ministry's first online workshop.

Tracking and Resolution of barriers to Foreign Investment' to find 'obstacles faced by those who want to invest or have already invested' and to identify 'obstacles that could develop into international investment disputes'.[209] Other agencies were reminded of the importance of '**early alerts about investment obstacles** that could result in International Investment Disputes' [emphasis in original].[210] Government officials would be taught so that 'they may try **to avoid or re-think some actions**' [emphasis in original].[211] In other words, in response to ISDS, the Colombian government was or is being reconfigured, both structurally and ideologically, to implement foreign investor protections at the expense of those whose interests—where embodied in laws, regulations, or other decisions—present 'obstacles' to investors.

I do not wish to pick on Colombia. Other countries have taken a similarly supine approach as they learned the hard way about their vulnerability to ISDS. Egypt reconfigured its processes in 2014; Peru did so in 2006; and Canada did so back in the 1990s, after its federal officials were caught off guard by early NAFTA claims.[212] The UN Conference on Trade and Development, with its sordid history of promoting the treaties, later pushed for ISDS-induced chill by providing advice to developing countries on how to reform their institutions to prevent ISDS disputes.[213] Chill is the next logical step after officials have been beguiled by promises of investment, educated by ISDS threats and claims, and frightened by the costs. Colombia's response is eminently sensible, if one accepts that the institutions representing everyone should be constrained by foreign investor protections. If one rejects this assumption, however, the reconfiguration of the state's governing apparatus reveals both the power of ISDS and the harmful impact of chill as predictable outcomes of special protections for the ultra-wealthy. Colombia's approach is thorough and dedicated and, as such, it shows how ISDS can cause sovereigns to genuflect to foreign investors.

[209] ibid.

[210] ibid.

[211] ibid.

[212] *For Egypt*: OECD, *Report—Investment Dispute Management and Prevention* (Cairo, 26–27 June 2018) 28 (strikingly identifying an Egyptian official, M El Behebity, as the deputy minister of justice for arbitration and international dispute, the head of a technical secretariat for the high committee for international arbitration and the ministerial committee for settlement of investment contract disputes and as also being an arbitrator at the ICC 'Court' of International Arbitration and a practising ISDS arbitrator and lawyer); 'Investment Disputes Committee Settles 27 Disputes' *Egypt Today* (3 January 2018); S Kebeich and N Abouelseoud, 'State–Investor Dispute Resolution Mechanisms under the Egyptian Investment Law' *Lexocology.com* (23 September 2018); *For Peru*: R Ampuero Llerena, 'Peru's State Coordination and Response System for International Investment Disputes' *Investment Treaty News* (14 January 2013); *For Canada*: Van Harten and Scott, 'Investment Treaties: A Case Study' (n 21); Van Harten and Scott, 'Investment Treaties: Further Findings' (n 15).

[213] In the late 1990s and early 2000s, UNCTAD's push for ISDS treaties went to the point of organized treaty-signing gatherings by negotiators from numerous countries in a Geneva hotel; LNS Poulsen, *Bounded Rationality and Economic Diplomacy: The Politics of Investment Treaties in Developing Countries* (CUP 2015) 92–99.

Advertisements and celebrations of chill

ISDS lawyers sometimes make claims about their ISDS wins for wealthy clients. This indicator of regulatory chill has its limits, since a self-promoting lawyer may embellish things, but it also seems unlikely that so many lawyers would misinform clients about how ISDS can help them. Also, since ISDS lawyers also often promote ISDS by denying chill, their celebrative claims about ISDS are all the more revealing.

There are many examples of this advertising for chill. Lawyers with the firm Steptoe and Johnson stated in 2015 that ISDS treaty protections 'may be a highly important tool for foreign investors and industry associations in advocating against legislative changes to renewable energy regulations' and that it may be possible 'to use such protections as a tool to assist lobbying efforts'.[214] The gigantic firm Freshfields noted on its website in 2016 that 'to be effective [ISDS treaty] claims need not result in years of arbitration' but instead 'can be used as leverage to compel the host state to enter into a favourable negotiated settlement'.[215] Lawyers with the firm Norton Rose Fulbright stated in 2017 that, when a country faces the possibility of a public award against it, '[t]he risk to the host state's reputation as a recipient of foreign investment may give an investor negotiating leverage'.[216] In a webinar in 2014, a lawyer from Freshfields asked rhetorically if the threat of ISDS has 'any real teeth' and answered that 75 per cent of ISDS settlements happen before a hearing on the merits, that many come 'right after the commencement of the arbitration', and that ICSID cases lead to 'more negotiating leverage' because they are 'publicly known'.[217] Several lawyers with the mega-firm Dentons stated in 2013 that, in considering whether to bring an ISDS claim, investors 'should bear in mind that around 30 to 40 per cent of investment disputes typically settle before a final award is issued' and that bringing a claim 'can create leverage to help the investor reach a satisfactory result'.[218] A lawyer from K&L Gates stated in 2013 that the treaties could be used by investors in the green energy sector 'as a tool of pressure against further governmental action' or 'as an exit strategy' and that, '[e]ffectively,

[214] M Coleman and others, 'Foreign Investors' Options to Deal with Regulatory Changes in the Renewable Energy Sector' (*Steptoe & Johnson Investor-State Arbitration Series*, 23 September 2014) <https://www.steptoe.com/en/news-publications/foreign-investors-options-to-deal-with-regulatory-changes-in-the-renewable-energy-sector-1.html> accessed 11 August 2019.

[215] This statement appears to have been removed from the Freshfields website and did not turn up in extensive online searches; I rely on contemporary notes taken by a research assistant for the quotation.

[216] Norton Rose Fulbright, 'Investor State Dispute Settlement in the Banking and Finance Sector' (November 2017) 10 Bank Finan Disp Rev 18.

[217] This statement also appears to have been removed from the Freshfields website and did not turn up in extensive online searches; I rely again on contemporary notes taken by a research assistant for the quotation.

[218] L Tout, M Bradfield, and L De Silva, 'The Latest Renewables Claim: Abengoa's Subsidiary Launches Investment Treaty Proceedings against Spain' (*Lexology.com* 29 November 2013).

the treaties have already been used in each of these ways by certain investors'.[219] In an industry magazine in 2012, lawyers from Milbank Tweed Hadley and McCloy (now Milbank LLP) stated that ISDS is useful 'as an ultimate option for achieving redress', but also 'by shifting the dynamics in negotiations between foreign investors and sovereigns if problems arise'.[220] The lawyers flagged that democratic countries could also be pressurized ('Adverse government actions do not have to take place only with autocratic rule. The populism that democracy can bring often is the catalyst for such actions'),[221] and pointed to 'regulations or taxes' as potential ISDS targets, noting that it may be unnecessary to file an actual claim, since the investor 'may decide to seek solely to renegotiate a new agreement with the host state, but against the backdrop of possible international legal proceedings'.[222] These examples show how many lawyers expect ISDS to achieve chill for their wealthy clients.

Sometimes the lawyers' claims are more specific. For instance, lawyers at Allen & Overy wrote in or around 2015 that a proposed Polish law on foreign exchange loans 'was ultimately abandoned after fierce resistance from major financial institutions, including warnings that they would seek protection in international investment arbitration'.[223] The lawyers said that '[f]oreign stockholders in other banks reminded [Poland's] Parliament that they are protected by international investment treaties' and that 'one major corporation ... declared that it intended to demand full compensation for the damage caused by the new legislation' and 'asked Poland to treat its letter as notice of a dispute under the relevant BITs'.[224] Facing this 'extraordinary external pressure', the upper house of the Parliament returned the proposed law to the lower house, where the majority party abandoned it.[225] A lawyer at Allen & Overy similarly stated in 2012 that ISDS treaty claims 'have been used to good effect when it comes to keeping pressure on States for the purposes of settlement'.[226] The lawyer pointed to the *Telefonica v Argentina* case, where the Spanish telecommunications multinational stayed an ISDS claim in 2006 after the Argentine government 'allowed certain tariffs to be increased and

[219] W Sadowski, 'International Investment Treaties as a Possible Shield against Government Cutbacks in Subsidies for the Green Energy Sector', *K&L Gates International Arbitration Alert* (10 January 2013).

[220] M Nolan and T Baldwin, 'Minimising Risk in the Face of Government Action' *Project Finance International* (16 May 2012) 49.

[221] ibid 47.

[222] ibid 48.

[223] Allen & Overy, 'Polish Banks Face Huge Losses under Proposed FX Loan Legislation' (*European Finance Litigation Review*, undated) <http://www.allenovery.com/publications/en-gb/european-finance-litigation-review/central-europe/Pages/Polish-banks-face-huge-losses-under-proposed-FX-loan-legislation.aspx> accessed 11 August 2019.

[224] ibid.

[225] ibid.

[226] A Welsh, 'The Strategic Importance of Investment Treaty Protections for Telecoms Operators' (*Allen & Overy*, 2012) <http://www.allenovery.com/SiteCollectionDocuments/Investment%20treaty%20protection.PDF> accessed 11 August 2019. Note that, as of 28 May 2020, this document appears subsequently to have been removed from the Allen & Overy website.

peak hours extended', and then withdrew the claim in 2009, 'when it reached a satisfactory settlement agreement with the Government'.[227] Assuming that the abandoned measures in these examples would have benefited others in the financial or telecommunications sector, the lawyers were celebrating regulatory chill.

Some lawyers made particularly dubious recommendations about how ISDS can be used to intensify pressure on a country. Lawyers with the firm Skadden Arps Slate Meagher & Flom stated in 2007, with respect to ISDS under the ECT, that '[i]f the investor's objective is to apply maximum pressure' then 'the prospect of multiple proceedings may contribute to that aim'.[228] Where an ISDS claim is legally possible under the ECT and another treaty, they said, the investor could 'start proceedings under both treaties and seek to have them heard by the same tribunal'.[229] The investor could also 'have the treaty claims heard by separate tribunals', which 'may add pressure to reach a settlement', since it 'may increase the chances of an adverse finding against the host state' and 'increase both sides' costs'.[230] Such candid advice reinforces how ISDS lawyers often characterize chill as a benefit for their clients, in spite of the expense or harm to others.

Conclusion

ISDS treaties provide powerful protections for foreign investors, who have used them to win major concessions from countries. A chemical company used ISDS to pollute in Canada. A health multinational received special treatment in the regulatory process in Colombia. An energy company won more lenient approvals for water releases and carbon emissions in Germany. Mining companies intimidated Indonesia into letting them continue to devastate one of the last great rainforests. In Romania, a mining company has kept hope alive for a ruinous open-pit mine. Tobacco firms stalled anti-tobacco laws aimed at reducing smoking and saving lives. Cumulatively, these concessions came at significant cost to millions of people.

By its design, ISDS anticipates these outcomes. The treaties create forums, processes, and remedies exclusively for foreign investors. They intensify incentives for governments to appease investors, requiring governments to choose between the interests of those protected by a policy and those who will pay for the state's costs in ISDS. Predictably, governments have responded by institutionalizing chill rather than simply waiting for actual claims. This step elevates foreign investor interests within the state, at yet more cost to the public. The reconfiguration of the governing apparatus creates immeasurable potential losses for those who do not own wealth

[227] ibid 5.

[228] D Herlihy and B Macaulay, 'Strategic Choices under the ECT' (2007) 2(2) Global Arbitration Review 26, 28.

[229] ibid 28.

[230] ibid 28.

abroad, as it privileges the ultra-wealthy within the institutions meant to represent and protect all.

The pressing question about regulatory chill at this stage is no longer whether it happens due to ISDS, as many ISDS promoters seek to debate.[231] The questions now are how often it happens, why sometimes and not others, how it impacts others, and how its negative impacts can be checked. Answering these questions comprehensively would be a major research undertaking to document chill in different countries, assess the backstory for thwarted proposals, and track the larger consequence of ISDS-induced change. Even so, it is reasonable to expect—based on the design of ISDS treaties, the evidence to date, and the surrounding confidentiality—that chill happens in all countries that are exposed to ISDS claims by wealthy investors and that have at least some institutional capacity to identify and manage ISDS risks.

[231] Those who deny regulatory chill typically do so by using an overly strict approach to causation, by applying an unrealistic evidentiary threshold, by declaring a lack of evidence of chill without having looked for it and without mentioning the evidence found by others, by clouding the picture with complex normative debates, or by actively hiding evidence of chill.

7
Fault Lines and the Future of ISDS

Foreign investor protections have been made into an exceptionally powerful component of international law that constrains governments to insulate the wealthy from sovereign choices designed to protect others. In turn, they disadvantage those whose life and future are rooted in one place. No one besides owners of high-value cross-border assets has a realistic prospect of using the protections, yet most people (as voters, taxpayers, or property owners) must assume the risks and the costs. Removing these protections from international law is a feasible, important, and perhaps necessary step to stem the concentration of wealth and reinvigorate state institutions that are needed to confront pressing concerns of humanity.

Foreign investor protections are embedded in hundreds of treaties, all hinging on investor–state dispute settlement (ISDS). The treaties were invented in the 1960s by officials of former colonial powers, and of the World Bank, for the purpose of disciplining and constraining newly independent countries. They put into law a stance of hostility towards self-determination where it was at odds with the post-colonialist assets of Western multinationals. Many of the early treaties were signed between a former colonial power and an authoritarian government that came to power violently. The attraction for most capital-importing countries, then as now, was that the treaties would bring foreign investment. In the 1990s, as the Soviet Union collapsed and Latin America was weakened by debt crises, most countries joined in the signing of hundreds of new treaties.

Around this time, specialized arbitration lawyers began activating ISDS. As counsel, they brought novel claims based on ambitious arguments. As arbitrators, they decided the claims adventurously. Over the course of the 1990s, the arbitrators handed a string of victories to investors, every one of which was premised on claimant-friendly, expansive interpretations. The investors' victories flowed from the legal innovation of the asymmetrical sovereign consent and from extending the concept of 'investment' beyond directly owned physical assets. Arbitrators allowed investors to bring claims using holding companies (including shell companies formed for the purposes of nationality shopping) or as partial owners of a local company. They allowed them to avoid national courts, even after the investor or a related company had agreed by contract to use them. Vague treaty assurances of 'fair and equitable treatment', compensation for 'indirect' expropriation, and 'most-favoured-nation' (MFN) treatment were read liberally to establish the arbitrators' power to order public compensation for asset owners. By 2000, the legal ground was set for a rapid expansion of claims.

Yet, as of 2000, ISDS was still only on the radar of a tiny group of lawyers and other specialists. There were just ten known treaty claims, compared to about 1,000 today.[1] By 2018, a beleaguered state-side lawyer would lament that 'virtually all new developments in this field go in the direction of expanding investor protection beyond anything imagined by the state that created the system'.[2] Tribunals have ordered billions for claimants, most of it benefiting huge companies and ultra-wealthy individuals. By a conservative estimate, the ISDS boom has also generated USD 7.8 billion in fees for ISDS lawyers and arbitrators up to 2019.[3] Repeat players in the ISDS industry dominate decision making, often after being appointed by the arbitration houses that recommend or appoint arbitrators by default in individual cases.[4] Repeat players have represented investors and governments, they have served as paid experts, they have recommended each other for appointment, they have worked in the arbitration houses or government trade ministries, they have written and cited texts on how to interpret the treaties, and they have advised governments on how to draft them. The ISDS industry, corporate lobbies, and trade officials still push for the last great expansion of ISDS, which would extend it widely among developed countries.[5] If they succeed, the protections will cover virtually all foreign-owned assets in the world and, by the same token, nearly all countries will have made themselves semi-independent in their relations with the wealthiest investors who benefit the most from ISDS.

The treaties offer an array of protections for the wealthy. Some of them are stated clearly in the treaties; many others have emerged from the arbitrators' creativity. All are backed by internationally enforceable orders against countries. Indeed, the treaties give investors access to the most powerful form of international

[1] UN Conference on Trade and Development (UNCTAD) Investment Dispute Settlement Navigator: <https://investmentpolicy.unctad.org/investment-dispute-settlement> accessed 9 November 2019 (reporting 983 treaty-based ISDS cases as of 31 July 2019).

[2] G Kahale III, 'ISDS: The Wild, Wild West of International Law and Arbitration', Brooklyn Lecture on International Business Law, Brooklyn Law School (3 April 2018) 9–10.

[3] The estimate is conservative because it does not include fees generated from unknown cases or from legal work that did not lead to an actual claim. The estimate comes from multiplying the 983 known treaty-based ISDS cases (n 1) by an Organisation for Economic Co-operation and Development (OECD) researchers' estimate of USD 8 million in average fees per case (derived from 143 available ISDS awards, of which 28 gave information on legal and arbitration costs, 81 gave some such information, and 62 gave no such information): D Gaukrodger and K Gordon, 'Investor-State Dispute Settlement: A Scoping Paper for the Investment Policy Community', Organisation for Economic Co-operation and Development Working Paper on International Investment 2012/03 (OECD 2013) 19.

[4] JA Fontoura Costa, 'Comparing WTO Panelists and ICSID Arbitrators: The Creation of International Legal Fields' (2011) 1 *Oñati Socio-Legal Series* 1, 14; J Pauwelyn, 'The Rule of Law without the Rule of Lawyers? Why Investment Arbitrators are from Mars, Trade Adjudicators are from Venus' (2015) 109 AJIL 761, 781–82; P Eberhardt and C Olivet, *Profiting from Injustice* (CEO and Transnational Institute 2012) 38; S Puig, 'Social Capital in the Arbitration Market' (2014) 25 EJIL 387, 415; M Langford, D Behn, and R Hilleren Lie, 'The Revolving Door in International Investment Arbitration' (2017) 20 JIEL 301, Table 6.

[5] G Van Harten, 'The European Commission's Push to Consolidate and Expand ISDS: An Assessment of the Proposed Canada–Europe CETA and Europe–Singapore FTA', Osgoode Legal Studies Research Paper Series 105 (2015); L Johnson, L Sachs, and J Sachs, 'Investor–State Dispute Settlement, Public Interest and US Domestic Law', Columbia Center on Sustainable Development Policy Paper (2015).

adjudication for any private party when challenging a sovereign. Further, investors can bring their claims in the absence of others who have conflicting interests, and the claims are decided by untenured adjudicators who depend on more claims for future business. The process is managed by arbitration houses whose work would also largely disappear if the claims did. The treaties thus harness competition among professionals to consolidate privileges for the rich.

Many pro-ISDS arguments seem like a product of deceptive public relations. Perhaps the strongest argument is the longstanding claim that the treaties will bring new investment to a country. Even if one accepts this claim as proven, the concessions by countries in ISDS treaties far outweigh the benefits. The treaties fortify inequality, they pit states against each other in the appeasing of investors, and they hamper sovereign action to respond to urgent social and environmental priorities. They do these things in a skewed and unfair way, at the direct expense of most of the world population. Beyond the cost of awards and litigation, ISDS deters governments from protecting any other constituency where doing so requires opposition to powerful investors. As a result of ISDS-induced chill, Canadians have been exposed to polluted air; Indonesians have had their communities ruined; Europeans have lost marine habitat and biodiversity; New Zealanders have been lured into tobacco addiction; Romanians have feared for their homes, cemeteries, and churches threatened by mining; and everyone in the world has been exposed to a higher risk of climate disruption. These consequences emerge from just a small number of ISDS cases, where established wealth has been protected at the expense of populations. ISDS lawyers celebrate how they can help their clients intimidate countries, as governments reconfigure their institutional processes to prioritize investors. The power of ISDS for the wealthy comes at a steep price for hundreds of millions of others.

Perhaps the most glaring demonstration of the severity of this price is climate disruption. The UN Intergovernmental Panel on Climate Change (IPCC) warns that global emissions of carbon dioxide need to fall by about 45 per cent from 2010 levels by 2030, reaching 'net zero' by about 2050, to avoid exceeding 1.5 °C in global warming.[6] On the current emissions trajectory, climate scientists Xu and Ramanathan peg the risk of 'dangerous' climate change at 50 per cent by 2050 and the risks of 'catastrophic' climate change at 50 per cent and 'beyond catastrophic' climate change at 5 per cent by 2100.[7] Here, 'catastrophic' entails widespread societal collapse and 'beyond catastrophic' is an existential threat to most of humanity.[8] From an 'investment' perspective, the fossil fuel industry owns USD tens of trillions in oil and gas deposits, much of which must stay in the ground as long-ago

[6] Intergovernmental Panel on Climate Change, *Summary for Policymakers of IPCC Special Report on Global Warming of 1.5 °C Approved by Governments* (IPCC 2018) 14.

[7] Y Xu and V Ramanathan, 'Well below 2 °C: Mitigation Strategies for Avoiding Dangerous to Catastrophic Climate Changes' (2017) 114 (39) Proc Nat'l Acad Sci 10315.

[8] ibid 5.

sequestered carbon.[9] Like Big Tobacco, fossil fuel companies and billionaires use deceptive tactics to defend their public subsidies and maintain profits.[10] In this context, governments face immense political obstacles to making the required changes to protect human society. The uncertainty, unfairness, and cost of foreign investor protections makes these changes even harder to achieve. By limiting government capacity to employ the policy levers recommended by scientists to protect us from vast climate-related damage, ISDS hampers states from acting in the face of a global emergency.[11]

Globalization has transformed society in many positive ways, but the mere fact of it does not justify allowing the ultra-wealthy to sidestep the institutions that otherwise govern all. It is not a reason to empower a multinational to sue a country outside of any court and to avoid responsibilities implicit in the ownership and conduct of business. In effect, ISDS gives the wealthy an enclave status, premised on their power to sue sovereigns in a skewed process and on protections that could never be funded for all. Globalization should not require this sacrificing of the interests of so many others to protect foreign investors.

A saving grace of the treaties might be that well-intentioned lawyers, especially when working as arbitrators, could take steps to lessen the imbalances in ISDS. They could moderate the treaties' pro-investor design and show restraint when reviewing legislatures and governments, even though doing so may undermine the ISDS industry. No doubt some are trying, but it seems most are unable or unwilling. The edifice is rotten and will not be fixed by a rounding of edges. A tribunal can give amicus status to an affected group, but it cannot remove the unfairness of denying one's right to be heard when one's interests are directly attacked in ISDS proceedings. Widespread and reasonable perceptions of bias in ISDS cannot be repaired by an arbitrator's reputation or a tribunal's careful wording. The omission of actionable responsibilities for foreign investors undermines the whole premise of protecting the vulnerable from abuse. ISDS should be rebuilt not renovated.

[9] McGlade and Ekins estimate that, globally, one-third of oil reserves, one-half of gas reserves, and over 80 per cent of current coal reserves 'should remain unused from 2010 to 2050 in order to meet the target of 2 °C in global warming': C McGlade and P Ekins, 'The Geographical Distribution of Fossil Fuel Unused when Limiting Global Warming to 2 °C' (2015) 517 *Nature* 187. B Tucker and A Doukas, 'Gas and the European Investment Bank: Why New Gas Infrastructure Investment is Incompatible with Climate Goals', Oil Change International Report (2019).

[10] T Zeltner and others, *Tobacco Company Strategies to Undermine Tobacco Control Activities at the World Health Organization*, Report of the Committee of Experts on Tobacco Industry Documents (WHO 2000) 18; D Michaels, *Doubt is their Product: How Industry's Assault on Science Threatens Your Health* (OUP 2008).

[11] The recommended levers, all needing to be deployed to avoid unacceptable risks of climate disruption, are (i) shift to a carbon-neutral economy by 2030; (ii) phase-out four super-pollutant greenhouse gases such as methane and black carbon by 2020; and (the most uncertain) (iii) development and scale-up of carbon extraction and sequestration technologies over the next several decades: Xu and Ramanathan (n 7). Lever (i) poses an existential threat to investments in the fossil fuel industry for the purpose of avoiding the existential threat to humanity from that 'investment'.

Since the 1990s, most countries have ill-advisedly subjected themselves to the constraints of ISDS. The treaties are often locked in for a decade or more.[12] To free sovereigns in the short term requires countries to agree to amend or terminate their treaties. The treaties bind countries only because governments, especially powerful ones, have prioritized the protection of investors over others whose position is more distant and diffuse in domestic politics (that is, until a foreign investor proposes an open-pit mine near one's community).

For most countries, whose people and companies do not own much abroad, any 'offensive' benefits of the treaties do not help them in a meaningful way. Meanwhile, the 'defensive' risks and costs become more and more severe. Why then do so many governments maintain ISDS? The reasons will no doubt vary but, beyond lack of knowledge and capacity, it seems fair to assume an important factor is the influence of multinationals and tycoons, both inside and outside government.[13] Bolstering this factor, many well-connected lawyers and arbitrators have staked their careers in ISDS and they often promote it avidly; in my experience, many seem actually to believe that whatever is good for ISDS is good for all. A more aware public could pressure governments to fix ISDS while still ensuring adequate protection for all from the dangers of uncompensated expropriation, evident discrimination, denials of justice, and obvious abuse by the state or a multinational. Yet it seems that most people in most countries are not at this stage, partly because ISDS is so complex and opaque.

In Europe, public pressure led governments and the European Union (EU), especially the EU Parliament, to pursue a genuine reform of ISDS.[14] The EU responded by modestly limiting the protections, affirming (somewhat vaguely) the state's right to regulate, and partially blocking nationality shopping, all of which seem likely to make some difference for key flaws in ISDS. Most importantly, the EU has sought to replace ISDS with an 'Investment Court System' (ICS) in its new economic agreements with Canada, Singapore, and Vietnam (for the latter two, in stand-alone bilateral investment treaties).[15] The ICS would have a higher

[12] I discuss the exceptionally long lock-in periods in ISDS treaties, often ranging from ten to twenty years (compared to six months to a year in other treaties), in G Van Harten, *Sold Down the Yangtze: Canada's Lopsided Investment Deal with China* (Lorimer 2015) ch 43.

[13] F Wettstein, *Multinational Corporations and Global Justice: Human Rights Obligations of a Quasi-Governmental Institution* (Stanford University Press 2009) ch 6; J Mayer, *Dark Money: The Hidden History of the Billionaires behind the Rise of the Radical Right* (Anchor Books 2016).

[14] I say 'genuine' to distinguish from largely fake reforms, such as those introduced earlier in the EU's Transatlantic Trade and Investment Partnership (TTIP) negotiating process, previously by North American governments, and recently in so-called progressive agreements such as the revamped Trans-Pacific Partnership: G Van Harten, 'A Parade of Reforms: The European Commission's Latest Proposal for ISDS', Osgoode Legal Studies Research Paper No 102 (2015).

[15] Comprehensive Economic and Trade Agreement between Canada and the European Union (CETA), signed 30 October 2016 (not fully in force), ch 8; EU–Singapore investment treaty, signed 15 October 2018; EU–Vietnam investment treaty, signed 30 June 2019. These agreements are available from UNCTAD International Investment Agreements Navigator: <https://investmentpolicy.unctad.org/international-investment-agreements> accessed 14 January 2020.

level of openness than ISDS and it would replace the for-profit arbitrators with roster-based adjudicators who are supported by more secure tenure, by an objective means of case assignment, and by further safeguards against conflicts of interest (although they will still depend on investor claims for some of their case-by-case remuneration).[16] The ICS also adds a quasi-judicial appellate body which, depending on who is appointed to it, could rein in the arbitrators' wildest interpretations.[17] The EU is likewise pushing for a multilateral investment court to replace ISDS in existing treaties.[18] This proposal is under discussion at the UN commission on international trade law (UNCITRAL), where a powerful group of countries—apparently led by Japan, Russia, and the United States—oppose the EU's proposed reforms to ISDS and where a weaker group of developing or transition countries, in contrast, see the EU's changes as insufficient.[19] In the EU debate, public pressure had a significant and meaningful impact on ISDS reform, informed and focused as it was by politicians, journalists, activists, and academics.

Linked to the EU politics of ISDS, the European Court of Justice (ECJ) in 2018 gave a red light to ISDS in treaties among EU countries, which could potentially be extended to EU countries' treaties outside the EU.[20] Yet, in 2019, the ECJ also gave a green light to the Investment Court System, and will presumably do the same for a multilateral court emerging from the UNCITRAL discussion.[21] While these ECJ decisions turned on byzantine issues of EU law, taken together they reject old school ISDS as an unacceptable encroachment on the role of the ECJ and other courts and on the principle of mutual trust among countries, while endorsing foreign investor protections via ICS.[22] Impressively, the 2018 judgment and the ICS proposal both overcame vigorous opposition by the ISDS industry, and both led to a great rending of hair among ISDS promoters.[23] The 2018 judgment also stands

[16] The clearest example of the ICS is in CETA (n 15) Articles 8.27, 8.30, and 8.36.

[17] ibid Articles 8.28.

[18] European Commission, 'The Multilateral Investment Court Project' (*European Commission News archive*, 21 December 2016, latest update 7 June 2019) <http://trade.ec.europa.eu/doclib/press/index.cfm?id=1608> accessed 14 January 2020; C Malmström, 'A Multilateral Investment Court: A Contribution to the Conversation about Reform of Investment Dispute Settlement', Speech by European Commissioner for Trade (Brussels, 22 November 2018).

[19] L Johnson, 'What Happened at UNCITRAL's April WG III Session? What Will Happen Next?' (*Columbia Center on Sustainable Development Blog*, 3 May 2019) <http://ccsi.columbia.edu/2019/05/03/what-happened-at-uncitral-april-1-5-what-will-happen-next/> accessed 14 January 2020; J Kelsey, Notes of UNCITRAL WG III session (April 2019) (on file with author).

[20] Case C-284/16, *Slovak Republic v Achmea BV* (6 March 2018) (European Court of Justice).

[21] Opinion 1/17 of the Court (Full Court) (30 April 2019) (European Court of Justice).

[22] See especially ECJ, Case-284/16 (n 20) [55]–[58].

[23] P Nikitin, 'The CJEU's Achmea Judgment: Getting Through the Five Stages of Grief' (*Kluwer Arbitration Blog*, 10 April 2018) <http://arbitrationblog.kluwerarbitration.com/2018/04/10/cjeus-achmea-judgment-getting-five-stages-grief/> accessed 14 January 2020. I witnessed some of the rending after presenting at the International Bar Association (IBA)'s annual conference in Washington, DC, in September 2016. I was invited to present at a session on the TTIP by members of the IBA European Law group, but I was able to attend sessions organized by the IBA Arbitration group and was struck by how the lawyers and arbitrators raged against even modest ISDS reforms like the ICS. At the session where I presented to a group of about thirty lawyers, one ISDS arbitrator stood up at the end to say, quite angrily, that he was shocked the panel did not have an ISDS lawyer to counter my criticisms

out, compared to high-level court decisions in North America, for example, as delivering a serious judicial study and critical scrutiny of ISDS.[24]

Nonetheless, the EU reforms leave the worst parts of ISDS intact by maintaining special privileges for the wealthy. Foreign investors will still enjoy vague protections that can be interpreted expansively by tribunals, especially if influenced by the tainted corpus of existing ISDS jurisprudence.[25] Foreign investors will also continue to avoid correspondingly actionable responsibilities, and appear very far from ever having to assume them, despite their powerful and exclusive protections.[26] The EU reforms do not include a clear right of standing for other affected parties, they do not reinstitute the customary duty of foreign investors to use national courts where reasonably available, and they do not oblige foreign investors to honour their contractual commitments to use the courts.[27] They retain retrospective compensation as the main remedy, and seem designed to worsen regulatory chill by directing adjudicators—when awarding compensation—to consider whether the rebuked country has withdrawn whatever decision the investor has attacked. The EU approach also promises to expand the reach of the protections by embedding them in new agreements, and it may well intensify them if ISDS hawks are appointed to the ICS roster or a multilateral court.[28] Notably, this key appointment power appears set to be given to national and EU trade ministries that have cultivated ISDS for decades.[29]

As for the idea of a multilateral investment court reform and the reform discussions at UNCITRAL, it is hard to say where they will go, but the background signals are not promising. For example, at the outset, a former ISDS lawyer and arbitrator (and former UNCTAD official), Anna Joubin-Bret, was appointed to lead the UNCITRAL department that is managing the discussions.[30] While at UNCTAD, Joubin-Bret was reportedly 'the lead organiser of UNCTAD's infamous mass signing parties where developing countries were lured into a room full of

and then wrongly said that ISDS arbitrators are required to dismiss claims if the state measure is not discriminatory or arbitrary or if there is an adequate remedy in domestic law. Partway through my reply to his question, I noticed he had already left the room!

[24] See eg *BG Grp, Plc v Republic of Argentina*, 134 S Ct 1198 (2014) (US); *Council of Canadians v Canada (Attorney General)*, 2006 CanLII 40222 (Court of Appeal for Ontario); *Hupacasath First Nation v Canada* (Attorney General), 2015 CanLII 4 (Federal Court of Appeal).

[25] G Van Harten, 'Investment Treaty Arbitration, Procedural Fairness, and the Rule of Law' in S Schill (ed), *International Investment Law and Comparative Public Law* (OUP 2010) 656–57.

[26] G Van Harten, 'ISDS in the Revised CETA: Positive Steps, But Is It a "Gold Standard"?', Centre for International Governance Innovation Commentary Series No 6 (20 May 2016).

[27] ibid; Council of the European Union, 'Negotiating Directives for a Convention Establishing a Multilateral Court for the Settlement of Investment Disputes' (20 March 2018).

[28] Kahale III (n 2) 19.

[29] CETA (n 15) Articles 8.27 and 26.1(1).

[30] International Arbitration Institute, 'Anna Joubin-Bret' (*International Arbitration Institute*, undated) <http://www.iaiparis.com/profile/anna.joubin-bret> accessed 14 January 2020; 'Bionote—Anna Joubin-Bret' (undated) <https://msal.ru/upload/medialibrary/ff5/Biograficheskaya_spravka.pdf> accessed 14 January 2020.

negotiators, leaving as signatories to dozens of investment treaties'.[31] Similarly, an 'academic' forum created alongside the government discussions was initially led by two members of the ISDS industry, including ISDS hawk Gabrielle Kaufmann-Kohler.[32] Work on ISDS reform by academics outside of the forum, including the present author, was not given equivalent access to the official UNCITRAL discussions.[33] In terms of the discussions themselves, the EU's reform proposals, despite their modesty, are opposed by other major governments,[34] and the arguments of developing countries for more ambitious reforms appear to have had little impact.[35] The situation is not hopeless, but at present it seems likely to maintain the deep favourtism toward the ultra-wealthy in ISDS treaties and unlikely to deliver much beyond a wider and stronger ICS.

I stress that the EU reforms are an important step forward, emerging from dedicated political efforts of many organizations and individuals, and ultimately from the courage and commitment of some governments to reject ISDS. One should celebrate this achievement while acknowledging its limitations. It has come in the face of strong opposition from many members of the ISDS industry who promote ISDS in misleading ways to the public and policy makers. As an academic who has criticized ISDS since completing my PhD on the topic in 2006, one gets accustomed to this ISDS industry lobbying and obfuscation. Many specialized legal 'academics', themselves part of the ISDS industry, have drawn on their scholarly credentials to speak against much-needed reforms.

For example, Christoph Schreuer—whose name has appeared multiple times in this book—is a longstanding academic specialist in the field, who works as an ISDS arbitrator and paid expert in the field. Amidst building momentum against ISDS in 2016, especially in Europe, Schreuer wrote against proposed reforms in a foreword penned for the Yearbook on International Investment Law and Policy.[36] His foreword was less than three pages long, but it packed in a string of sweeping assertions against reform, with scant reasoning and no empirical evidence or references

[31] Eberhardt and Olivet (n 4) 29.

[32] The other was Kaufmann-Kohler's law firm colleague Michele Potestà. Under pressure from some of its members, the forum in late 2018 expanded its list of organizers and steering committee to include various academics alongside the ISDS lawyers: PluriCourts, 'Academic Forum on ISDS' (*University of Oslo Faculty of Law*, 8 May 2019) <https://www.jus.uio.no/pluricourts/english/projects/leginvest/academic-forum/> accessed 14 January 2020.

[33] The European Union has indicated that the forum will be consulted during the government discussions, whereas other academic submissions were not accepted by UNCITRAL for dissemination to government participants and instead posted in an inconspicuous online 'Bibliography of recent writings related to the work of UNCITRAL': Kelsey (n 19); email exchanges between G Van Harten and C Nicholas and J Sung Lee of UNCITRAL (on file with author); UNCITRAL Working Group III, 'Bibliography of Recent Writings related to the Work of UNCITRAL' (*UNCITRAL*, undated) <https://www.zotero.org/groups/282978/bibliography_of_recent_writings_related_to_the_work_of_uncitral/items/collectionKey/CTC8J7YE/order/creator/sort/asc> accessed 14 January 2020.

[34] These include Japan, Russia, and the US: Johnson (n 19); Kelsey (n 19).

[35] Kelsey (n 19).

[36] C Schreuer, 'Foreword' in AK Bjorklund (ed), *Yearbook on International Investment Law and Policy 2014–2015* (OUP 2016) xxix.

to support them. Most significantly, Schreuer condemned the idea of institutional safeguards of independence for ISDS (which obviously are a business risk for arbitrators like Schreuer), claiming that permanent courts and semi-permanent tribunals are 'unlikely to advance either independence or uniformity', that set salaries for judges 'would add costs with no guarantee that appointees will actually serve in a dispute', and that permanent courts will 'inevitably generate international bureaucracies, further adding to costs'.[37] In stating these conclusions, he neglected to discuss the well-documented reasons for such institutional safeguards in courts, such as the doubtfulness that for-profit arbitration ensures as much public confidence in the adjudicator's impartiality, how set salaries could reduce costs if they amounted to less than ISDS arbitrator fees, or how bureaucracies at the arbitration houses have grown immensely in the post-2000 ISDS litigation boom. In his foreword, Schreuer condemned ISDS critics too, especially those with worries about regulatory chill, which he called (without elaborating) '*for the most part* hypothetical' [emphasis added].[38] Schreuer likened ISDS critics to unspecified others who, according to Schreuer, object to '*judicial* scrutiny of state action', '*[j]udicial* control of public administration and regulation', '*judicial* restraint on administrative discretion', and 'international *judicial* control of state action', or who are 'at odds with the acceptance of international human rights *courts*' [emphasis added].[39] This misleading tactic of conflating for-profit ISDS with public and independent courts has been used by other ISDS promoters, such as leading hawk Charles Brower, with the effect of deflecting from the glaring absence of judicial safeguards in ISDS.[40] Along similar lines, Scheuer also criticized the push for an appellate body in ISDS, claiming (again without supporting evidence) that it would contradict 'finality'—meaning unreviewable arbitrator power—and, '[i]nevitably, appeal would lead to a further increase in the cost of proceedings'.[41] In ISDS, though, both the International Centre for Settlement of Investment Disputes (ICSID) annulments and UNCITRAL set-aside proceedings also increase the cost of proceedings, except they do so without judges in the case of ICSID and, in both contexts, with much more leeway for arbitrator error than a typical appeals mechanisms would allow.[42] Schreuer also criticized the prudent idea of allowing states to make joint interpretations of their ISDS treaties, which then bind tribunals. Schreuer noted that such interpretations could affect pending proceedings, which 'gives rise to serious concerns about the fairness of the procedure' and is 'highly problematic'.[43] For this assertion, Schreuer cited a procedural fairness rule against bias (known in the

[37] ibid xxxi.
[38] ibid xxxi.
[39] ibid xxx.
[40] CN Brower and SW Schill, 'Is Arbitration a Threat or a Boon to the Legitimacy of International Investment Law?' (2009) 9 Chi J Int'l L 471.
[41] Schreuer (n 36) xxx.
[42] ibid xxx.
[43] ibid xxx.

common law as *nemo judex in sua causa*) without also mentioning the companion rule (known as *audi alteram partem*). As discussed in Chapter 4, the latter rule is neglected in ISDS itself, as others are denied the right to be heard even when a case affects their interests very profoundly.[44] Schreuer's foreword illustrates how academic credentials can be used to deliver a one-sided and vacuous pitch for ISDS.

By the way, the volume of the Yearbook in which Schreuer's foreword was published was edited by another pro-ISDS academic, Andrea Bjorklund, who holds a chair in international arbitration and international commercial law (at McGill University in Canada) that is named after leading hawk Yves Fortier.[45] The Yearbook's advisory board for the relevant volume included, among its members, leading ISDS hawks Gabrielle Kaufmann-Kohler, Francisco Orrego Vicuña, and Stephen Schwebel, as well as various other repeat players: Ahmed El Kosheri, who was encountered in Chapter 3 of this book; Jan Paulsson, who was encountered in Chapter 6 and will be again in the Appendix; Daniel M Price, who was encountered in Chapter 2; and Schreuer himself, who was encountered in Chapters 3 and 5 as tribunals cited his work to support pro-investor interpretations. Schreuer's foreword thus also indicates how purportedly academic venues can be used as platforms for ISDS promotion and how ISDS reform can be hampered by academics, lawyers, arbitrators, and other experts who have an apparent financial interest in the outcome of the reform debate.

In a surprising twist in 2018, conservative nationalism within the Trump Administration led to more significant reform of ISDS in North America than in Europe.[46] Once finalized, the renegotiated North American Free Trade Agreement (NAFTA) would remove ISDS entirely between the United States and Canada and curtail its reach considerably between the United States and Mexico.[47] In the old NAFTA, ISDS had been tweaked before, in the early 2000s, when the NAFTA governments issued a joint interpretation of NAFTA's investment chapter that supported transparency and amicus participation and that tried to contain the meaning of some of the agreement's investor protections (most notably by trying, with limited success, to rein in the arbitrators' readings of 'fair and equitable

[44] ibid xxx.

[45] Bjorklund is also presently one of three deputy chairs of the UNCITRAL academic forum (n 32) and, in 2015, she posted on her university website an open pro-ISDS letter signed by various ISDS practitioners and academics: P Akhavan and others, 'An Open Letter about Investor–State Dispute Settlement' (*McGill Fortier Chair in International Arbitration and International Commercial Law*, April 2015) <https://www.mcgill.ca/fortier-chair/isds-open-letter> accessed 14 January 2020.

[46] In the Trump Administration, US Trade Representative Robert Lighthizer appears to have played a key role: R Lighthizer, 'Testimony to House Ways and Means Committee' (*C-Span*, 21 March 2018) <https://www.c-span.org/video/?c4719932/brady-lighthizer-isds-discussion> accessed 14 January 2020.

[47] United States–Mexico–Canada trade agreement, signed 30 November 2018 (not in force), ch 14, annexes 14-C and 14-D, available from UNCTAD International Investment Agreements Navigator (n 15).

treatment').[48] Yet the NAFTA governments did not at the time address the lack of independence in ISDS, question the premise of one-way investor privileges, or re-establish the duty to exhaust local remedies. In contrast to this earlier reform, the handling of ISDS in the renegotiated NAFTA is a huge step forward. Above all, it eliminates the oldest example of ISDS between developed countries and greatly limits ISDS between the largest capital exporter and its closest Latin American neighbour. As a model for other developing countries, Mexico's position in the renegotiated NAFTA would be one of the best in relation to ISDS, beyond the ideal of withdrawing from ISDS completely.[49]

The renegotiated NAFTA also highlights the failures of many other countries. Outside Europe, Japan is apparently a diehard for ISDS arbitrator power, having pushed for it in the Trans-Pacific Partnership when that agreement was re-kindled after the United States withdrew from the negotiations.[50] Australia and New Zealand have opposed ISDS, but inconsistently.[51] China now pushes ISDS to protect its companies' assets abroad. In a particularly strange case, Canada conceded to a lopsided ISDS treaty with China in 2012, but then accepted the ICS reform in the Canada–EU trade deal in 2016, only to agree to old ISDS in the rebranded Trans-Pacific Partnership in early 2018.[52] Canada then signed the renegotiated NAFTA, dropping ISDS with the United States, in late 2018.[53] Once the Canada–EU deal is implemented, Canada will be one of the most ISDS-constrained countries in the world—until ISDS is removed from NAFTA, at which point Canada

[48] Free Trade Commission (NAFTA), *Notes of Interpretation of Certain Chapter 11 Provisions* (NAFTA 31 July 2001); M Kinnear and R Hansen, 'The Influence of NAFTA Chapter 11 in the BIT Landscape' (2005) 12 UC Davis J Int'l L Pol 111. These adjustments were included, albeit inconsistently, in subsequent treaties of each country; as an example of the inconsistency, Canada pulled back from its anti-secrecy ISDS position in 2014 by agreeing in the Canada–China BIT to allow the host state to an arbitration claim to withhold all documents other than awards from disclosure at the host state's discretion: Canada–China investment treaty, signed 9 September 2012, UN Conference on Trade and Development (UNCTAD), International Investment Agreements Navigator: <https://investmentpolicy.unctad.org/international-investment-agreements> accessed 14 January 2020.

[49] L Johnson, J Coleman, and B Güven, 'Withdrawal of Consent to Investor–State Arbitration and Termination of Investment Treaties' *Investment Treaty News* (24 April 2018); T Voon and AD Mitchell, 'Ending International Investment Agreements: Russia's Withdrawal from Participation in the Energy Charter Treaty' (2017) 111 AJIL Unbound 461.

[50] Y Fukunaga, 'ISDS under the CPTPP and Beyond: Japanese Perspectives' (*Kluwer Arbitration Blog*, 30 May 2018) <http://arbitrationblog.kluwerarbitration.com/2018/05/30/isds-cptpp-beyond-japanese-perspectives/> accessed 14 January 2020.

[51] A Kawharu, 'Renouncing Investor–State Dispute Settlement in Australia, Then New Zealand: Déjà Vu', Sydney Law School Research Paper No 18/03 (2 February 2018).

[52] China–Canada investment treaty, signed 9 September 2012; Comprehensive and Progressive Agreement for Trans-Pacific Partnership (CPTPP), signed 8 March 2018, ch 9. Both agreements are available from UNCTAD International Investment Agreements Navigator (n 15). In the case of the CPTPP, Canada did not follow the example of Australia and New Zealand, which agreed to side agreements excluding the CPTPP's ISDS provisions as between each other and, in New Zealand's case, with several other CPTPP countries. See eg Exchange of letters between S Ciobo and D Parker (New Zealand Ministry of Foreign Affairs and Trade, 8 March 2018) <https://www.mfat.govt.nz/assets/CPTPP/New-Zealand-Australia-ISDS-Trade-Remedies-and-Relationship-with-Other-Agreements.pdf> accessed 18 August 2019.

[53] US–Mexico–Canada trade agreement (n 47).

will be free, after more than twenty-five years, from the worst concession of a developed country's sovereignty to ISDS in history, while having shortly before made similar concessions in its relationships with China, Japan, and Western Europe. It is hard to be confidently optimistic about ISDS reform based on that record.

By far the most effective responses to ISDS constraints have come from developing or transition countries that have withdrawn outright from the treaties. These include most clearly South Africa, Ecuador, and Indonesia, followed by Bolivia, the Czech Republic, and Venezuela. India has withdrawn from existing treaties in pursuit of ISDS reforms that fall short of the EU reform model.[54] To its credit, Brazil never accepted ISDS at all.[55] Yet none of these countries can change the system fundamentally, they can only save themselves, and it remains exceptional for most countries to terminate their ISDS treaties, thereby avoiding the dilemma of having to appease investors or risk being ordered to pay them a vast sum. The more countries are punished for regulating the rich, the more they may see the value of escaping ISDS, but for now most are still on the road to regulatory chill, financial liability, and sovereign decline.

A grander alternative might be to create an international forum to adjudicate major disputes arising from the international ownership of assets, based on principles of balanced rights and responsibilities, respect for national institutions, procedural fairness, and judicial independence. Such a forum would need to allow for claims against the misconduct, as well as the mistreatment, of foreign investors.[56] To avoid a deluge of claims, most claimants would still need to go to national courts first, based on a duty to exhaust reasonably available local remedies. In contrast to ISDS, the forum would have actual judges, it would allow access by all directly affected parties, and it would be open to the public. No such forum exists and, while some countries are moving in a good direction, the core pillars of balance in the allocation of rights and responsibilities and of respect for national institutions seem anathema to the priorities of many powerful governments. For this reason, it would be advisable for other governments, if possible, to strengthen their position in the discussion of ISDS reform by terminating their existing ISDS treaties.

ISDS treaties are part of the architecture of global inequality. They are comparable to other concessions to the ultra-wealthy, such as tax cuts, prohibitions on unions, and lax regulation. All are linked to the ability of multinationals and tycoons to allocate resources, maximize returns, and influence countries in a global economy. Yet ISDS treaties are more fundamental because they catch governments

[54] India, 'Model Text for the Indian Bilateral Investment Treaty' (undated) available from UNCTAD International Investment Agreements Navigator (n 15).

[55] D Campello and L Barreiro Lemos, 'The Non-Ratification of Bilateral Investment Treaties in Brazil: A Story of Conflict in a Land of Cooperation' (2015) Rev Int'l Pol Econ 22.

[56] N Bernasconi and others, 'Harnessing Investment for Sustainable Development: Inclusion of Investor Obligations and Corporate Accountability Provisions in Trade and Investment Agreements', Background document for the expert meeting co-hosted by the International Institute for Sustainable Development and Friedrich Ebert Stiftung (9 January 2018).

in the web spun by all of the other concessions, reaching to the heart of sovereign capacity. Foreign investor protections shift power from countries without creating new international institutions to counter the dilution of national democracy, regulation, and courts. National institutions instead become subject to international tribunals that are under the sway of investors. Yet sovereigns can protect the wealthy from risk only to the point when other pressures, economic or environmental, engulf their budgets and institutions. A predicable outcome of maintaining ISDS may be the collapse of society.

Imagine a world supreme court. Its judges can review anything a country does in its sovereign role. Upon condemning a country, they can order public compensation for those harmed. If the country does not pay, their orders are enforceable against the country's assets worldwide. Such a supreme court would be the most powerful in history. Few know that a version of it already exists, but only to protect foreign investors. Fewer still know that it is not a court, as commonly understood, but rather a network of lawyers working as arbitrators, whose careers in the field typically turn on how lucrative their decisions are for the ultra-wealthy. The world supreme court has a dull name, ISDS, but its selective protections and skewed design are a clear symbol and guarantor of the gilded age of international law.

APPENDIX

Leading Hawks of ISDS

In this appendix, I elaborate on arbitrators who are described in the book as 'leading hawks' of investor–state dispute settlement (ISDS). From a comprehensive review[1] of ISDS rulings, these arbitrators emerged as having appeared to have done the most, over the first twenty years of ISDS, to interpret ISDS treaties in ways that expanded its compensatory promise for claimants, its corresponding risks for states, and the power and opportunities it created for the ISDS industry. To illustrate the role of repeat players in promoting ISDS, I also highlight two examples of pro-ISDS advocacy on the part of such arbitrators.

A. Comprehensive review

The review from which the leading hawks emerged covered all public rulings by ISDS tribunals from 1990 to 2010. It focused on whether the arbitrators on the tribunal joined in the resolution of contested legal issues under the treaties in ways that expanded the compensatory promise of ISDS for foreign investors and, in turn, the power of arbitrators to review and discipline states. The following contested issues were reviewed.[2]

Issue 1: Claims by corporate 'foreign' investors

The review of rulings for this issue asked whether arbitrators had addressed the question of whether an ISDS claim should be allowed when ownership of the investment ran through a chain of companies, via one or more third states, from the host state to the nominal home state under the relevant treaty.[3] An expansive approach to this issue permitted the claim to proceed regardless of the point at which the investor claimed foreign nationality in the multi-state chain of ownership, whereas a restrictive approach put limitations on such claims. The expansive approach thus tended to facilitate legal planning by wealthy companies and individuals to organize their affairs in ways that make it more difficult to regulate them in any state because of the obscurity of who owns what and where. An expansive approach could also facilitate companies and individuals choosing from among different nationalities in their strategies to avoid regulation or pursue litigation against states. As summarized

[1] For more information on this review, see G Van Harten, 'Arbitrator Behaviour in Asymmetrical Adjudication: An Empirical Study of Investment Treaty Arbitration' (2012) 50 Osgoode Hall LJ 211; G Van Harten, 'Arbitrator Behaviour in Asymmetrical Adjudication (Part Two): An Examination of Hypotheses of Bias in Investment Treaty Arbitration' (2016) 53 Osgoode Hall LJ 540; and G Van Harten, 'Leaders in the Expansive and Restrictive Interpretation of Investment Treaties: A Descriptive Study of ISDS Awards to 2010' (2018) 29 EJIL 507.

[2] For an explanation of how these issues were identified and how the rulings were reviewed, see Van Harten, 'Arbitrator Behaviour' (n 1) 225–33; Van Harten, 'Arbitrator Behaviour (Part Two)' (n 1) 549–54; and Van Harten, 'Leaders' (n 1) 539.

[3] T Voon, AD Mitchell, and J Munro, 'Legal Responses to Corporate Manoeuvring in International Investment Arbitration' (2014) 5 J Int'l Disp Settlement 41.

Table 1. Expansive or restrictive resolutions per issue

Issue	No of issue resolutions	Resolution of issue (%)	
		Expansive	Restrictive
1—corporate person investor	72	85	15
2—natural person investor	6	0	100
3—concept of investment	119	70	30
4—minority shareholder interest	75	92	8
5—permissibility of investment	27	67	33
6—parallel claims	162	84	16
7—scope of MFN treatment	60	50	50
8—national treatment	60	35	65
9—fair and equitable treatment (autonomous standard)	56	73	27
10—fair and equitable treatment (content)	137	83	17
11—full protection and security	51	57	43
12—indirect expropriation	120	72.5	27.5
13—umbrella clause	32	91	9
14—national security exception	24	75	25
Cumulative	**1,001**	**73.5**	**26.5**

in Table 1, arbitrators were found to have resolved the issue expansively or restrictively on seventy-two occasions in ISDS awards, tending heavily towards expansive approaches.

Issue 2: Claims by natural person 'foreign' investors

This issue arose from ambiguity in many treaties about how the nationality of some natural persons—as distinct from the companies and other legal persons in Issue 1 above—should be determined. It arose in particular where natural persons sought to bring ISDS claims against their own state in their own name, instead of through a holding company or other vehicle. Would arbitrators allow such claims or bar them on grounds that the investor was not sufficiently 'foreign'? More specifically, would they allow the claim when the investor was a natural person who was a national of the host state? An expansive approach answered yes to this question; a restrictive approach no. As it turned out, virtually no cases raised this issue and so almost no data—six resolutions, all restrictive—was generated. ISDS claims in which an investor appeared to be suing his or her own state typically were not brought in the name of a natural person, but instead through holding companies used by (very wealthy) individuals to obtain ostensibly foreign nationality.[4]

[4] See eg G Van Harten and P Malysheuski, 'Who Has Benefited Financially from Investment Treaty Arbitration? An Evaluation of the Size and Wealth of Claimants', Osgoode Hall Law School Legal Studies Research Paper No 14 (2016) 5–7.

Issue 3: Concept of 'investment'

The issue examined was whether 'investment' should be limited to situations in which certain indicators—commitment of capital for a certain period, expectation of gain, assumption of risk, and contribution to the host economy—are present. These indicators are often called the *Fedax* criteria[5] in ISDS, after they were adopted by that early tribunal to guide the assessment of short-term or non-risky activity, for example, when applying the concept of investment. Arbitrators who applied the *Fedax* criteria were taken to have adopted a restrictive approach on this issue; those who did not, an expansive approach. The issue was found to have been resolved by ISDS arbitrators on 119 occasions and they tended towards expansiveness.

Issue 4: Claims by minority shareholders

What should happen in ISDS if the foreign owner of a domestic company—the shares of which are themselves the foreign investor's 'investment'—owns only a small part of that company?[6] One might expect that the foreign investor, as a minority shareholder of the company, should be able to seek compensation in ISDS only for the portion of the company that the investor actually owns, and not the whole company. Yet some arbitrators have allowed foreign minority shareholders to bring claims on behalf of the whole company they partly own, effectively expanding ISDS arbitrators' authority to award compensation. For this issue, a restrictive approach limited minority shareholder claims to the minority interest; an expansive approach allowed such claims on behalf of the whole company. The issue was found to have been resolved by arbitrators on seventy-five occasions and they tended heavily towards the expansive approach.

Issue 5: Claims involving questionable investments

In some ISDS cases, there are doubts about the legitimacy of the investment that led to the dispute with the host state. For example, it may be alleged that the investment was secured by corrupt dealings or that it did not comply with domestic rules of entry for foreign investments.[7] Where the ISDS claim related to an investment made in allegedly suspect circumstances, the issue reviewed was whether the foreign investor or the respondent state should have the onus of establishing that the ISDS claim should be allowed or prohibited. An expansive approach put the onus on the state, a restrictive approach put it on the investor. As it turned out, the issue was found not to have arisen much. It was resolved on twenty-seven occasions and the resolutions tended towards expansiveness.

[5] *Fedax NV v Republic of Venezuela* (Award, 11 July 1997), 37 ILM 1378; *Salini v Morocco* (Award, 23 July 2001), 42 ILM 609.

[6] D Gaukrodger, 'Investment Treaties and Shareholder Claims for Reflective Loss: Insights from Advanced Systems of Corporate Law', Organisation for Economic Co-operation and Development Working Paper on International Investment 2014/02 (2014).

[7] J Yackee, 'Investment Treaties and Investor Corruption: An Emerging Defence for Host States?' (2012) 52 Virginia J Int'l L 723.

Issue 6: Claims that run parallel to another forum

This issue related to a complicated but important aspect of the foreign investor protection system. It raised the question of whether ISDS can displace other forums for dispute resolution, such as the domestic state courts or forums agreed upon by foreign investors in their contracts with state entities. Faced with another forum, domestic and international courts often show restraint by requiring litigants to use the forum most connected to the dispute. Many ISDS tribunals, in contrast, have favoured allowing parallel ISDS proceedings, thus expanding the compensatory promise of the treaties for investors.[8] This issue was reviewed by asking whether a parallel ISDS claim should be allowed in circumstances where the investor had agreed under a contract to use another forum, where the investor is required by the treaty to use domestic courts, or where the investor has brought a claim for compensation in another international forum. An expansive approach allowed the ISDS claim to proceed in such circumstances, whereas a restrictive approach did not. The issue was found to have been resolved more often than any other issue, on 162 occasions, and the resolutions tended heavily towards expansive approaches.

Issue 7: Claims based on 'most-favoured-nation treatment'

Many ISDS treaties give foreign investors a broad right to treatment from the state that is at least as favourable as the treatment received by foreign investors from other states. The most-favoured-nation (MFN) treatment clause raises complex issues of interpretation. For example, should MFN treatment be limited to the substantive treatment of foreign investors or should it extend to procedural and institutional questions, such as the ability to bring an ISDS claim under another treaty where the host state's treaty with the foreign investor's home state does not allow ISDS?[9] For the purposes of the comprehensive review, an expansive approach to this question extended MFN treatment to encompass more favourable dispute settlement provisions in other treaties, whereas a restrictive approach declined to do so. The issue was found to have been resolved on sixty occasions, with an even split between expansive and restrictive approaches.

Issue 8: Scope of 'national treatment' rights

Through MFN treatment, foreign investors are protected from discrimination—more precisely from less favourable treatment—in comparison to foreign investors from other states. With the right of national treatment, they are protected from less favourable treatment in comparison to domestic investors. Though such 'non-discrimination' may sound straightforward, national treatment also raises complex issues in the analysis of how investors are compared.[10] For present purposes, the issue was whether national treatment should be interpreted in a variety of flexible ways that would favour foreign investor claims. For example, can a foreign investor compare itself to a domestic investor, even if the two are not

[8] Y Shany, 'Contract Claims vs Treaty Claims: Mapping Conflicts between ICSID Decisions on Multisourced Investment Claims' (2005) 99 AJIL 835.

[9] A Faya Rodriguez, 'The Most-Favored-Nation Clause in International Investment Agreements—A Tool for Treaty Shopping?' (2008) 25 J Int'l Arb 89.

[10] J Kurtz, 'The Use and Abuse of WTO Law in Investor–State Arbitration: Competition and its Discontents' (2009) 20 EJIL 749.

'in like circumstances' in their businesses? An expansive approach took a flexible approach to this or other aspects of national treatment; a restrictive approach did not. Overall, the issue was found to have been resolved on sixty occasions and the resolutions tended toward restrictiveness.

Issue 9: Tethering of 'fair and equitable treatment' to customary international law

ISDS arbitrators, when finding states in violation of an investment treaty, have relied on the concept of 'fair and equitable treatment' more often than any other foreign investor protection.[11] The concept has been controversial because of how flexibly and variably it has been interpreted.[12] For example, in many cases governments have argued that the concept was limited to characterizations of the 'minimum standard of treatment' for foreign nationals in customary international law. Yet investment treaties did not state this limiting condition in clear and express terms, leaving space for arbitrators to decide whether the term should be tethered to custom in this way.[13] An expansive approach treated fair and equitable treatment as a protection that was autonomous from customary international law, whereas a restrictive approach limited the concept to the customary minimum standard. Arbitrators were found to have resolved the issue on fifty-six occasions and to have tended towards an expansive approach.

Issue 10: Scope of 'fair and equitable treatment'

A more fundamental question about fair and equitable treatment is how broadly the arbitrators interpreted its content, regardless of whether they approached it as autonomous from customary international law. Broadly, this question involved whether arbitrators chose to characterize the vaguely worded protection as a source of broad-ranging rights for investors and corresponding powers of review for the arbitrators or, alternatively, as a last-resort protection against egregious abuse not covered by other foreign investor protections in the treaties.[14] In the comprehensive review, various terms drawn from customary sources[15]—such as 'outrage', 'bad faith', 'wilful disregard of due process of law', and 'wilful neglect of duty'—were used as markers of a restrictive approach to fair and equitable treatment. An expansive approach went beyond these markers, using more far-reaching language to review states' decisions, such as 'idiosyncratic', 'unreasonable', 'legitimate expectations', 'stability of the legal or business framework', and 'affirmative transparency'. This issue was the second most frequently resolved issue by arbitrators, with 137 resolutions, and they tended heavily toward expansiveness.

[11] UN Conference on Trade and Development (UNCTAD), *Fair and Equitable Treatment* (United Nations 2012) 10–15.

[12] R Kläger, 'Fair and Equitable Treatment: A Look at the Theoretical Underpinnings of Legitimacy and Fairness' (2010) 11 J World Invest Trade 435; R Kläger, *'Fair and Equitable Treatment' in International Investment Law* (CUP 2011).

[13] MC Porterfield, 'A Distinction without a Difference? The Interpretation of Fair and Equitable Treatment under Customary International Law by Investment Tribunals' *ITN Quarterly* (March 2013).

[14] ibid.

[15] *Neer Claim (United States v Mexico)* (1926) 4 RIAA 60; *Elettronica Sicula SpA (ELSI) (United States v Italy)* [1989] ICJ Rep 4, ICJ Rep 15.

Issue 11: Scope of 'full protection and security'

Another ambiguous foreign investor protection is full protection and security.[16] Although not to the same extent as fair and equitable treatment, this protection has also lent itself to expansive interpretations.[17] The main hinge for this expansion has been to swing the standard beyond the issue of physical security of investors and their assets to include broader notions of economic or legal security. Indeed, since the ISDS litigation boom began, some states have clarified in their treaties that the standard should be limited to physical security.[18] Under those treaties, the arbitrators' resolutions on the point would not be counted in the comprehensive review because the issue would be judged to have been resolved clearly and specifically in the treaty. In reviewing ISDS decisions under those treaties that left the issue open, interpretations that limited full protection and security to physical security were treated as restrictive; those that extended it to economic or legal security were classified as expansive. Arbitrators were found to have resolved the issue on fifty-one occasions and the resolutions modestly favoured the expansive approach.

Issue 12: Scope of 'indirect' expropriation

Investment treaties give investors protection against expropriation. This protection goes beyond direct expropriations to also include situations of indirect expropriation that leave the foreign investor's formal ownership intact.[19] Indirect expropriation is an uncertain concept, open to the interpretation that public compensation must be paid to investors even for incidental economic costs of general, non-discriminatory laws and regulations that serve a public purpose.[20] In our study, a decision was seen as reflecting a restrictive approach where, for example, arbitrators decided that a law or regulation, if it did not transfer ownership of the relevant assets, would have to amount to a 'near-complete' taking of the assets' value before compensation was owed. An expansive approach required compensation of the investor when a law or regulation had only a 'significant' or 'substantial' effect on the value of its assets. Arbitrators resolved issues of indirect expropriation often, on 120 occasions, and the resolutions tended to be expansive.

Issue 13: Scope of umbrella clause protections

Some treaties include a provision that protects foreign investors, not just under the treaty's protections, but also in relation to other legal relationships with a state.[21] In the extreme, these 'umbrella clauses' could transform all of a state's domestic legal obligations to foreign

[16] G Cordero Moss, 'Full Protection and Security' in A Reinisch (ed), *Standards of Investment Protection* (OUP 2008) 131.

[17] M Malik, 'The Full Protection and Security Standard Comes of Age: Yet Another Challenge for States in Investment Treaty Arbitration?', International Institute for Sustainable Development Best Practices Series (2011), a short paper/report.

[18] See eg Comprehensive Economic and Trade Agreement (CETA) between Canada and the European Union, signed 30 October 2016 (not fully in force), Article 8.10(5).

[19] AK Hoffman, 'Indirect Expropriation' in A Reinisch (ed), *Standards of Investment Protection* (OUP 2008) 151.

[20] MC Porterfield, 'International Expropriation Rules and Federalism' (2004) 23 Stan Envt'l LJ 3.

[21] J Crawford, 'Treaty and Contract in Investment Arbitration' (2008) 24 Arb Int'l 351.

investors—such as in contracts—into international obligations and make them enforceable in ISDS.[22] Expansive interpretations of other foreign investor protections, such as fair and equitable treatment, can have a similar effect, but the presence of an umbrella clause makes it easier for ISDS to be characterized as a substitute for other forums for resolving disputes. In reviewing this issue, a restrictive approach limited the impact of umbrella clauses to situations in which a state, in its treatment of investors, was involved in sovereign or regulatory conduct as opposed to private or commercial conduct. An expansive approach applied the umbrella clauses without that constraint. The issue was found to have been resolved on thirty-two occasions and the resolutions tended overwhelmingly towards expansiveness.

Issue 14: Availability of national security exception

In some ISDS cases, the sued state argued that its actions, having caused economic loss to an investor, were justified by a national emergency arising from a severe economic or political crisis.[23] Legally, this argument was based on essential security exceptions in the treaties.[24] An expansive approach refused to extend this essential security exception to circumstances of economic and financial emergency; a restrictive approach allowed it to be extended that way, at least to some degree. The issue was found to have been resolved on twenty-four occasions and the resolutions tended towards expansiveness.

In the comprehensive review of how arbitrators resolved these contested issues, various arbitrators stood out for their high number of expansive resolutions and for tending towards expansive resolutions more than other arbitrators. As highlighted in Table 2, these were Yves Fortier, Francisco Orrego Vicuña, Charles Brower, Marc Lalonde, Stephen Schwebel, and Gabrielle Kaufmann-Kohler.[25] Some of these individuals also stood out for having adopted many expansive resolutions while serving as presiding arbitrator of a tribunal or for having almost universally favoured expansive resolutions of the contested issues.[26] All of them

[22] J Wong, 'Umbrella Clauses in Bilateral Investment Treaties: Of Breaches of Contract, Treaty Violations, and the Divide between Developing and Developed Countries in Foreign Investment Disputes' (2006) 14 George Mason L Rev 137.

[23] Organisation for Economic Co-operation and Development (OECD), 'Essential Security Interests under International Investment Law' in *International Investment Perspectives: Freedom of Investment in a Changing World* (OECD 2007) 93–105; WW Burke-White, 'The Argentine Financial Crisis: State Liability under BITs and the Legitimacy of the ICSID System' (2008) 3 Asian J WTO and Int'l Health L Pol 199.

[24] See eg United States–Argentina investment treaty, signed 14 November 1991, Article XI, UN Conference on Trade and Development (UNCTAD) International Investment Agreements Navigator: <https://investmentpolicy.unctad.org/international-investment-agreements>.

[25] I have omitted from the individualized backgrounds below a seventh arbitrator, Andrés Rigo Sureda, who stood out similarly to other leading hawks, although his record generated somewhat fewer expansive resolutions over fewer cases than the other six. Briefly, Rigo Sureda is a Spanish national who was a lawyer at the World Bank between 1973 and 2000, and its Deputy General Counsel for the last eight years of this term, when ISDS treaties were expanding rapidly. His entry into ISDS arbitration came in early claims against Argentina. Shortly after he retired from the Bank, the Bank's President chose him as president arbitrator in *Azurix Corpn v Argentine Republic* (Awards, 8 December 2003 and 14 July 2006), and in 2002, again as presiding arbitrator in *Siemens AG v Argentine Republic* (Awards, 3 August 2004 and 6 February 2007). In both cases, the tribunal adopted a series of expansive interpretations and awarded compensation to the investor. In 2007, Rigo Sureda was appointed by ICSID as presiding arbitrator in *Railroad Development Corporation v Republic of Guatemala* (Award, 18 May 2010), ICSID Case No ARB/07/23, where the tribunal also issued various expansive interpretations on the way to awarding compensation.

[26] Fortier and Orrego Vicuña stood out additionally for their interpretations in the role as presiding arbitrator, whereas Brower, Lalonde, and Schwebel stood out more for their near-universal adoption

Table 2. Leading arbitrators, based on total expansive resolutions and proportion of expansive-to-restrictive resolutions of contested ISDS treaty issues

Arbitrator	Total resolutions (expansive or restrictive)	Expansive resolutions	Restrictive resolutions	Share of resolutions that were expansive (%)
Francisco Orrego-Vicuña	53	44	9	83
Yves Fortier	44	33	11	75
Marc Lalonde	38	34	4	90
Gabrielle Kaufmann-Kohler	34	31	3	91
Stephen Schwebel	25	24	1	96
Charles Brower	24	22	2	92
Andrés Rigo Sureda	22	21	1	96
All other arbitrators	761	525	236	69

emerged as having contributed more than other arbitrators to the expansion of ISDS arbitration by adopting interpretations of the treaties that generally favour the legal position of investors at the expense of states,[27] and on this basis I have called them 'leading hawks' of ISDS for the relevant period.

B. Six leading hawks based on the review

I offer in this section some further background of the repeat arbitrators who emerged as leading hawks, including some examples of their investor-friendly records. The aim is to shed light on who was allocated power under the treaties to make the case-by-case interpretive decisions about ambiguities in the treaties that in turn drove the expansion of ISDS from the 1990s until at least 2010, the end year of the comprehensive review.

Yves Fortier

Before Yves Fortier became an ISDS arbitrator, he was a commercial arbitrator and partner at the large Canadian law firm Ogilvy Renault. He has sat on the corporate boards of major companies such as TransCanada and DuPont, some of which have since used ISDS to sue

of expansive instead of restrictive interpretations. Kaufmann-Kohler stood out for both additional reasons: Van Harten, 'Leaders' (n 1) 539.

[27] Together, the seven arbitrators (including Rigo Sureda: n 25) generated 240 of all 1,001 expansive or restrictive resolutions of the fourteen analysed issues in the dataset. They adopted an expansive rather than a restrictive resolution for 209 of the 240 resolutions, for an expansive tendency of 87 per cent compared to 69 per cent for the 199 arbitrators across the other 761 resolutions. Strikingly, they accounted for 209 (28 per cent) of the 736 expansive resolutions among all arbitrators and just thirty-one (12 per cent) of the 265 restrictive resolutions: Van Harten, 'Leaders' (n 1).

countries. From 1988 to 1992, Fortier was Canada's ambassador to the United Nations (UN) under the conservative federal government of Prime Minister Brian Mulroney. In this period, incidentally, the federal government negotiated the North American Free Trade Agreement (NAFTA), including its ground-breaking investment chapter, which set the stage for Canada to become the first—and still only—Western developed country to have accepted ISDS with the United States. As an arbitrator, Fortier was a tribunal member for momentous rulings in ISDS history.[28] Most notably, he presided over the tribunal in *Yukos v Russia*, having been chosen for this role by officials at the Permanent Court of Arbitration (PCA), where he was joined by another leading hawk, Stephen Schwebel.[29] The tribunal issued a string of rulings based on expansive interpretations of the pertinent treaty on the way to a shockingly huge award of USD 50 billion against Russia.[30] These expansive interpretations included the tribunal's resolution of issues concerning the definition of 'investment', the ability of investors to bring a treaty claim in parallel to other proceedings, the ability of minority shareholders to bring claims on behalf of the full company in which they own shares, and the ability of investors to use a corporation or other legal vehicle to nationality-shop among treaties. Facilitated by the tribunal's approach to this last issue, in particular, its decision appears to have enabled several Russian oligarchs to use the named claimants—holding companies or other legal vehicles in Cyprus or the Isle of Man—to bring an ISDS claim against their country of origin. As an aside, the case also stands out for the massive cost of the arbitration itself: about USD 80 million in costs for the investor and USD 40 million for Russia, plus over EUR 5 million in arbitration fees and expenses.[31] For his part, Fortier billed about EUR 1.7 million in fees and 52,000 in expenses (and Schwebel about EUR 2 million and 85,000, respectively), among the highest amounts ever billed by an ISDS arbitrator.[32] The tribunal ordered Russia to pay these fees.

Francisco Orrego Vicuña

Francisco Orrego Vicuña was a Chilean arbitrator and professor. Notably, during the Chilean dictatorship of General Augusto Pinochet in the mid-1980s, he was Chile's ambassador to the UK. As ISDS litigation was getting started in the 1990s, Orrego Vicuña was a commercial arbitrator at the International Chamber of Commerce (ICC) and London Court of International Arbitration and a member of the World Bank's Administrative Tribunal (which decides employment disputes between the Bank's management and staff), eventually

[28] Fortier appears to have been a favourite of the law firm Freshfields, whose clients picked him as the investor-side or, in one case, as the state-side arbitrator in *Saluka v Czech Republic* (Award, 7 May 2004); *Oko v Estonia* (Award, 19 November 2007), ICSID Case No ARB/04/6; *Bureau Veritas v Paraguay* (Award, 29 May 2009), ICSID Case No ARB/07/9; and the mega-claim of *ConocoPhillips v Venezuela* (Award, 8 March 2019), ICSID Case No ARB/07/30.

[29] Schwebel was Russia's arbitrator in what proved a very poor choice.

[30] The award remains under review in Dutch courts, having been set aside in the first instance by a Dutch trial court: *Russian Federation v Veteran Petroleum Limited, Russian Federation v Yukos University Limited,* and *Russian Federation v Hulley Enterprises Limited* (20 April 2016) (The Hague District Court).

[31] *Yukos Universal Limited (Isle of Man) v Russia* (Award, 30 November 2009), 22(2) World Trade and Arb Mat 279 [1847] and [1856].

[32] The investor's arbitrator (Dan Price and then Charles Poncet) billed a combined EUR 1,617,417.50 in fees and EUR 89,228.63 in expenses: *Yukos* (n 31) [1860] to [1862].

becoming its president.[33] The Bank and its International Centre for Settlement of Investment Disputes also gave Orrego Vicuña his start as an ISDS arbitrator by appointing him as president of the early tribunals in *Fedax v Venezuela* and *Maffezini v Spain*. Both tribunals issued investor-friendly rulings, as discussed in Chapters 3 and 5 of this book.[34] Thanks to another World Bank appointment, Orrego Vicuña was also President of the *CMS v Argentina* tribunal, which took a highly permissive approach to claims by minority shareholders and to claims that ran parallel to the investor's contractually agreed forum.[35] These interpretations led to the tribunal's order of USD 151 million against Argentina based on further expansive interpretations of its obligations to ensure 'fair and equitable treatment' and compensate for 'indirect' expropriation.[36] The *CMS* ruling was subsequently condemned by an ICSID annulment committee for 'manifest errors of law' and 'lacunae and elisions', but the annulment committee nevertheless left the ruling in place, noting the annulment committee's 'narrow and limited mandate' under the ICSID Convention.[37] Besides *CMS*, Orrego Vicuña presided over various tribunals that issued pro-investor interpretations in ISDS cases against Argentina after the country's 2001–02 economic crisis.[38] He later presided over *Oxy v Ecuador*, where the tribunal decided adventurously that Ecuador's approach to taxing an oil multinational could be compared to its approach to taxing Ecuadorean flower exporters, even when the two were not in 'like circumstances', on the way to a huge award for Oxy.[39] Based on these and other rulings, Orrego Vicuña emerged from the comprehensive review as a leading early adopter of expansive interpretations, usually as the tribunal's presiding arbitrator.

Charles Brower

Charles Brower is a US national with a long history with the corporate law firm White and Case. He was a lawyer there from 1961 to 1969 and, after a stint as a legal advisor at the US state department, he was a partner or special counsel at the firm on and off from 1973 to 2005. His corporate practice came to be dominated by international arbitration work and, in 1983, he was appointed by the Reagan Administration to the Iran–United States claims tribunal, which was established to hear claims by US nationals against Iran in the aftermath of

[33] F Orrego Vicuña, 'CV' (*Francisco Orrego Vicuña*, 10 August 2005) <http://forrego.blogspot.com/> accessed 18 January 2020.

[34] *Fedax NV v Republic of Venezuela* (Award, 11 July 1997), 37 ILM 1378, 5 ICSID Rep 186; *Maffezini (Emilio Agustín) v Kingdom of Spain* (Award, 25 January 2000), 16 ICSID Rev 212, 124 ILR 9, 5 ICSID Rep 396.

[35] *CMS Gas Transmission Company v Argentine Republic* (Award, 17 July 2003), 42 ILM 788, [56].

[36] *CMS Gas Transmission Company v Argentine Republic* (Award, 12 May 2005), 44 ILM 1205, [1] to [6].

[37] *CMS Gas Transmission Company v Argentine Republic* (Annulment Decision, 25 September 2007), ICSID Case No ARB/01/18, [158] to [163].

[38] After *CMS*, Orrego Vicuña was appointed, either fully or partly by ICSID, as presiding arbitrator in *Enron Corpn and Ponderosa Assets v Argentine Republic* (Award, 14 January 2004), ICSID Case No ARB/01/3; *Sempra Energy International v Argentine Republic* (Award, 11 May 2005), ICSID Case No ARB/02/16; and *Camuzzi International SA v Argentine Republic* (Award, 11 May 2005), ICSID Case No ARB/03/2; in each case, the tribunal took an expansive approach to the concept of investment, minority shareholder claims, and parallel claims in the course of allowing the claim to go ahead and ultimately awarding compensation.

[39] The tribunal took a highly permissive approach to the requirement that foreign investors be in 'like situations' to domestic investors for the purposes of non-discrimination; *Occidental Exploration and Production Company v Ecuador* (Award, 1 July 2004), 138 ILR 35, [168] and [173]–[178].

the 1979 revolution. Since becoming an ISDS arbitrator, Brower has avidly promoted ISDS, as discussed below. His first appointment to an ISDS tribunal was *Ethyl v Canada*, the first NAFTA claim against Canada, where he sat with another leading hawk, Marc Lalonde.[40] Brower was chosen for the tribunal by the US multinational Ethyl Corporation. After the tribunal's surprising ruling allowing Ethyl's claim to proceed against a proposed law, the Canadian government agreed to a concessionary settlement.[41] A few years later, Brower was chosen for the *Siemens v Argentina* tribunal by the German multinational claimant.[42] The tribunal ruled for Siemens after taking pro-investor approaches on various issues, including the meaning of 'fair and equitable treatment', 'full protection and security', compensation for 'indirect' expropriation, and 'most-favoured-nation' treatment.[43] Awkwardly, not long before Siemens was swept up in an international corruption scandal, the *Siemens* tribunal had declined to hear Argentina's arguments that Siemens won the contract for the project that generated its ISDS dispute with Argentina through corruption.[44] A decade later, it was confirmed in separate US legal proceedings that a Siemens executive had 'engaged in a decade-long scheme to pay tens of millions of dollars in bribes to Argentine government officials' in connection with the project.[45] Having declined to consider Argentina's submissions on the matter, the tribunal ordered over USD 200 million in compensation for Siemens, including about half of the company's arbitration costs.[46] Siemens subsequently settled the case, reportedly for an insignificant amount, after the corruption scandal had erupted.[47]

Marc Lalonde

Marc Lalonde is the second of two Canadians among the leading hawks who emerged from the comprehensive review. Before becoming an arbitrator, he had a long political career, primarily as a parliamentarian and minister from 1972 to 1984 in the Liberal governments of Prime Minister Pierre Trudeau. After the Liberals were defeated in 1984, Lalonde became a partner at the large law firm Stikeman Elliot and worked for about two decades as a commercial arbitrator. Like other leading hawks, he has also been a board member for large corporations such as Citibank Canada and Sherritt International Corporation and has been active in the International Council for Commercial Arbitration, which promotes the arbitration industry. Lalonde's first appointment in ISDS was in *Ethyl v Canada*, where he was Canada's arbitrator and served alongside Charles Brower. After this case, Lalonde appears to have become a favourite appointee of multinationals and their lawyers, especially in early

[40] The presiding arbitrator was Karl-Heinz Böckstiegel.

[41] See the discussion of *Ethyl v Canada* in Chapter 6.

[42] *Siemens AG v Argentine Republic* (Award, 3 August 2004), 44 ILM 138, [3].

[43] ibid [103]; *Siemens AG v Argentine Republic* (Award, 6 February 2007), 19(2) World Trade and Arb Mat 103, [271], [273], [298]–[300], [303], and [308].

[44] US Securities and Exchange Commission, 'SEC Charges Siemens AG for Engaging in Worldwide Bribery' (*US SEC*, 15 December 2008) <https://www.sec.gov/news/press/2008/2008-294.htm> accessed 18 January 2020; F Marshall, 'Siemens AG v Republic of Argentina' in N Bernasconi-Osterwalder and L Johnson (eds), *International Investment Law and Sustainable Development: Key Cases from 2000–2010* (International Institute for Sustainable Development, 2011) 132.

[45] US Department of Justice, 'Former Siemens Executive Pleads Guilty to Role in $100 Million Foreign Bribery Scheme' (*US Department of Justice*, 15 March 2018) <https://www.justice.gov/opa/pr/former-siemens-executive-pleads-guilty-role-100-million-foreign-bribery-scheme> accessed 18 January 2020.

[46] *Siemens* (6 February 2007) (n 43), [402]–[423].

[47] S Rubenfeld, 'Former Siemens Executive Pleads Guilty in Argentina Bribery Case' *Wall Street Journal* (New York, 15 March 2018).

cases against Argentina, where tribunals took expansive approaches to key issues and issued large awards to claimants.[48] He was the investor's arbitrator in *CMS v Argentina*, *Sempra v Argentina*, and *Azurix v Argentina*; he also sat on early tribunals in *MTD Equity v Chile* and *Walter Bau v Thailand*, which also adopted expansive interpretations in the course of ruling for the investor.[49] Lalonde thus emerged as a highly consistent and early adopter of investor-friendly interpretations.[50]

Stephen Schwebel

Stephen Schwebel, a US national, began his work as an ISDS arbitrator after a long career as an academic, diplomat, and US-appointed international judge. In the 1950s, he worked at the law firm White and Case and, from 1967 to 1981, was a professor at John Hopkins University and legal advisor to the US State Department; from 1977 to 1980, he was a member of the UN Commission on International Trade Law (UNCITRAL). In 1981, he was appointed by the Reagan Administration to the International Court of Justice (ICJ), where he served until 2000.[51] While an ICJ judge, he worked as an arbitrator on a tribunal to decide a dispute between British Petroleum Company and Iran, and then on other international commercial arbitration tribunals. As an aside, the practice of ICJ judges taking on simultaneous work as arbitrators was recently prohibited by the ICJ after several judges had repeatedly accepted appointments as ISDS arbitrators.[52] Schwebel himself entered ISDS arbitration in the early 2000s after leaving the ICJ, as the investor's arbitrator in *CME v Czech Republic*.[53] The *CME* tribunal is notorious for ordering a huge amount of compensation for a Dutch company owned by US billionaire Ralph Lauder after the Dutch company had sued under a Netherland–Czech ISDS treaty; the award of compensation came ten days after an earlier ISDS tribunal, appointed to hear the same factual dispute, had dismissed Lauder's claims as a US national in a parallel case under a United States–Czech treaty.[54] Allowing the parallel ISDS claims gave Lauder two bites at the apple in the dispute with Czech regulators of his media business. In the second case (*CME*)—which Lauder won, via his Dutch corporate persona, and where Schwebel was the investor's arbitrator—the tribunal's interpretations

[48] These were *CMS* (n 35 and 36); *Azurix Corpn v Argentine Republic* (8 December 2003; 14 July 2006); *Camuzzi* (n 38); and *Sempra v Argentina* (Award, 11 May 2005; Award, 28 September 2007). In the latter three cases, the tribunal took expansive approaches to 'investment' and parallel claims; in *Azurix* and *Sempra* to 'fair and equitable treatment' and 'full protection and security'; in *Sempra* and *Camuzzi* to minority shareholder claims; in *Azurix* to corporate forum shopping and 'indirect' expropriation; and in *Camuzzi* to most-favoured-nation (MFN) treatment. In *CMS*, the tribunal did the same for various issues. In each of *CMS*, *Azurix*, and *Sempra*, the tribunal issued a large award against Argentina, whereas *Camuzzi* appears to have settled confidentially.

[49] ibid. *MTD Equity Sdn Bhd & MTD Chile SA v Republic of Chile* (Award, 25 May 2004), 44 ILM 91; *Walter Bau v Thailand* (Award, 1 July 2009), 22(4) World Trade and Arb Mat 681. In *CMS*, Lalonde was appointed by a corporate claimant represented by Freshfields. In *Azurix* (n 25), *Camuzzi* (38), and *Sempra* (38), he was appointed by corporate claimants represented by King and Spalding.

[50] See Table 2.

[51] Schwebel continues to use the title 'judge' when working as an arbitrator based on his previous position as a judge at the ICJ.

[52] 'Judges of the International Court of Justice Decide to No Longer Participate as Arbitrators in ISDS Cases' *Investment Treaty News* (21 December 2018); N Bernasconi-Osterwalder and MD Brauch, 'Is "Moonlighting" a Problem? The Role of ICJ Judges in ISDS', International Institute for Sustainable Development Commentary (November 2017).

[53] *CME v Czech Republic* (Award, 13 September 2001), 14(3) World Trade and Arb Mat 109; *CME v Czech Republic* (Award, 14 March 2003), 15(4) World Trade and Arb Mat 83 and 245.

[54] *Lauder v Czech Republic* (Award, 3 September 2001), 4 World Trade and Arb Mat 35.

went heavily and sweepingly towards the investor.[55] With this ruling, Schwebel became an early adopter of expansive approaches to 'fair and equitable treatment', 'full protection and security', and 'indirect' expropriation. On the wider record, he emerged as a leading hawk due to his near-universal adoption of expansive, pro-investor interpretations.[56]

Gabrielle Kaufmann-Kohler

Gabrielle Kaufmann-Kohler, a Swiss national, is the only woman among the leading hawks and by far the youngest, aged forty-eight in 2000 (compared to seventy-one for Lalonde and Schwebel, sixty-five for Brower and Fortier, and fifty-eight for Orrego-Vicuña). For much of her career, she worked in private practice and as a professor at the University of Geneva. She has been honorary president of the Swiss Arbitration Association and a member of the ICC's International 'Court' of Arbitration.[57] She has her own arbitration firm and a thriving business in ISDS, while also sitting regularly on corporate boards. In this last respect, incidentally, Kaufmann-Kohler was criticized by an ICSID annulment committee for not having investigated and disclosed a conflict of interest arising from her having been a board member at the Swiss bank UBS while arbitrating an ISDS claim by a company in which UBS owned shares.[58] Despite the conflict, the ruling in that ISDS case (against Argentina) was upheld by the annulment committee, partly because of 'the extraordinary length of the present case' and, according to the committee, the 'overriding principle that all litigation must come to an end unless there are strong reasons for it to continue'.[59]

Kaufmann-Kohler's origins as an arbitrator in ISDS are hard to track due to a lack of official information. She was the presiding arbitrator in various early cases, but it is unclear from the awards whether officials at the arbitration house chose her for that role or whether the disputing investor and state did so. Her earliest ruling in *PSEG v Turkey* is perhaps revealing. Kaufmann-Kohler was appointed to the tribunal by Turkey in 2002, alongside Yves Fortier as the investor's arbitrator and Francisco Orrego Vicuña as the president.[60] Turkey was represented in the case by the law firm Sidley Austin, where Stephen Schwebel acted as Turkey's lead counsel and Dan Price, also prominent in the ISDS industry, as its co-counsel. The *PSEG* tribunal went on to adopt a series of investor-friendly interpretations, including on the definition of 'investment', the ability of minority shareholders to bring claims, the ability of investors to bring parallel claims, and the state's obligations to ensure 'fair and equitable treatment' for investors and to compensate for 'indirect' expropriation. Based on these interpretations, Turkey was ordered to pay USD 15 million (plus USD 13.6 million in legal and arbitration costs) to a US multinational. After that case, Kaufmann-Kohler was appointed as the investor's arbitrator in several ISDS cases brought by other multinationals

55 I recall reading the tribunal's reasoning as a doctoral student; it struck me then as exceptionally poorly reasoned and rambling, and gave me the impression that the arbitrators were intent to rule for the investor on every significant issue.

56 Van Harten, 'Leaders' (n 1).

57 The scare quotes are meant to emphasize that the ICC's 'Court' is an arbitration house, not a court with independent judges in the usual meaning of the term.

58 *Vivendi v Argentina (No 2): Compañia de Aguas del Aconquija SA and Vivendi Universal SA v Argentine Republic* (Annulment decision, 10 August 2010), ICSID Case No ARB/97/3, [204] and [217]–[228].

59 ibid [241].

60 *PSEG Global Inc v Turkey* (Award, 4 June 2004), 44 ILM 465.

against Argentina.[61] In each of these cases, the tribunal likewise took expansive approaches to the treaty before issuing (or apparently issuing) a large award to the investor. This context aside, Kaufmann-Kohler emerged as a leading hawk because, overall, she adopted many expansive interpretations with a high tendency towards expansiveness, often as the presiding arbitrator.[62]

C. Examples of pro-ISDS advocacy

Members of the ISDS industry often advocate for ISDS in misleading ways. Many early arbitrators were particularly active in promoting and justifying the growth of ISDS litigation in its boom phase from 2000 on, while also opposing proposals to reform ISDS up to the present. An example of dubious pro-ISDS advocacy by Christoph Schreuer was offered in Chapter 7; two more are highlighted here from among the leading hawks.

1. Yves Fortier's speech on 'Investment Protection and the Rule of Law'

In a speech in 2009 to the British Institute for International and Comparative Law (of which Fortier and other ISDS industry members arbitrators were 'patrons'), Fortier argued that 'the emergence of [bilateral investment treaties] has fostered a far more secure and fair investment environment and, indeed, a greater respect for the rule of law'.[63] The speech showcased common claims by ISDS promoters. For example, Fortier claimed that, without bilateral investment treaties (BITs), foreign investors 'were limited to the host country laws alone for the protection of their investments'.[64] That was wrong; foreign investors can obtain similar arbitration protections by negotiating them in their contracts with the state or can use political risk insurance, diplomatic support, and domestic courts to protect themselves. They are not limited to host country laws alone. Further, Fortier claimed that the advent of BITs '[n]aturally ... has been pivotal in the encouragement ... of foreign investment', but gave no evidence to support the claim, which was contradicted at the time by published studies.[65]

For his own sources, Fortier referred mostly to other ISDS repeat players, citing Stephen Schwebel, for example, for the position that international investment law had witnessed the 'dethroning' of the state 'from its status as the sole subject of international law'.[66] Fortier also cited Schwebel's presentation of the view that ISDS treaties have altered customary international law by their 'immense number' (although they only cover

[61] *AWG Group Ltd v Argentine Republic* (Award, 3 August 2006), ICSID Case No ARB/03/19; *EDF International SA v Argentine Republic* (Award, 8 March 2019), ICSID Case No ARB/07/30; and *Vivendi (No 2)* (n 58).

[62] Van Harten, 'Leaders' (n 1).

[63] Y Fortier, 'Investment Protection and Rule of Law: Change or Decline?' British Institute of International and Comparative Law, 50th Anniversary Event Series (17 March 2009) 5.

[64] ibid 6.

[65] ibid 8; see egM Hallward-Driemeier, 'Do Bilateral Investment Treaties Attract Foreign Direct Investment? Only a Bit ... and They Could Bite', World Bank Policy Research Working Paper (2003); KP Gallagher and MBL Birch, 'Do Investment Agreements Attract Investment? Evidence from Latin America' (2006) 7 J World Invest Trade 961.

[66] Fortier (n 63) 4, citing SM Schwebel, 'A BIT about ICSID' (2008) 23 ICSID Review—FILJ 4.

about 20 per cent of bilateral relationships among states), by 'the virtual universality of their adherence' (although most countries have only concluded ISDS treaties with approximately two dozen other countries), and by 'the predominant consistency of their terms' (although key provisions of the treaties have been interpreted divergently by tribunals).[67] As is common among ISDS promoters, Fortier also asserted that the treaties promote the rule of law by depoliticizing disputes and dealing with them 'as part of the commercial arbitration' field.[68] Yet it is inconsistent to argue that a tribunal which lacks institutional safeguards of independence also promotes the rule of law or is insulated from politics when executive officials can choose the arbitrators after learning who sued whom and in what political context, and likewise to approach the sovereign's role as if it were simply a private party in a commercial relationship. However, Fortier asserted sweepingly that these characteristics of ISDS treaties were 'key to ensuring that "the infrastructure of international law can sustain a robust global economy"',[69] again without supporting evidence.

Fortier also criticized the tentative moves at the time towards more openness in ISDS, warning that the costs and benefits of transparency 'are not necessarily apportioned equally among the system's participants'.[70] He did not mention the related point that most people have no right to access ISDS at all, even if it affects them directly, but warned instead that greater transparency and inclusion of other parties could undermine ISDS as 'neutral, non-political dispute resolution'.[71] Fortier thus ignored how ISDS is lopsided in favour of investors, when others are denied the right to protect their own interests in proceedings, and how it is inescapably politicized when safeguards of independence are absent. It would be more accurate to say that more transparency and inclusion in ISDS could challenge its politicized favouritism toward the ultra-wealthy.

Fortier also spoke against proposals to allow for judicial review of ISDS arbitrators, lamenting that 'every now and then critics clamour for the creation of an appellate structure' to encourage consistency in the interpretation of the treaties.[72] He warned that an appellate mechanism 'will not be implemented easily' and noted that 'perfect coherence' is not a part of any national judicial system.[73] Citing another repeat player, Jan Paulsson, Fortier claimed that the proposed reforms in ISDS '"would fare no better"',[74] rallying the audience to 'take heart' from his belief that ISDS was only 'living through a period of "growing pains"' and would emerge 'with even greater vitality'.[75] Fortier's speech is one example among many of how ISDS lawyers and arbitrators have presented or rehashed broad assertions, without offering any serious evidence or careful analysis, to undermine proposals for ISDS reform and maintain its deep imbalances and institutional failings.

[67] Fortier (n 63) 4, citing Schwebel (n 66) 4.

[68] Fortier (n 63) 10.

[69] Fortier (n 63) 11, citing DP Price, 'Chapter 11—Private Party vs Government, Investor–State Dispute Settlement: Frankenstein or Safety Valve?' (2000) 26 Canada–US LJ 107, 112.

[70] Fortier (n 63) 15, citing N Rubins, 'Opening the Investment Arbitration Process: At What Cost, for What Benefit?' in R Hoffman and C Tams (eds), *The International Convention on the Settlement of Investment Disputes (ICSID): Taking Stock after 40 Years* (Nomos 2007) 222.

[71] Fortier (n 63) 15, citing Rubins (n 70).

[72] Fortier (n 63) 16.

[73] ibid 17, citing E Lauterpacht, 'Aspects of the Administration of International Justice', Hersch Lauterpacht Memorial Lectures No 9 (1991).

[74] Fortier (n 63) 17, citing J Paulsson, 'Avoiding Unintended Consequences' in K Sauvant and M Chiswick-Patterson (eds), *Appeals Mechanism in International Investment Disputes* (OUP 2008) 245.

[75] Fortier (n 63) 21–22.

2. Francisco Orrego Vicuña's speech on 'Carlos Calvo, Honorary NAFTA Citizen'

The late Francisco Orrego Vicuña promoted ISDS treaties publicly from the early days. An example is his speech in 2002 to New York University law school, mockingly called 'Carlos Calvo, Honorary NAFTA Citizen'.[76] The speech criticized Canada, Mexico, and the United States for having issued a joint statement that reacted to early NAFTA tribunal rulings by making clear their shared understanding that NAFTA's minimum standard of treatment did not go beyond the deferential approach to sovereigns that is reflected in customary international law. For Orrego Vicuña, this step by the NAFTA governments evoked Carlos Calvo, the nineteenth-century Argentine jurist who is much maligned by ISDS promoters for his position that international law should oblige countries to give foreign investors the same protection as domestic investors, but not more.[77] Orrego Vicuña's remarks also forecast the reasoning of later tribunals, which undermined the NAFTA governments' joint statement by arguing that the content of customary international law is unclear and has 'dramatically evolved' in the context of ISDS treaties.[78]

In his speech, Orrego Vicuña promoted his own early investor-friendly rulings in *Fedax* and *Maffezini* (discussed in Chapters 3 and 5). He described the former ruling as having addressed the 'new reality of financial markets' and noted that the concept of MFN treatment was capable 'of improving the treatment accorded to its beneficiary [the investor] by comparing rights under different treaties', as in the latter ruling.[79] He also defended the then-recent ruling of the *Metalclad* tribunal, which had taken a highly expansive approach to 'fair and equitable treatment' and 'indirect' expropriation.[80] He claimed—again without evidence—that it was wrong to worry that developing countries did not appreciate the risks of ISDS treaties when they concluded them, a claim he found 'paternalistic' and dismissive of developing country lawyers as 'dummies'—as if all such lawyers were somehow immune from the pressures and incentives to favour multinationals and tycoons.[81]

As reflecting in the title of his speech, Orrego Vicuña joined the debates at the time about the use of ISDS in NAFTA. He objected to proposals that ISDS should be taken out of NAFTA or excluded from the then-proposed Free Trade Area of the Americas.[82] He spoke against limiting access by corporations and individuals to 'international claims procedures', noting that the ICJ's 'obstacles' to investor protection in the *Barcelona Traction* ruling of 1970 had 'fallen apart' because of decisions by arbitrators at the Iran–United States claims tribunal and the UN Compensation Commission.[83] Incidentally, Orrego Vicuña himself had sat on the latter body, and another leading hawk, Charles Brower, had sat on the former. Orrego Vicuña did not mention that both bodies have less stature as a source of international law than the ICJ. Perhaps most outlandish of all, Orrego Vicuña claimed in this speech that '[t]here is no reason to believe that foreign investments are detrimental to the environment'![84] Presumably he had not lived in the vicinity of a foreign-owned mine whose tailings pond has leaked.

[76] F Orrego Vicuña, 'Carlos Calvo, Honorary NAFTA Citizen', Keynote remarks to the Conference on Regulatory Expropriations in International Law, New York University School of Law (26 April 2002).
[77] See Chapter 3.
[78] Orrego Vicuña, 'Carlos Calvo' (n 76) 11.
[79] ibid 21.
[80] ibid 14–15.
[81] ibid 17.
[82] ibid 17–18.
[83] ibid 19–20.
[84] ibid 18.

Fortier and Orrego Vicuña are two of many dozens of promoters of ISDS in the arbitration industry. Even among leading hawks, both are probably eclipsed by Charles Brower, whose promotional work would warrant a chapter of its own. In my experience as an academic who has followed the ascendance of ISDS, the industry's role in promoting the treaties has been a crucial source of misinformation for policy makers and the public. Over and over, members of the industry have repeated dubious pro-ISDS assertions, even after the treaties' weaknesses and the risks for countries were readily apparent. They advocated for ISDS in ways that benefited themselves or their clients, without adequate attention to fundamental values such as principles of fairness and independence and to the wider impact on countries.

Bibliography

Agreement on Internal Trade (Canada), *Report of the Article 1704 Panel Concerning the Dispute between Alberta and Canada regarding the Manganese-Based Fuel Additives Act* (Agreement on Internal Trade (Canada) 2 June 1998).

Aisbett E, 'Bilateral Investment Treaties and Foreign Direct Investment: Correlation versus Causation' in KP Sauvant and LE Sachs (eds), *The Effect of Treaties on Foreign Direct Investment: Bilateral Investment Treaties, Double Taxation Treaties, and Investment Flows* (OUP 2009).

Akhavan P and others, 'An Open Letter about Investor–State Dispute Settlement' (*McGill Fortier Chair in International Arbitration and International Commercial Law*, April 2015) <https://www.mcgill.ca/fortier-chair/isds-open-letter>accessed 14 January 2020.

Akinremi O, 'An Empirical Analysis of the Bilateral Investment Treaties of the Top Ten GDP Producing African States', JD Student Paper for International Investment Law course, Osgoode Hall Law School (2014).

Allee T and Peinhardt C, 'Contingent Credibility: The Impact of Investment Treaty Violations on Foreign Direct Investment' (2011) 65 Int'l Org 401.

Allen & Overy, 'Polish Banks Face Huge Losses under Proposed FX Loan Legislation' (*European Finance Litigation Review*, undated) <http://www.allenovery.com/publications/en-gb/european-finance-litigation-review/central-europe/Pages/Polish-banks-face-huge-losses-under-proposed-FX-loan-legislation.aspx> accessed 11 August 2019.

Alvaredo F and others, *World Inequality Report 2018* (World Inequality Lab 2017).

Álvarez-Correa Glen C (Colombian Minister of Commerce, Industry, and Tourism), Letter of 4 December 2014 responding to questions from Jorge Enrique Robledo (Colombian Senator) (on file with author).

American Cancer Society, 'Report: Big Tobacco is Targeting the World's most Vulnerable to Increase Profits' (American Cancer Society 2018).

Ampuero Llerena R, 'Peru's State Coordination and Response System for International Investment Disputes' *Investment Treaty News* (14 January 2013).

Appleton B, 'Municipalities and the MAI', Brief by Appleton and Associates (1998).

Appleton B, 'The Song is Over: Why It's Time to Stop Talking about an International Investment Arbitration Appellate Body' (2013) 107 ASIL Proc 23.

Arcuri A, 'The Great Asymmetry and the Rule of Law in International Investment Arbitration' in L Sachs, L Johnson, and J Coleman (eds), *Yearbook on International Investment Law and Policy 2018* (OUP 2019).

Atkinson J, 'Case 3: Barisan Gold Mine', Oxfam National Policy Coordinator and Mining Ombudsman for Community Aid Abroad (2000).

Avery B, 'MMT Not an Issue in U.S.' *Edmonton Journal* (Edmonton, AL, 22 November 1996).

Ayine D and others, 'Lifting the Lid on Foreign Investment Contracts: The Real Deal for Sustainable Development', Sustainable Markets Briefing Paper No 1 (International Institute for Environment and Development 2005).

Azpiazu D, Basualdo EM, and Nochteff HJ, 'Menem's Great Swindle: Convertibility, Inequality and the Neoliberal Shock', North American Congress on Latin America Report on the Americas (25 September 2007).

Baker McKenzie, 'Withdrawal from Investment Treaties: An Omen for Waning Investor Protection in AP?' *Lexology* (12 May 2017).

Bambaci J, Saront T, and Tommasi M, 'The Political Economy of Economic Reforms in Argentina' (2002) 5 Policy Reform 75.

Barlow M and Clarke T, *MAI: The Multilateral Agreement on Investment and the Threat to Canadian Sovereignty* (Stoddart 1997).

Batifort S and Benton Heath J, 'The New Debate on the Interpretation of MFN Clauses in Investment Treaties: Putting the Brakes on Multilateralization' (2017) 111 AJIL 873.

Berger A and others, 'More Stringent BITs, Less Ambiguous Effects on FDI? Not a Bit!', World Trade Organization Staff Working Paper ERSD-2010-10 (2010).

Berkeley B, 'Zaire: An African Horror Story' *The Atlantic* (August 1993).

Bernasconi N, 'Vattenfall v. Germany Arbitration', International Institute for Sustainable Development background paper (2009).

Bernasconi N and others, 'Harnessing Investment for Sustainable Development: Inclusion of Investor Obligations and Corporate Accountability Provisions in Trade and Investment Agreements', Background document for the expert meeting co-hosted by the International Institute for Sustainable Development and Friedrich Ebert Stiftung (2018).

Bernasconi-Osterwalder N and Brauch MD, 'Is "Moonlighting" a Problem? The Role of ICJ Judges in ISDS', International Institute for Sustainable Development Commentary (November 2017).

Biber E, 'The Importance of Resource Allocation in Administrative Law' (2008) 60 Admin L Rev 1.

Biondi A and Farley M, *The Right to Damages in European Law* (Wolters Kluwer 2009).

'Bionote—Anna Joubin-Bret' (undated) <https://msal.ru/upload/medialibrary/ff5/Biograficheskaya_spravka.pdf> accessed 14 January 2020.

Biucovic L, 'Impact of the Adoption of the Model Law in Canada: Creating a New Environment for International Arbitration' (1998) 30 Can Bus LJ 376.

Bland B and Donnan S, 'Indonesia to Terminate More than 60 Bilateral Investment Treaties' *Financial Times* (London, 26 March 2014).

Blum W, *Killing Hope: US Military and CIA Interventions since World War II* (Black Rose Books 1998).

Blumberg K and Walsh MP, *Status Report concerning the Use of MMT in Gasoline* (International Council on Clean Transportation 2004).

Blythe SE, 'The Advantages of Investor–State Arbitration as a Dispute Resolution Mechanism in Bilateral Investment Treaties' (2013) 47 Int'l Lawyer 273.

Boase M, 'A Genealogy of Censurable Conduct: Antecedents for an International Minimum Standard of Investor Conduct' in SW Schill, CJ Tams, and R Hofmann (eds), *International Investment Law and History* (Edward Elgar 2018).

Bonnell M and others, 'Strike 1: Rights of Investors against Indonesian Mining Laws' (King & Wood Mallesons, 28 August 2014).

Boone Barrera E, 'The Case for Removing the Fair and Equitable Treatment Standard from NAFTA', Centre for International Governance Innovation Paper No 128 (2017).

Boras A, 'Ethyl Fights Ban on MMT' *Calgary Herald* (Calgary, AL, 22 January 1997).

Borchard EM, 'The "Minimum Standard" of the Treatment of Aliens' (1940) 38 Mich L Rev 445.

Boseley S, 'Threats, Bullying, Lawsuits: Tobacco Industry's Dirty War for the African Market' *The Guardian* (London, 12 July 2017).

Bradner E and Biskupic J, 'How the Supreme Court could Shape the 2020 Presidential Race' (*CNN*, 23 January 2019).

Braithwaite J and Drahos P, *Global Business Regulation* (CUP 2000).

Brand RA, 'Enforcement of Foreign Money Judgments in the United States: In Search of Uniformity and International Acceptance' (1991) 67 Notre Dame L Rev 253.

Bratton WW and others, 'Introduction: Regulatory Competition and Institutional Evolution' in WW Bratton and others (eds), *International Regulatory Competition and Coordination* (Clarendon 1996).

Brauch MD, 'Exhaustion of Local Remedies in International Investment Law', International Institute for Sustainable Development Best Practices Series (2017).

Brewin S, 'Security for Costs', International Institute for Sustainable Development Best Practices Series (2018).

Breytenbach W and others, 'Conflicts in the Congo: From Kivu to Kabila' (2010) 8 African Security Rev 33.

Brierly JEC, 'Canadian Acceptance of International Commercial Arbitration' (1988) 40 Maine L Rev 287.

British Columbia Legislature, *Report on the Multilateral Agreement on Investment: Transcripts of Proceedings* (1998).

Broad R, 'Remembering the "Tokyo No" Fifty Years Later' (*Triple Crisis*, 5 December 2014) <http://triplecrisis.com/remembering-the-tokyo-no-fifty-years-later/>accessed 14 January 2020.

Broches A, 'Bilateral Investment Protection Treaties and Arbitration of Investment Disputes' in JC Schultsz and AJ van den Berg (eds), *The Art of Arbitration* (Kluwer 1982).

Broches A, 'Selected Essays: World Bank, ICSID, and other Subjects of Public and Private International Law' (M Nijhoff 1995).

Brower CN and Schill SW, 'Is Arbitration a Threat or a Boon to the Legitimacy of International Investment Law?' (2009) 9 Chi J Int'l L 471.

Brown JG, 'International Investment Agreements: Regulatory Chill in the Face of Litigious Heat' (2013) 3 Western J Legal Stud (Article 3).

Burke-White WW, 'The Argentine Financial Crisis: State Liability under BITs and the Legitimacy of the ICSID System' (2008) 3 Asian J WTO and Int'l Health L Pol 199.

Burnett HG and Beess und Chrostin J, 'Interim Measures in Response to the Criminal Prosecution of Corporations and their Employees by Host States in Parallel with Investment Arbitration Proceedings' (2015) 30 Md J Int'l L 31.

Calvo C, *Le Droit International* (5th edn, A Rousseau 1896).

Campaign for Tobacco-Free Kids, *US Chamber of Commerce: Blowing Smoke for Big Tobacco* (July 2015).

Campaign for Tobacco-Free Kids, 'Research Evidence' in *Plain Packaging of Tobacco Products Toolkit* (2016).

Campello D and Barreiro Lemos L, 'The Non-Ratification of Bilateral Investment Treaties in Brazil: A Story of Conflict in a Land of Cooperation' (2015) Rev Int'l Pol Econ 22.

Cave T and Rowell A, *A Quiet Word: Lobbying, Crony Capitalism and Broken Politics in Britain* (The Bodley Head 2014).

Center for International Environmental Law and others, *Whose Resources? Whose Common Good? Towards a New Paradigm of Environmental Justice and the National Interest in Indonesia* (2002).

Chipty T, 'Addendum to Study of the Impact of the Tobacco Plain Packaging Measure on Smoking Prevalence in Australia' (Australian Government Department of Health, 19

May 2016) <https://www1.health.gov.au/internet/main/publishing.nsf/content/study-pp-measure>accessed 14 January 2020.

Ciobanu C, 'Romania to Withdraw Rosia Montana UNESCO Application' (*BlogActiv*, 31 August 2017) <https://guests.blogactiv.eu/2017/08/31/romania-to-withdraw-rosia-montana-unesco-application/> accessed 14 January 2020.

Cole T, *The Structure of Investment Arbitration* (Routledge 2013).

Coleman M and others, 'Foreign Investors' Options to Deal with Regulatory Changes in the Renewable Energy Sector' (*Steptoe & Johnson Investor–State Arbitration Series*, 23 September 2014) <https://www.steptoe.com/en/news-publications/foreign-investors-options-to-deal-with-regulatory-changes-in-the-renewable-energy-sector-1.html> accessed 11 August 2019.

Colombia (Consejo Nacional de Política Económica y Social República), *Fortalecimiento de la Estrategia del Estado Para Prevención y Atención de Controversias Internacionales de Inversión*, Conpes Doc 3684 (author's translation) (19 October 2010).

Colombia (Ministry of Commerce, Industry, and Tourism), 'Managing Investment Disputes in Colombia', Power Point presentation (on file with author) (14 March 2012).

Cordero Moss G, 'Full Protection and Security' in A Reinisch (ed), *Standards of Investment Protection* (OUP 2008).

Corporate Accountability International, Southeast Asia Tobacco Control Alliance (SEATCA), and Global Center for Good Governance in Tobacco Control, *Anti-Corruption and Tobacco Control* (SEATCA 2017).

Corporate Europe Observatory and Friends of the Earth Europe, 'Lawyers Subverting the Public Interest: Lobby Group EFILA's Stake in Investment Arbitration', Briefing report (2015).

Costa R, 'Trump Will Nominate David Malpass, a Treasury Official, to Lead World Bank' *The Washington Post* (Washington DC, 4 February 2019).

Cotula L, *Investment Contracts and Sustainable Development: How to Make Contracts for Fairer and More Sustainable Natural Resource Investments* (International Institute for Environment and Development 2010).

Council of the European Union, 'Negotiating Directives for a Convention Establishing a Multilateral Court for the Settlement of Investment Disputes' (20 March 2018).

Crawford J, 'Treaty and Contract in Investment Arbitration' (2008) 24 Arb Int'l 351.

Credit Suisse Research Institute, *Global Wealth Databook 2018* (2018).

Credit Suisse Research Institute, *Global Wealth Report 2018* (Credit Suisse Research Institute 2018).

Crosbie E and Thomson G, 'Why Did it Take 53 Months for NZ to Introduce Plain Cigarette Packs?' *Noted* (14 June 2018).

Crowell & Moring, 'Government Affairs' (*Crowell & Moring*, undated) <https://www.crowell.com/Practices/Government-Affairs> accessed 14 January 2020.

Daele K, *Challenge and Disqualification of Arbitrators in International Arbitration* (Kluwer Law International 2012).

D'Ascoli S and Scherr KM, 'The Rule of Prior Exhaustion of Local Remedies in the International Law Doctrine and Its Application in the Specific Context of Human Rights Protection', European University Institute Working Paper LAW No 2007/02 (2007).

Dayen D, 'A Monster Payday in Argentina Shows a Flaw in Trump's NAFTA Renegotiation' *The Intercept* (28 July 2017).

De la Fuente M, 'A Personal View: The Water War in Cochabamba, Bolivia: Privatization Triggers an Uprising' (2003) 23 Mountain Res Dev 98.

De Smith SA, 'The Right to a Hearing in English Administrative Law' (1955) 68 Harv L Rev 569.

Delaume GR, 'Sovereign Immunity and Transnational Arbitration' (1987) 3 Arb Int'l 28.

Lord Denning, 'The Independence of the Judges', Presidential Address to the Holdsworth Club of the University of Birmingham (1949–50).

DePalma A, 'Nafta's Powerful Little Secret; Obscure Tribunals Settle Disputes, but Go Too Far, Critics Say' *New York Times* (New York, 11 March 2001).

Department of Trade and Industry (South Africa), 'Bilateral Investment Treaty Policy Framework Review', Government Position Paper (2009).

Dezalay Y, 'Between the State, Law, and the Market: The Social and Professional Stakes in the Construction and Definition of a Regulatory Arena' in WW Bratton and others (eds), *International Regulatory Competition and Coordination* (Clarendon 1996).

Dezalay S and Dezalay YM, 'Professionals of International Justice: From the Shadow of State Diplomacy to the Pull of the Market of Arbitration' in J d'Aspremont and others (eds), *International Law as a Profession* (CUP 2017).

Dezalay Y and Garth BG, *Dealing in Virtue: International Commercial Arbitration and the Construction of a Transnational Legal Order* (University of Chicago Press 1996).

Diehl A, *The Core Standard of International Investment Protection: Fair and Equitable Treatment* (Kluwer Law International 2012).

Dingle L and Bates D, 'A Conversation with Judge Stephen M Schwebel' (*University of Cambridge Squire Law Library*, 13 May 2009) <https://www.squire.law.cam.ac.uk/eminent-scholars-archivejudge-stephen-m-schwebel/conversation-judge-stephen-m-schwebel> accessed 14 January 2020.

Dobbin M, *The Myth of The Good Corporate Citizen* (James Lorimer and Co 2003).

Donner R, *The Regulation of Nationality in International Law* (2nd edn, Transnational Publishers 1994).

Drope J and Schluger AW (eds), *Tobacco Atlas* (6th edn, American Cancer Society and Vital Strategies 2018).

Duffy A, 'Canada Drops Ban on Gas Additive: MMT Now Permitted' *Ottawa Citizen* (Ottawa, ON, 21 July 1998).

Eagleton C, *The Responsibility of States in International Law* (NYU Press 1928).

Eberhardt P and Olivet C, *Profiting from Injustice* (CEO and Transnational Institute 2012).

Ebert BP, *Forum Shopping in International Investment Law* (Mohr Siebeck 2017).

Echeverria G, 'Redressing Torture: A Genealogy of Remedies and Enforcement' (2006) 16 Torture 152.

Edwards R and Hoek J, 'Protect our Children: Standardise Tobacco Packaging Now', *Aspire2025* (7 October 2017).

El-Kosheri A, 'Curriculum Vitae' (Kosheri, Rashed & Riad, undated) <http://www.krr-law.com/assets/det-ver-of-dr-ahmed-cv.pdf> accessed 14 January 2020.

Epstein L, Knight J, and Shvetsova O, 'Comparing Judicial Selection Systems' (2001) 10 Wm & Mary Bill Rts J 7.

European Commission, 'Natura 2000' (*European Commission Environment*, undated) <http://ec.europa.eu/environment/nature/natura2000/index_en.htm> accessed 14 January 2020.

European Commission, 'Environment: Commission Refers Germany to Court over Coal Power Plant in Moorburg', Press release (*European Commission Press corner*, 25 March 2015) <http://europa.eu/rapid/press-release_IP-15-4669_en.htm> accessed 14 January 2020.

European Commission, 'The Multilateral Investment Court Project' (*European Commission News archive*, 21 December 2016, latest update 7 June 2019) <http://trade.ec.europa.eu/doclib/press/index.cfm?id=1608> accessed 14 January 2020.

EU Council, Directive 92/43/EEC of 21 May 1992 on the conservation of natural habitats and of wild fauna and flora, Official Journal of the European Communities No L 206/7 (22 July 1992).

Fasken, 'Government Relations and Strategy' (*Fasken*, undated) <https://www.fasken.com/en/solution/practice/government-relations-and-strategy/#sort=%40fclientworksortdate75392%20descending> accessed 14 January 2020.

Faya Rodriguez A, 'The Most-Favored-Nation Clause in International Investment Agreements—A Tool for Treaty Shopping?' (2008) 25 J Int'l Arb 89.

Fernholz T, 'First, a US Hedge Fund Tried to Seize Argentina's Boat, then Its Rockets—Now It's After a Person' *Quartz* (5 November 2014).

Feschuk S, 'Marchi Advocates Ban on MMT' *Globe and Mail* (26 September 1996).

Finnegan W, 'Leasing the Rain' *The New Yorker* (New York, 31 March 2002).

Fleming S, 'Corporate Power on the Agenda at Jackson Hole' *Financial Times* (London, 17 August 2018).

Fletcher G, 'U.S. Bans It; Canada Burns It' *National Post* (6 September 2002).

Foley B, *Deference and the Presumption of Constitutionality* (Institute of Public Administration 2008).

Fontoura Costa JA, 'Comparing WTO Panelists and ICSID Arbitrators: The Creation of International Legal Fields' (2011) 1 Oñati Socio-Legal Ser 1.

Forest Watch Indonesia, World Resources Institute, and Global Forest Watch, *The State of the Forest: Indonesia* (2002).

Fortier Y, 'Investment Protection and Rule of Law: Change or Decline?' British Institute of International and Comparative Law, 50th Anniversary Event Series (17 March 2009).

Franck SD, 'Foreign Direct Investment, Investment Treaty Arbitration, and the Rule of Law' (2007) 19 Global Bus Dev't LJ 337.

Free Trade Commission (NAFTA), *Notes of Interpretation of Certain Chapter 11 Provisions* (NAFTA 31 July 2001).

Fukunaga Y, 'ISDS under the CPTPP and Beyond: Japanese Perspectives' (Kluwer Arbitration Blog, 30 May 2018) <http://arbitrationblog.kluwerarbitration.com/2018/05/30/isds-cptpp-beyond-japanese-perspectives/> accessed 14 January 2020.

'Gabriel Resources Pushes Arbitration Case over Gold Mine Rosia Montana Romania' *Mining See* (12 April 2016).

Gallagher KP, 'The New Vulture Culture: Sovereign Debt Restructuring and Trade and Investment Treaties', IDEAs Working Paper No 02/2011 (2011).

Gallagher KP and Birch MBL, 'Do Investment Agreements Attract Investment? Evidence from Latin America' (2006) 7 J World Invest Trade 961.

Garcia FJ, 'Third Party Funding as Exploitation of the Investment Treaty System', Boston College Law School Faculty Paper (2018).

Gaukrodger D, 'Investment Treaties and Shareholder Claims for Reflective Loss: Insights from Advanced Systems of Corporate Law', Organisation for Economic Co-operation and Development Working Paper on International Investment 2014/02 (2014).

Gaukrodger D, 'Appointing Authorities and the Selection of Arbitrators in Investor–State Dispute Settlement: An Overview', Organisation for Economic Co-operation and Development Consultation Paper (2018).

Gaukrodger D and Gordon K, 'Investor–State Dispute Settlement: A Scoping Paper for the Investment Policy Community', Organisation for Economic Co-operation and Development Working Paper on International Investment 2012/03 (2013).

George S and Sabelli F, *Faith and Credit: The World Bank's Secular Empire* (Penguin 1994).

Gilman N, 'The New International Economic Order: A Reintroduction' (2015) 6(1) Humanity 1.

Giorgetti C, 'The Arbitral Tribunal: Selection and Replacement of Arbitrators' in C Giorgetti (ed), *Litigating Investment Disputes: A Practitioner's Guide* (Brill 2014).

Global Justice Now, 'Ending Corporate Impunity: The Struggle to Bring About a Binding UN Treaty on Transnational Corporations and Human Rights', Raw data on 2017 revenues of governments and corporations (2018).

Goldhaber MD, 'Arbitration Scorecard 2011: The Biggest Cases You Never Heard Of' *American Lawyer* (New York, 6 July 2011).

Gómez MA, 'The Global Chase: Seeking the Recognition and Enforcement of the Lago Agrio Judgment outside of Ecuador' (2013) 1 Stan J Complex Litig 429.

Gómez-Pinzón, 'Firm Profile' (Chambers and Partners, undated) <https://chambers.com/profile/organisation/3304?publicationTypeId=2> accessed 14 January 2020.

Gordon K, 'Investment Guarantees and Political Risk Insurance: Institutions, Incentives and Development', OECD Investment Policy Perspective 2008 (OECD 2008).

Griffin P, *The Carbon Majors Database: CDP Carbon Majors Report 2017* (Carbon Disclosure Project 2017).

Grimmer S, 'The Determination of Arbitrator Challenges by the Secretary-General of the Permanent Court of Arbitration' in C Giorgetti (ed), *Challenges and Recusals of Judges and Arbitrators in International Courts and Tribunals* (Brill 2015).

Grinspun R and Kreklewich R, 'Consolidating Neoliberal Reforms: "Free Trade" as a Conditioning Framework' (1994) 43 Stud Pol Econ 33.

Grishko E, '4 Ways to Identify and Mitigate the Political Risks of Global Business' (*TradeReady Blog*, 17 May 2018) <http://www.tradeready.ca/2018/topics/international-trade-finance/4-ways-mitigate-political-risks/> accessed 14 January 2020.

Gross SG, 'Inordinate Chill: BITs, Non-NAFTA MITS, and Host-State Regulatory Freedom—An Indonesian Case Study' (2003) Mich J Int'l L 894.

Güven B and Johnson L, 'The Policy Implications of Third-Party Funding in Investor–State Dispute Settlement', Columbia Center on Sustainable Investment Paper (2019).

Guzman M and Stiglitz JE, 'Creating a Framework for Sovereign Debt Restructuring That Works' in M Guzman, JA Ocampo, and JE Stiglitz (eds), *Too Little, Too Late: The Quest to Resolve Sovereign Debt Crises* (Columbia University Press 2016).

Hafner-Burton EM, Puig S, and Victor DG, 'Against Secrecy: The Social Cost of International Dispute Settlement' (2017) 42 Yale J Int'l L 279.

Hallward-Driemeier M, 'Do Bilateral Investment Treaties Attract Foreign Direct Investment? Only a Bit … and They Could Bite', World Bank Policy Research Working Paper (2003).

Hamby C, 'The Secret Threat that Makes Corporations More Powerful than Countries' *BuzzFeed News* (30 August 2016).

Hepburn J, 'Final Costs Details are Released in Philip Morris v. Australia Following Request by IA Reporter' *IAReporter* (California, IL, 21 March 2019).

Herlihy D and Macaulay B, 'Strategic Choices under the ECT' (2007) 2(2) Global Arbit Rev 26.

Heron M, 'Government Confident It Can Send Tobacco Companies Packing' *RadioNZ* (9 September 2016).

Hershey A, 'The Calvo and Drago Doctrines' (1907) 1 AJIL 26.

Hertz DB and Thomas H, *Risk Analysis and Its Applications* (John Wiley & Sons 1983).

Hochschild A, *King Leopold's Ghost: A Story of Greed, Terror, and Heroism in Colonial Africa* (Mariner Books 1998).

Hoffman AK, 'Indirect Expropriation' in A Reinisch (ed), *Standards of Investment Protection* (OUP 2008).

Hood M, *Gunboat Diplomacy 1895–1905* (George Allen & Unwin 1975).

Houde M-F, 'Most-Favoured-Nation Treatment in International Investment Law', Organisation for Economic Co-operation and Development Working Paper on International Investment No 2004/2 (OECD 2004).

Hudson MO, *International Tribunals* (Carnegie Endowment for International Peace and the Brookings Institution 1944).

'ICC Left Reeling as Arbitration Court Chairman Tercier Resigns' *The Lawyer* (31 March 2008).

Imai S, Mehranvar L, and Sander J, 'Breaching Indigenous Law: Canadian Mining in Guatemala' (2007) 6 Indigenous LJ 101.

India, 'Model Text for the Indian Bilateral Investment Treaty' (undated), available from UNCTAD International Investment Agreements Navigator: < https://investmentpolicy.unctad.org/international-investment-agreements > accessed 14 January 2020.

Intergovernmental Panel on Climate Change, *Summary for Policymakers of IPCC Special Report on Global Warming of 1.5°C Approved by Governments* (IPCC 2018).

International Arbitration Institute, 'Anna Joubin-Bret' (*International Arbitration Institute*, undated) <http://www.iaiparis.com/profile/anna.joubin-bret> accessed 14 January 2020.

International Bank for Reconstruction and Development and International Development Association, 'Annual Address by George D. Woods, President of the Bank and its Affiliates', 1964 Annual Meetings of the Boards of Governors (Tokyo, 7–11 September 1964).

International Centre for Settlement of Investment Disputes (ICSID), *Rules of Procedure for Arbitration Proceedings*, revised 26 September 1984 and 1 January 2003 (original rules 1968), reprinted in *Convention, Regulations and Rules* (ICSID 2003).

ICSID, *Rules Governing the Additional Facility for the Administration of Proceedings by the Secretariat of the International* Centre *for Settlement of Investment Disputes*, revised 1 January 2003 and 10 April 2006 (original rules 1978) 1 ICSID Rep 213.

ICSID, 'Schedule of Fees' (*ICSID*, 1 July 2017) <https://icsid.worldbank.org/en/Pages/icsiddocs/Schedule-of-Fees.aspx> accessed 14 January 2020.

ICSID, 'Panels of Arbitrators and of Conciliators' (*ICSID*, 27 June 2019) <https://icsid.worldbank.org/en/Pages/about/Panels-of-Arbitrators-and-Conciliators.aspx> accessed 14 January 2020.

International Council on Monuments and Sites (ICOMOS), *Evaluations of Nominations of Cultural and Mixed Properties*, Report for the World Heritage Committee (ICOMOS 2018).

International Court of Justice (ICJ), 'Declarations Recognizing the Jurisdiction of the Court as Compulsory' (*ICJ*, undated) <https://www.icj-cij.org/en/declarations> accessed 14 January 2020.

International Crisis Group, *Indonesian Natural Resources and Law Enforcement*, Asia Report No 29 (2000).

International Energy Agency, *World Energy Outlook 2018: Electricity Database* (2018).

International Law Commission, 'Draft Articles on Responsibility of States for Internationally Wrongful Acts', *Report of the International Law Commission on the Work of Its Fifty-Third Session*, UN GAOR, 56th Sess, Supp No 10, annex, UN Doc A/56/10 (2001).

International Monetary Fund (IMF), *Balance of Payments Manual* (6th edn, IMF 2009).

IMF, 'The Liberalization and Management of Capital Flows: An Institutional View', IMF Policy Paper (14 November 2012).

IMF, 'Sovereign Debt Restructuring—Recent Developments and Implications for the Fund's Legal and Policy Framework', IMF Policy Paper (2013).

International Union against Tuberculosis and Lung Disease, 'Uruguay Becomes the First Country to Require Plain Packaging of Tobacco Products in Latin America' (*The Union*, 9 August 2018) <https://www.theunion.org/news-centre/news/uruguay-becomes-the-first-country-to-require-plain-packaging-of-tobacco-products-in-latin-america> accessed 14 January 2020.

'Investment Disputes Committee Settles 27 disputes' *Egypt Today* (3 January 2018).

Investment Treaty Working Group of the International Arbitration Committee of the American Bar Association Section on International Law, 'Initial Task Force Discussion Paper: Executive Summary & Conclusions and Recommendations', Discussion Paper (2016).

Ireland R, 'The Tobacco Plain Packaging Wars Continue Following Appeal of WTO Ruling' (*Regulating for Globalization*, 12 September 2018) <http://regulatingforglobalization.com/2018/09/12/tobacco-plain-packaging-wars-continue-following-appeal-wto-ruling/> accessed 14 January 2020.

Isayev UT, 'Session VII: Foreign Investment during the Transition: How to Attract It, and How to Make the Best Use of It', Presentation to the International Monetary Fund–Kyrgyz Republic Conference on Challenges to Economies in Transition: Stabilization, Growth, and Governance (Bishkek, 27–28 May 1998).

Jacobson P, 'Revealed: Australian Miner Used Arbitration Threat to Upend Indonesian Environmental Law' *Mongabay* (15 September 2016).

Jamasmie C, 'Romania Wants City of Rosia Montana Application to be Pulled from UNESCO List' *Mining.com* (30 August 2017).

Jennings R and Watts A (eds), *Oppenheim's International* Law, vol I (9th edn, Longman 1992).

Johnson L, 'What Happened at UNCITRAL's April WG III Session? What Will Happen Next?' (*Columbia Center on Sustainable Development Blog*, 3 May 2019) <http://ccsi.columbia.edu/2019/05/03/what-happened-at-uncitral-april-1-5-what-will-happen-next/> accessed 14 January 2020.

Johnson L, Sachs L, and Sachs J, 'Investor–State Dispute Settlement, Public Interest and US Domestic Law', Columbia Center on Sustainable Development Policy Paper (2015).

Johnson L, Coleman J, and Güven B, 'Withdrawal of Consent to Investor–State Arbitration and Termination of Investment Treaties' *Investment Treaty News* (24 April 2018).

Joseph S, 'Protracted Lawfare: The Tale of Chevron Texaco in the Amazon' (2012) 3 J Human Rights and Env't 70.

'Judges of the International Court of Justice Decide to No Longer Participate as Arbitrators in ISDS Cases' *Investment Treaty News* (21 December 2018).

Kahale III G, 'ISDS: The Wild, Wild West of International Law and Arbitration', Brooklyn Lecture on International Business Law, Brooklyn Law School (3 April 2018).

Karrer PA, 'Curriculum Vitae' (Pierre Karrer, undated) <http://www.pierrekarrer.com/curriculum.html> accessed 14 January 2020.

Kawharu A, 'Renouncing Investor–State Dispute Settlement in Australia, Then New Zealand: Déjà Vu', Sydney Law School Research Paper No 18/03 (2 February 2018).

Kebeich S and Abouelseoud N, 'State–Investor Dispute Resolution Mechanisms under the Egyptian Investment Law' *Lexocology.com* (23 September 2018).

Keenan G, 'Car Dealers Join Fight to Ban Gas Additive MMT' *Globe and Mail* (27 September 1996).

Kellow A, 'Multi-Level and Multi-Arena Governance: The Limits of Integration and the Possibilities of Forum Shopping' (2012) 12 Int'l Envt'l Agreements: Pol, L Econ 327.

Kelly JM, 'Audi Alteram Partem' (1964) 9 Nat'l L Forum 103.

Kelsey J, 'Regulatory Chill: Learning from New Zealand's Plain Packaging Tobacco Law' (2017) 17 QUT L Rev 21.

Kelsey J, Notes of UNCITRAL WG III session (April 2019) (on file with author).

Kierstead S, 'Referral to Arbitration under Article 8 of the UNCITRAL Model Law: The Canadian Approach' (1999) 31 Can Bus LJ 98.

Kim J, 'US Covert Action in Indonesia in the 1960s: Assessing the Motives and Consequences' (2002) 9 J Int'l Area Stud 63.

King JA, 'The Justiciability of Resource Allocation' (2007) 70 MLR 197.

Kinnear M and Hansen R, 'The Influence of NAFTA Chapter 11 in the BIT Landscape' (2005) 12 UC Davis J Int'l L Pol 111.

Kirkpatrick C and others, *A Trade SIA Relating to the Negotiation of a Comprehensive Economic and Trade Agreement (CETA) between the EU and Canada*, Final Report (2011).

Kitman JL, 'The Secret History of Lead' *The Nation* (2 March 2000).

Kläger R, 'Fair and Equitable Treatment: A Look at the Theoretical Underpinnings of Legitimacy and Fairness' (2010) 11 J World Invest Trade 435.

Kläger R, *'Fair and Equitable Treatment' in International Investment Law* (CUP 2011).

Knauer S, 'Vattenfall vs Germany: Power Plant Battle Goes to International Arbitration' *Spiegel Online* (15 July 2009).

Kosheri, Rashed & Riad, 'Company Profile' (*Kosheri, Rashed & Riad*, undated) <http://www.krr-law.com/#companyprofile> accessed 14 January 2020.

Kosheri, Rashed & Riad, 'Founders' (*Kosheri, Rashed & Riad*, undated) <http://www.krr-law.com/#founders> accessed 14 January 2020.

Kruk ME and others, 'Mortality Due to Low-Quality Health Systems in the Universal Health Coverage Era: A Systematic Analysis of Amenable Deaths in 137 Countries' (2018) 392 *The Lancet* 2203.

Kurtz J, 'The Use and Abuse of WTO Law in Investor–State Arbitration: Competition and its Discontents' (2009) 20 EJIL 749.

Langford M, Behn D, and Hilleren Lie R, 'The Revolving Door in International Investment Arbitration' (2017) 20 JIEL 301.

Latore RM, 'Coming Out of the Dark: Achieving Justice for Victims of Human Rights Violations by South American Military Regimes' (2002) 25 BC Int'l Comp L Rev 419.

Lauterpacht E, 'Aspects of the Administration of International Justice', Hersch Lauterpacht Memorial Lectures No 9 (1991).

Lavopa F, 'Crisis, Emergency Measures and the Failure of the ISDS System: The Case of Argentina', South Centre Investment Policy Brief No 2 (2015).

Lavranos N, 'After Philip Morris II: The "Regulatory Chill" Argument Failed—Yet Again' (*Kluwer Arbitration Blog*, 18 August 2016) <http://arbitrationblog.kluwerarbitration.com/2016/08/18/after-philipp-morris-ii-the-regulatory-chill-argument-failed-yet-again/> accessed 14 January 2020.

Lavrijssen S, Gerbrandy A, and Essens O, 'European and National Standards of Review: Differentiation or Convergence' in O Essens, A Gerbrandy, and S Lavrijssen (eds), *National Courts and the Standard of Review in Competition Law and Economic Regulation* (Europa 2009).

League of Nations Conference for the Codification of International Law, *Responsibility of States for Damage Caused in their Territory to the Person or Property of Foreigners*, Bases of Discussion, vol 3, LN Doc C.75.M.69.1929.V (1929) 15.

Lee LJ, 'Barcelona Traction in the Twenty-First Century: Revisiting its Customary and Policy Underpinnings 35 Years Later' (2006) 42 Stanford J Int'l L 237.

Legal Information Institute, 'Sovereignty' (*Cornell Law School*, undated) <https://www.law.cornell.edu/wex/sovereignty> accessed 14 January 2020.

Levine E, '*Amicus Curiae* in International Investment Arbitration: The Implications of an Increase in Third-Party Participation' (2012) 29 Berkeley J Int'l L 200.

Lighthizer R, 'Testimony to House Ways and Means Committee' (*C-Span*, 21 March 2018) <https://www.c-span.org/video/?c4719932/brady-lighthizer-isds-discussion> accessed 14 January 2020.

Lowrey A, 'The US Doesn't Deserve the World Bank Presidency' *The Atlantic* (12 February 2019).

Luiz JM and Ruplal M, 'Foreign Direct Investment, Institutional Voids, and the Internationalization of Mining Companies into Africa' (2014) 49 Emerging Markets Fin Trade 113.

Luttikhuis B and Moses AD, 'Mass Violence and the End of the Dutch Colonial Empire in Indonesia' (2012) 14 J Genocide Res 257.

Luttrell S, *Bias Challenges in International Commercial Arbitration: The Need for a 'Real Danger' Test* (Wolters Kluwer 2009).

MacArthur E, 'Regulatory Competition and the Growth of International Arbitration in Singapore' (2018) 23 Appeal 165.

Maffry A, 'Direct Versus Portfolio Investment in the Balance of Payments' (1954) 44 American Econ Rev 614.

Main D, 'In Transylvania, A Fierce Battle Over Gold and Roman History' *National Geographic* (Washington, DC, 12 July 2018).

Malik M, 'The Full Protection and Security Standard Comes of Age: Yet Another Challenge for States in Investment Treaty Arbitration?', International Institute for Sustainable Development Best Practices Series (2011).

Malleson K and Russell PH (eds), *Appointing Judges in an Age of Judicial Power: Critical Perspectives from Around the World* (University of Toronto Press 2006).

Malmström C, 'A Multilateral Investment Court: A Contribution to the Conversation about Reform of Investment Dispute Settlement', speech by European Commissioner for Trade (Brussels, 22 November 2018).

Manea S, 'The Dispute over the Rosia Montana Mining Project Represents an Opportunity to Reshape Romania's Sustainable Development Policy' (*LSE European Institute European Politics and Policy*, 28 November 2013) <http://blogs.lse.ac.uk/europpblog/2013/11/28/the-dispute-over-the-rosia-montana-mining-project-represents-an-opportunity-to-reshape-romanias-sustainable-development-policy-2/> accessed 14 January 2020.

Maniruzzaman AFM, 'The Pursuit of Stability in International Energy Investment Contracts: A Critical Appraisal of the Emerging Trends' (2008) 1 J World Energy L & Bus 121.

Mann FA, 'The Protection of Shareholders' Interests in the Light of the Barcelona Traction Case' (1973) 67 AJIL 259.

Mann ME, 'The Serengeti Strategy: How Special Interests Try to Intimidate Scientists, and How Best to Fight Back' (2015) 71 Bull Atomic Scientists.

Marboe I, *Calculation of Compensation and Damages in International Investment Law* (OUP 2009).

Marboe I, 'State Responsibility and Comparative State Liability for Administration and Legislative Harm to Economic Interests' in SW Schill (ed), *International Investment Law and Comparative Public Law* (OUP 2010).

Marica I, 'UNESCO Postpones Evaluation of Rosia Montana Nomination for World Heritage List' *Romania Insider* (2 July 2018).

Markusen JR, 'Commitment to Rules on Investment: The Developing Countries' Stake' (2001) 9 Rev Int'l Pol Econ 287.

Marshall F, 'Siemens AG v Republic of Argentina' in N Bernasconi-Osterwalder and L Johnson (eds), *International Investment Law and Sustainable Development: Key cases from 2000–2010* (International Institute for Sustainable Development, 2011).

Mayer J, *Dark Money: The Hidden History of the Billionaires behind the Rise of the Radical Right* (Anchor Books 2016).

McDermott Will & Emery, 'Dr Sabine Konrad' (*McDermott Will & Emery*, undated) <https://www.mwe.com/people/konrad-sabine/> accessed 5 August 2019.

McGlade C and Ekins P, 'The Geographical Distribution of Fossil Fuel Unused when Limiting Global Warming to 2 °C' (2015) 517 *Nature* 187.

McGregor K, 'Mass Violence in the Indonesian Transition from Sukarno to Suharto' (2013) 15 Global Dialogue 134.

Menon S, 'The Transnational Protection of Private Rights: Issues, Challenges, and Possible Solutions' (2015) 108 ASIL Proc 219.

Meredith I and Tanner C, 'Investment Treaties: Taking Advantage of the Protections on Offer' *Practical Law* (15 September 2006).

Merle R, 'How One Hedge Fund Made $2 Billion from Argentina's Economic Collapse' *Washington Post* (Washington, DC, 29 March 2016).

Michaels D, *Doubt is their Product: How Industry's Assault on Science Threatens Your Health* (OUP 2008).

Miles K, *The Origins of International Investment Law: Empire, Environment and the Safeguarding of Capital* (CUP 2013).

Miller SK, 'Piercing the Corporate Veil among Affiliated Companies in the European Community and in the US: A Comparative Analysis of US, German, and UK Veil-Piercing Approaches' (1998) 36 Am Bus LJ 73.

Miller S and Hicks GN, 'Investor–State Dispute Settlement: A Reality Check', Report of the CSIS Scholl Chair in International Business (Center for Strategic and International Studies) (2015).

'Mining Bane: Stir over Fresh Threat to Indonesian Forests' *DowntoEarth News* (4 July 2015).

Mohamadieh K and Uribe D, 'The Rise of Investor–State Dispute Settlement in the Extractive Sectors: Challenges and Considerations for African Countries', South Centre Research Paper (2016).

Montt S, *State Liability in Investment Treaty Arbitration: Global Constitutional and Administrative Law in the BIT Generation* (Hart Publishing 2009).

Morón G, *A History of Venezuela* (George Allen & Unwin 1964).

Mouawed C and Silbert E, 'A Guide to Interim Measures in Investor–State Arbitration' (2013) 29 Arb Int'l 381.

Ndikumana L and Boyce JK, 'Congo's Odious Debt: External Borrowing and Capital Flight in Zaire' (1998) 29 Dev Change 195.

New Zealand Cancer Society, 'What are the Smokefree Laws in New Zealand?' (*Cancer Society*, undated) <https://auckland-northland.cancernz.org.nz/reducing-cancer-risk/what-you-can-do/smoking-and-cancer/tobacco-control-nz/what-are-the-smokefree-laws-in-new-zealand/?divisionId=17&centreId=1> accessed 14 January 2020.

New Zealand House of Representatives (Māori Affairs Committee), *Inquiry into the Tobacco Industry in Aotearoa* and *the Consequences of Tobacco Use for Māori*, Report 1.10A (2010).

New Zealand Parliament, 'Smoke-Free Environments (Controls and Enforcement) Amendment Bill, Progress of the Bill' (*New Zealand Parliament*, undated) <https://www.parliament.nz/en/pb/bills-and-laws/bills-proposed-laws/document/00DBHOH_BILL10487_1/smoke-free-environments-controls-and-enforcement-amendment> accessed 14 January 2020.

New Zealand Parliament, 'Smoke-Free Environments (Tobacco Standardised Packaging Amendment Bill), Progress of the Bill' (*New Zealand Parliament*, undated) <https://www.parliament.nz/en/pb/bills-and-laws/bills-proposed-laws/document/00DBHOH_BILL12969_1/smoke-free-environments-tobacco-standardised-packaging> accessed 14 January 2020.

Newcombe A and Paradell L, *Law and Practice of Investment Treaties: Standards of Treatment* (Kluwer Law International 2009).

Nial H, 'Selected Problems of Public International Law' (1968) 3 Acad Droit Int'l, Recueil de Cours 316.

Nikièma SH, 'The Most-Favoured-Nation Clause in Investment Treaties', International Institute for Sustainable Development Best Practices Series (2017).

Nikitin P, 'The CJEU's Achmea Judgment: Getting through the Five Stages of Grief' (*Kluwer Arbitration Blog*, 10 April 2018) <http://arbitrationblog.kluwerarbitration.com/2018/04/10/cjeus-achmea-judgment-getting-five-stages-grief/> accessed 14 January 2020.

Nolan M and Baldwin T, 'Minimising Risk in the Face of Government Action' *Project Finance International* (16 May 2012).

Norton Rose Fulbright, 'Investor State Dispute Settlement in the Banking and Finance Sector' (2017) 10 Bank Finan Disp Rev 18.

Nriagu JO, 'The Rise and Fall of Leaded Gasoline' (1990) 92 Sci Total Environ 13.

Obermayer B and Obermaier F, *The Panama Papers: Breaking the Story of How the Rich & Powerful Hide their Money* (Oneworld 2016).

Okawa P, 'Admissibility and the Law on International Responsibility' in MD Evans (ed), *International Law* (2d edn, OUP 2006).

Oliver RW, 'A Conversation with Aron Broches', California Institute of Technology, Division of the Humanities and Social Sciences (7 November 1985).

Olson DL and Wu D, *New Frontiers in Enterprise Risk Management* (Springer-Verlag 2008).

Organisation for Economic Co-operation and Development (OECD), *The MAI Negotiating Text* (OECD 1998).

OECD, 'Essential Security Interests under International Investment Law' in *International Investment Perspectives: Freedom of Investment in a Changing World* (OECD 2007).

OECD, *Report—Investment* Dispute *Management and Prevention* (Cairo, 26–27 June 2018).

Orrego Vicuña F, 'Interim Report on the Changing Law of Nationality of Claims', International Law Association Committee on Diplomatic Protection of Persons and Property, London Conference (2000).

Orrego Vicuña F, 'Carlos Calvo, Honorary NAFTA Citizen', Keynote remarks to the Conference on Regulatory Expropriations in International Law, New York University School of Law (26 April 2002).

Orrego Vicuña F, 'C.V.' (*Francisco Orrego Vicuña*, 10 August 2005) <http://forrego.blogspot.com/> accessed 18 January 2020.

Oxfam, 'An Economy for the 1%: How Privilege and Power in the Economy Drive Extreme Inequality and How This Can be Stopped', Oxfam Briefing Paper (18 January 2016).

Oxford Pro Bono Publico, 'Obstacles to Justice and Redress for Victims of Corporate Human Rights Abuse', Comparative submission prepared for Professor John Ruggie

(UN Secretary-General's Special Representative on Business and Human Rights) (3 November 2008).

Palan R, 'Tax Havens and Commercialization of State Sovereignty' (2003) 56 Int'l Org 151.

Palmer R, 'Coalition Calls for Ban on Additive MMT' *Calgary Herald* (Calgary, AL, 19 September 1996).

Pan American Health Organization (PAHO), 'Tobacco Facts', Press release (*PAHO*, undated) <https://www.paho.org/hq/index.php?option=com_content&view=article&id=1318:about-tobacco-control-program&Itemid=1187&lang=en> accessed 14 January 2020.

Parra AR, *The History of ICSID* (OUP 2012).

Parra AR, 'Remembering Aron Broches' (*Investment Claims*, 14 October 2016) <https://oxia.ouplaw.com/page/icsid-aron-broches> accessed 14 January 2020.

Paulsson J, 'Arbitration without Privity' (1995) 10 ICSID Rev—FILJ 232.

Paulsson J, 'Avoiding Unintended Consequences' in K Sauvant and M Chiswick-Patterson (eds) *Appeals Mechanism in International Investment Disputes* (OUP 2008).

Paulsson J, 'Moral Hazard in International Dispute Resolution', Inaugural Lecture as Holder of the Michael R Klein Distinguished Scholar Chair, University of Miami School of Law (29 April 2010).

Pauwelyn J, 'The Rule of Law without the Rule of Lawyers? Why Investment Arbitrators Are from Mars, Trade Adjudicators Are from Venus' (2015) 109 AJIL 761.

Permanent Court of Arbitration (PCA), 'Schedule of Fees and Costs' (PCA, undated) <https://pca-cpa.org/fees-and-costs/> accessed 14 January 2020.

Peter W, *Arbitration and Renegotiation of International Investment Agreements* (Kluwer Law International 1995).

Peterson LE, 'Early Investment Arbitrations against "Improper" Use of Environmental Laws Uncovered' *Investment Law and Policy Weekly News Bulletin* (International Institute for Sustainable Development, 5 January 2004).

Peterson LE, 'Challenge to Arbitrator Schwebel Rejected by Belgian Court, Poland Seeks Appeal' *Investment Treaty News* (17 January 2007).

Peterson LE, 'Argentine Crisis Arbitration Awards Pile Up, but Investors Still Wait for a Payout' *Law.com* (25 June 2009).

Picciotto S, *International Business Taxation* (Weidenfeld and Nicolson 1992).

PluriCourts, 'Academic Forum on ISDS' (*University of Oslo Faculty of Law*, 8 May 2019) <https://www.jus.uio.no/pluricourts/english/projects/leginvest/academic-forum/> accessed 14 January 2020.

Porterfield MC, 'International Expropriation Rules and Federalism' (2004) 23 Stan Envt'l LJ 3.

Porterfield MC, 'A Distinction without a Difference? The Interpretation of Fair and Equitable Treatment under Customary International Law by Investment Tribunals' *ITN Quarterly* (March 2013).

Porterfield MC, 'Aron Broches and the Withdrawal of Unilateral Offers of Consent to Investor–State Arbitration' *Investment Treaty News* (11 August 2014).

Posirca O, 'It's Official: Romania's Government Backs Move to Delay Rosia Montana Inclusion in UNESCO World Heritage Network' *Business Review* (28 June 2018).

Poulsen LNS, 'The Importance of BITs for Foreign Direct Investment and Political Risk Insurance: Revisiting the Evidence' in KP Sauvant (ed), *Yearbook on International Investment Law and Policy 2009–2010* (OUP 2010).

Poulsen LNS, *Bounded Rationality and Economic Diplomacy: The Politics of Investment Treaties in Developing Countries* (CUP 2015).

Powers A, 'Settlement Colonialism: Compensatory Justice in United States Expansion, 1903–1941' (PhD thesis, Columbia University, 2017).

Price DP, 'Chapter 11—Private Party vs. Government, Investor–State Dispute Settlement: Frankenstein or Safety Valve?' (2000) 26 Canada–US LJ 107.

Prieto G, 'The Colombian Constitutional Court Judgment C-252/19: A New Frontier for Reform in International Investment Law' (*EJIL Talk! Blog*, 29 July 2019). <https://www.ejiltalk.org/the-colombian-constitutional-court-judgment-c-252-19-a-new-frontier-for-reform-in-international-investment-law/> accessed 14 January 2020.

Prosser T, *The Regulatory Enterprise* (OUP 2003).

PT Newmont Nusa Tenggara, 'PTNNT Discontinues and Withdraws Arbitration Claim in Anticipation of Formal MoU Negotiations with Indonesia' (*Newmont*, 26 August 2014) <https://s2.q4cdn.com/575378270/files/doc_news/archive/Final-NNT-News-Release-26-August-2014-PTNNT-Discontinues-and-Withdraws-Arb_v001_w0g1d7.pdf> accessed 14 January 2020.

PT Newmont Nusa Tenggara, 'PTNNT to Resume Operations and Copper Concentrate Exports' (*Newmont*, 4 September 2014) <https://www.newmont.com/document/ptnnt-to-resume-operations-and-copper-concentrate-exports/> accessed 14 January 2020.

Puig S, 'Social Capital in the Arbitration Market' (2014) 25 EJIL 387.

PwC, *Mining in Indonesia—Investment and Taxation Guide* (7th edn, 2015).

Quinn JJ, 'Diffusion and Escalation in the Great Lakes Region: The Rwandan Genocide, the Rebellion in Zaire, and Mobutu's Overthrow' in SE Lobell and P Mauceri (eds), *Ethnic Conflict and International Politics: Explaining Diffusion and Escalation* (Palgrave Macmillan 2004).

Redfern A and Hunter A, *Law and Practice of International Commercial Arbitration* (Sweet & Maxwell 2004).

Reguly E, 'Gabriel Threatens Romania with Billion-Dollar Lawsuit' *Globe and Mail* (11 September 2013).

Reguly E, 'Peter Munk: The Extraordinary Life of a Business Legend, Philanthropist and National Champion' *Globe and Mail* (29 March 2018).

Reinisch A, 'How Narrow are Narrow Dispute Settlement Clauses in Investment Treaties?' (2011) 2 J Int'l Disp Settlement 115.

Ripinsky S and Williams D, *Damages in International Investment Law* (British Institute of International and Comparative Law 2015).

Rogers WP, 'The Rule of Law and the Settlement of International Disputes' (1970) 64 AJIL 285.

Rosert D, 'The Stakes are High: A Review of the Financial Costs of Investment Treaty Arbitration', International Institute for Sustainable Development Research Report (2014).

Rubenfeld S, 'Former Siemens Executive Pleads Guilty in Argentina Bribery Case' *Wall Street Journal* (New York, 15 March 2018).

Rubins N, 'Opening the Investment Arbitration Process: At What Cost, for What Benefit?' in R Hoffman and C Tams (eds), *The International Convention on the Settlement of Investment Disputes (ICSID): Taking Stock after 40 Years* (Nomos 2007).

Ryan CM, 'Discerning the Compliance Calculus: Why States Comply with International Investment Law' (2009) 38 Ga J Int'l & Comp L 63.

Sadowski W, 'International Investment Treaties as a Possible Shield against Government Cutbacks in Subsidies for the Green Energy Sector', *K&L Gates International Arbitration Alert* (10 January 2013).

St John T, *The Rise of Investor–State Arbitration* (OUP 2018).

Salazar A, 'Defragmenting International Investment Law to Protect Citizen-Consumers: The Role of *Amici Curiae* and Public Interest Groups', Osgoode Hall Law School Comparative Research in Law & Political Economy Research Paper No 6/2013 (2013).

Saloojee Y and Dagli E, 'Tobacco Industry Tactics for Resisting Public Policy on Health' (2000) 78(7) Bull WHO 902.

Samples TR, 'Winning and Losing in Investor–State Dispute Settlement' (2019) 56 Am Bus LJ 115.

Save Roşia Montană, 'All about Rosia Montana Mining Project' (*Salvaţi Roşia Montană*, undated) <https://www.rosiamontana.org/node/1825?language=en> accessed 14 January 2020.

Saunders S, 'Barrick Gold Founder Peter Munk Leaves a Tarnished Legacy' *NOW Magazine* (25 April 2018).

Schill SW, 'Fair and Equitable Treatment under Investment Treaties as an Embodiment of the Rule of Law', NYU School of Law Institute for International Law and Justice Working Paper 2006/6 (2006).

Schill SW, *The Multilateralization of International Investment Law* (CUP 2009).

Schill SW, 'Reforming Investor–State Dispute Settlement (ISDS): Conceptual Framework and Options for the Way Forward', E15 Task Force on Investment Policy Think Piece (2015).

Schneiderman D, 'Investment Rules and the New Constitutionalism' (2000) 25 Law & Social Inquiry 757.

Schneiderman D, *Constitutionalizing Economic Globalization: Investment Rules and Democracy's Promise* (CUP 2008).

Schneiderman D, Tienhaara K, and Van Harten G, 'Reply to EFILA' (*Investor–State Dispute Settlement*, 6 July 2015) <https://gusvanharten.wordpress.com> accessed 14 January 2020.

Schram E, 'Newmont Escaped Indonesian Law via Investment Treaty' *Mines and Communities* (28 December 2015).

Schreuer C, 'Commentary on the ICSID Convention. Article 25' (1997) 12 ICSID Rev—FILJ 59.

Schreuer C, *The ICSID Convention: A Commentary* (CUP 2001).

Schreuer C, 'Interaction of International Tribunals and Domestic Courts in Investment Law' in AW Rovine (ed), *Contemporary Issues in International Arbitration and Mediation: The Fordham Papers 2010* (Brill 2011).

Schreuer C, 'Foreword' in AK Bjorklund (ed), *Yearbook on International Investment Law and Policy 2014–2015* (OUP 2016).

Schumacher J, Trebesch C, and Enderlein H, 'Sovereign Defaults in Court', European Central Bank Working Paper No 2135 (2018).

Schwebel SM, 'A BIT about ICSID' (2008) 23 ICSID Rev—FILJ 4.

Scott PD, 'The United States and the Overthrow of Sukarno, 1965–1967' (1985) 58 Pacific Affairs 239.

Scott PD and Marshall J, *Cocaine Politics: Drugs, Armies, and the CIA in Central America* (University of California Press 1991).

Seidl-Hohenveldern I, 'Die Entwicklung der diplomatischen Protektion für juristische Personen', Lecture to the European Institute of the University of Saarland, Saarbrücken (27 June 1991).

Shany Y, 'Contract Claims vs Treaty Claims: Mapping Conflicts between ICSID Decisions on Multisourced Investment Claims' (2005) 99 AJIL 835.

Shea DR, *The Calvo Clause* (University of Minnesota Press 1955).

Shihata IFI, 'The Settlement of Disputes regarding Foreign Investment: The Role of the World Bank, with Particular Reference to ICSID and MIGA' (1986) 1 Am U Int'l L Rev 97.

Shrybman S, Letter to DR Cass and LV Fortier re: *United Parcel Service of America Inc v Government of Canada* (*ICSID*, 3 November 2005) <http://icsidfiles.worldbank.org/icsid/ICSIDBLOBS/OnlineAwards/C5546/DC8845_En.pdf> accessed 14 January 2020.

Simmons BA, 'Bargaining over BITs, Arbitrating Awards: The Regime for Protection and Promotion of International Investment' (2014) 66 World Pol 12.

Smith HM, 'Sex Trafficking: Trends, Challenges, and the Limitations of International Law' (2011) 12 Human Rights Rev 271.

Sornarajah M, *The Pursuit of Nationalized Property* (Martinus Nijhoff 1986).

Sornarajah M, *The International Law on Foreign Investment* (CUP 2010).

Stadler J and others, 'New Visionaries and the Chinese Century: Billionaires' Insights 2018' (UBS and PricewaterhouseCoopers 2018).

Stern B, [title unknown] (1990) 117 J Droit Int'l 3.

Stockholm Chamber of Commerce Arbitration Institute, Arbitration Rules 2017 (SCC Rules).

Stone Sweet A and Grisel F, *The Evolution of International Arbitration: Judicialization, Governance, Legitimacy* (OUP 2017).

Strange S, *The Retreat of the State* (CUP 1996).

'Suharto Tops Corruption Rankings' *BBC News* (25 March 2004).

Tansey R, *Blaming the Messenger: The Corporate Attack on the Movement for Trade Justice* (Corporate Europe Observatory and LobbyControl 2017).

Taylor M and Supriatna Y, 'Newmont Withdraws Mining Arbitration Case against Indonesia' *Reuters* (26 August 2014).

Thom WG, 'Congo–Zaire's 1996–97 Civil War in the Context of Evolving Patterns of Military Conflict in Africa in an Era of Independence' (1999) 19 J Conflict Stud.

Tienhaara K, *The Expropriation of Environmental Governance: Protecting Foreign Investors at the Expense of Public Policy* (CUP 2009).

Tienhaara K, 'Regulatory Chill in a Warming World: The Threat to Climate Policy Posed by Investor–State Dispute Settlement' (2018) 7 Transnat'l Env L 229.

Tienhaara K and Ranald P, 'Australia's Rejection of Investor–State Dispute Settlement: Four Potential Contributing Factors' *Investment Treaty News* (12 July 2011).

Tietje C, Baetens F, and Ecorys, 'The Impact of Investor–State Dispute Settlement (ISDS) in the Transatlantic Trade and Investment Partnership', Study prepared for the Minister for Foreign Trade and Development Cooperation and the Ministry of Foreign Affairs of the Netherlands (2014).

Timberg S, 'International Combines and National Sovereigns' (1947) 95 U Penn L Rev 575.

Tout L, Bradfield M, and De Silva L, 'The Latest Renewables Claim: Abengoa's Subsidiary Launches Investment Treaty Proceedings against Spain' *Lexology.com* (29 November 2013).

Trading Economics, 'Republic of the Congo GDP per Capita' (*Trading Economics*, undated) <https://tradingeconomics.com/republic-of-the-congo/gdp-per-capita> accessed 14 January 2020.

Traynor K, 'How Canada Became a Shill for Ethyl Corporation' (1998) 23 Intervenor (Canadian Environmental Law Association) 3.

Treasury Board of Canada Secretariat, *Guidelines on International Regulatory Obligations and Cooperation* (Treasury Board of Canada 2007).

Tucker B and Doukas A, 'Gas and the European Investment Bank: Why New Gas Infrastructure Investment is Incompatible with Climate Goals', Oil Change International Report (2019).

Tupman WM, 'Challenge and Disqualification of Arbitrators in International Commercial Arbitration' (1989) 38 ICLQ 26.

UBS and PricewaterhouseCoopers, *New Visionaries and the Chinese Century: Billionaires' Insights 2018* (USB and PricewaterhouseCoopers 2018) 24.

United Nations (UN), *Resolution on Permanent Sovereignty over Natural Resources*, GA Res 1803, UN GAOR, 17th Sess, Supp No 17, UN Doc A/5217 (1962) 15, 57 AJIL 710.

UN, *Arbitration Rules of the United Nations Commission on International Trade Law*, UN GA Res 31/98, UN GAOR, 31st Session, Supp No 17, UN Doc A/31/17, c V, s C (1976).

UN, Report of the Secretary-General: Analytical Commentary on Draft Text of a Model Law on International Commercial Arbitration, UN Doc A/CN.9/264 (25 March 1985) 16 Ybk UNCITRAL 104.

UN (Food and Agriculture Organization and others), *The State of Food Security and Nutrition in the World 2018: Building Climate Resilience for Food Security and Nutrition* (FAO 2018).

UN, *The Sustainable Development Goals Report 2018* (UN 2018).

UN Commission on International Trade Law (UNCITRAL), *Model Law on International Commercial Arbitration*, 21 June 1985, UN Doc A/40/17, Annex I, 24 ILM 1302.

UNCITRAL, *Rules on Transparency in Treaty-Based Investor–State Arbitration* (UN 2014).

UNCITRAL Working Group III, 'Bibliography of Recent Writings related to the Work of UNCITRAL' (*UNCITRAL*, undated) <https://www.zotero.org/groups/282978/bibliography_of_recent_writings_related_to_the_work_of_uncitral/items/collectionKey/CTC8J7YE/order/creator/sort/as> accessed 14 January 2020.

UN Conference on Trade and Development (UNCTAD), *Taxation*, UNCTAD Series on Issues in International Investment Agreements (UN 2000).

UNCTAD, *The Role of International Investment Agreements in Attracting Foreign Direct Investment to Developing Countries*, UNCTAD Series on International Investment Policies for Development (UN 2009).

UNCTAD, *Investor–State Disputes: Prevention and Alternatives to Arbitration* (UN 2010).

UNCTAD, 'Most-Favoured-Nation Treatment', UNCTAD Series on Issues in International Investment Agreements II (UN 2010).

UNCTAD, *Best Practices in Investment for Development: How to Prevent and Manage Investor–State Disputes: Lessons from Peru* (UN 2011).

UNCTAD, *Fair and Equitable Treatment* (UN 2012).

UNCTAD, 'Special Update on Investor–State Dispute Settlement: Facts and Figures', IIA Issues Note (2017).

UNCTAD, 'Investor–State Dispute Settlement: Review of Developments in 2017', IIA Issues Note (2018).

UNCTAD, *World Investment Report 2019* (UN 2019).

UN Educational, Scientific and Cultural Organization (UNESCO) Institute for Statistics, 'Literacy Rates Continue to Rise from One Generation to the Next', Fact Sheet No 45 (2017).

US Chamber of Commerce, '13 Myths about Investment Agreements and Investor–State Dispute Settlement (ISDS)' (*US Chamber of Commerce*, 13 April 2015) <https://www.uschamber.com/sites/default/files/13_myths_about_investment_agreements_and_isds.pdf> accessed 14 January 2020.

US Department of Justice, 'Former Siemens Executive Pleads Guilty to Role in $100 Million Foreign Bribery Scheme' (*US Department of Justice*, 15 March 2018) <https://www.justice.gov/opa/pr/former-siemens-executive-pleads-guilty-role-100-million-foreign-bribery-scheme> accessed 18 January 2020.

US Securities and Exchange Commission, 'SEC Charges Siemens AG for Engaging in Worldwide Bribery' (*US SEC*, 15 December 2008) <https://www.sec.gov/news/press/2008/2008-294.htm> accessed 18 January 2020.

Velásquez Ruiz MA, 'The Colliding Vernaculars of Foreign Investment Protection and Transitional Justice in Colombia: A Challenge for the Law in a Global Context', (PhD thesis, Osgoode Hall Law School of York University, 2016).

van Aaken A, 'Primary and Secondary Remedies in International Investment Law and National State Liability: A Functional and Comparative View' in SW Schill (ed), *International Investment Law and Comparative Public Law* (OUP 2010).

van den Herik L and Černič JL, 'Regulating Corporations under International Law: From Human Rights to International Criminal Law and Back Again' (2010) 8 J Int'l Crim Justice 725.

van der Pas H and Damanik R, *Netherlands–Indonesia Bilateral Investment Treaty Rolls Back Implementation of New Indonesian Mining Law: The Case of Newmont Mining vs Indonesia*, Briefing report (Indonesia for Global Justice, Transnational Institute, and EU–ASEAN FTA Network 2014).

Van Harten G, *Investment Treaty Arbitration and Public Law* (OUP 2007).

Van Harten G, 'A Case for an International Investment Court', Society of International Economic Law Inaugural Conference Paper (2008).

Van Harten G, 'Investment Provisions in Economic Partnership Agreements' (*Social Science Research Network*, 1 March 2008) <https://papers.ssrn.com/sol3/papers.cfm?abstract_id=1461110> accessed 14 January 2020.

Van Harten G, 'Investment Treaty Arbitration, Procedural Fairness, and the Rule of Law' in S Schill (ed) *International Investment Law and Comparative Public Law* (OUP 2010).

Van Harten G, 'Arbitrator Behaviour in Asymmetrical Adjudication: An Empirical Study of Investment Treaty Arbitration' (2012) 50 Osgoode Hall LJ 211.

Van Harten G, *Sovereign Choices and Sovereign Constraints: Judicial Restraint in Investment Treaty Arbitration* (OUP 2013).

Van Harten G, 'Comments on the European Commission's Approach to Investor–State Arbitration in TTIP and CETA', Osgoode Legal Studies Research Paper No 59 (2014).

Van Harten G, 'A Parade of Reforms: The European Commission's Latest Proposal for ISDS', Osgoode Legal Studies Research Paper No 102 (2015).

Van Harten G, 'The European Commission's Push to Consolidate and Expand ISDS: An Assessment of the Proposed Canada–Europe CETA and Europe–Singapore FTA', Osgoode Legal Studies Research Paper Series No 105 (2015).

Van Harten G, '"International Law Experts" Release Misleading Promo of ISDS' (*Investor-State Dispute Settlement*, 3 May 2015) <https://gusvanharten.wordpress.com> accessed 14 January 2020.

Van Harten G, *Sold Down the Yangtze: Canada's Lopsided Investment Deal with China* (Lorimer 2015).

Van Harten G, 'Arbitrator Behaviour in Asymmetrical Adjudication (Part Two): An Examination of Hypotheses of Bias in Investment Treaty Arbitration' (2016) 53 Osgoode Hall LJ 540.

Van Harten G, 'ISDS in the Revised CETA: Positive Steps, But Is It a "Gold Standard"?', Centre for International Governance Innovation Commentary Series No 6 (20 May 2016).

Van Harten G, 'Leaders in the Expansive and Restrictive Interpretation of Investment Treaties: A Descriptive Study of ISDS Awards to 2010' (2018) 29 EJIL 507.

Van Harten G and Malysheuski P, 'Who Has Benefited Financially from Investment Treaty Arbitration? An Evaluation of the Size and Wealth of Claimants', Osgoode Hall Law School Legal Studies Research Paper No 14 (2016).

Van Harten G and Scott DN, 'Investment Treaties and the Internal Vetting of Regulatory Proposals: A Case Study from Canada' (2016) 7 J Int'l Disp Settlement 92.

Van Harten G and Scott DN, 'Investment Treaties and the Internal Vetting of Regulatory Proposals: Further Findings from a Case Study from Canada' in LE Sachs and L Johnson (eds), *Yearbook on International Investment Law and Policy 2015–2016* (OUP 2018).

van Os R and Knottnerus R, *Dutch Bilateral Investment Treaties—A Gateway to "Treaty Shopping" for Investment Protection by Multinational Companies* (SOMO 2011).

Vandevelde KJ, 'A Brief History of International Investment Agreements' (2005) 12 UC Davis J Int'l L and Pol 157.

Vasagar J and Oliver C, 'German Fear of Tribunals Threatens EU–US Trade Deal' *Financial Times* (London, 28 January 2015).

Vasani BS and Palmer SA, 'Challenge and Disqualification of Arbitrators at ICSID: A New Dawn?' (2015) 30 ICSID Rev—FILJ 194.

Vázquez Pimentel DA, Macías Aymar I, and Lawson M, *Reward Work, Not Wealth: Methodology Note* (Oxfam International 2018).

Velásquez Ruiz MA, 'The Colliding Vernaculars of Foreign Investment Protection and Transitional Justice in Colombia: A Challenge for the Law in a Global Context' (PhD thesis, Osgoode Hall Law School of York University, 2016).

Verheyen R, 'The Coal-Fired Power Plant Hamburg–Moorburg, ICSID Proceedings by Vattenfall under the Energy Charter Treaty and the Result for Environmental Standards' (*Greenpeace*, 11 April 2012) <https://www.greenpeace.de/sites/www.greenpeace.de/files/publications/icsid_case_regarding_the_vattenfall_coal-fired_power_plant_hamburg-moorburg.pdf> accessed 14 January 2020.

Vetulli E and Kaufman EE, 'Is Argentina Looking for Reconciliation with ISDS?' (*Kluwer Arbitration Blog*, 13 October 2016) <http://arbitrationblog.kluwerarbitration.com/2016/10/13/is-argentina-looking-for-reconciliation-with-isds/> accessed 14 January 2020.

Viñuales JE and Bentolila D, 'The Use of Alternative (Non-Judicial) Means to Enforce Investment Awards against States' in L Boisson de Chazournes, M Kohen, and JE Viñuales (eds), *Diplomatic and Judicial Means of Dispute Settlement: Assessing their Interactions* (Brill 2012).

Vivekananda N and Menezes JJ, 'Singapore as a Seat for Investor–State Disputes' (*SIAC*, nd) <https://www.siac.org.sg/newsite/index.php/70-articles/169-singapore-as-a-seat-for-investor-state-disputes > accessed 14 January 2020.

Voon T and Mitchell AD, 'Ending International Investment Agreements: Russia's Withdrawal from Participation in the Energy Charter Treaty' (2017) 111 AJIL Unbound 461.

Voon T, Mitchell AD, and Munro J, 'Legal Responses to Corporate Manoeuvring in International Investment Arbitration' (2014) 5 J Int'l Disp Settlement 41.

Wang H, 'A Deeper Look at China's "Going Out" Policy', Centre for International Governance Innovation Commentary (2016).

Wasco MD, 'When Less is More: The International Split Over Expanded Judicial Review in Arbitration' (2010) 62 Rutgers L Rev 599.

Wealth-X, *World Ultra Wealth Report 2018* (2018).

Weisz G, Schwarzkopf NE, and Panitch M, 'Selected Issues in Sovereign Debt Litigation' (1991) 12 U Pa J Int'l Bus L 1.

Wellhausen R, 'Recent Trends in Investor–State Dispute Settlement' (2016) 7 J Int'l Disp Settlement 117.

Welsh A, 'The Strategic Importance of Investment Treaty Protections for Telecoms Operators' (*Allen & Overy*, 2012) <http://www.allenovery.com/SiteCollectionDocuments/Investment%20treaty%20protection.PDF> accessed 11 August 2019.

Wettstein F, *Multinational Corporations and Global Justice: Human Rights Obligations of a Quasi-Governmental Institution* (Stanford University Press 2009).

Wheat A, 'Toxic Shock in a Mexican Village' (1995) 16 Multinat'l Monitor 5.

Wicke L, 'Either with CCS or Not at All' (2008) 58(11) Energiewirthschaftliche Tagesfragen 8.

Wieland P, 'Why the Amicus Curia Institution is Ill-Suited to Address Indigenous Peoples' Rights before Investor–State Arbitration Tribunals: *Glamis Gold* and the Right of Intervention' (2011) 3 Trade, L & Dev't 334.

Wilkinson SM, 'NAFTA, Mexico and Metalclad: Understanding the Normative Framework of International Trade Law' (LLM thesis, University of British Columbia 2002).

Williams D, 'Vattenfall's Hamburg Coal-Fired Power Unit Finally Set to Activate' *Power Engineering International* (25 February 2015).

Wilson D, 'Bloomberg Backs Uruguay's Anti-Smoking Laws' *New York Times* (New York, 15 November 2010).

Wong J, 'Umbrella Clauses in Bilateral Investment Treaties: Of Breaches of Contract, Treaty Violations, and the Divide between Developing and Developed Countries in Foreign Investment Disputes' (2006) 14 George Mason L Rev 137.

Woolhouse S, 'Seats of Corporate Convenience and International Investment Law', (PhD thesis, University of Waterloo 2016).

World Bank, *Indonesia: Environment and Natural Resource Management in a Time of Transition* (World Bank 2001).

World Health Organization (WHO), *Report on the Global Tobacco Epidemic, 2011: Warning about the Dangers of Tobacco* (WHO 2011).

WHO, 'Tobacco and the WHO Framework Convention on Tobacco Control: Online Q&A' (*WHO*, May 2017) <https://www.who.int/features/qa/tobacco/en/> accessed 14 January 2020.

WHO, 'Drinking-Water' (*WHO*, 7 February 2018) <https://www.who.int/news-room/fact-sheets/detail/drinking-water> accessed 14 January 2020.

WHO (Western Pacific Region), 'Tobacco Factsheet' (WHO, 21 June 2016).

WHO and International Bank for Reconstruction and Development/World Bank, Tracking Universal Health Coverage: 2017 Global Monitoring Report (WHO 2017).

World Trade Organization (WTO) Appellate Body, EC *Measures concerning Meat and Meat Products (Hormones)* (Decision, 16 January 1998).

WTO Dispute Settlement Body, *Australia—Certain Measures concerning Trademarks, Geographical Indications and other Plain Packaging Requirements Applicable to Tobacco Products and Packaging*, Reports of the Panels, WT/DS435/R, WT/DS441/R, WT/DS458/R, WT/DS467/R (28 June 2018).

Wulandari F, 'Indonesia to Allow Underground Mining in Forests' *Reuters* (21 April 2009).

Xu Y and Ramanathan V, 'Well below 2 °C: Mitigation Strategies for Avoiding Dangerous to Catastrophic Climate Changes' (2017) 114 (39) Proc Nat'l Acad Sci 10315.

Yackee J, 'Investment Treaties and Investor Corruption: An Emerging Defence for Host States?' (2012) 52 Virginia J Int'l L 723.

Yackee JW, 'Do Investment Treaties Work—In the Land of Smiles?' in J Chaisse and L Nottage (eds) *International Investment Treaties and Arbitration across Asia* (Brill/Nijhoff 2017).

Yamin AE and Parra-Vera O, 'How Do Courts Set Health Policy? The Case of the Colombian Constitutional Court' (2009) 6(2) PLoS Med.

Zarocostas J, 'Australia's Proposals on Plain Packaging Set New Global Benchmark in Anti-Smoking Efforts' (2011) BMJ 342.

Zarra G, 'The Interference of ICSID Provisional Measures with National Criminal Proceedings' (2017) 26 Italian Ybk Int'l L 83.

Zeltner T and others, *Tobacco Company Strategies to Undermine Tobacco Control Activities at the World Health Organization*, Report of the Committee of Experts on Tobacco Industry Documents (WHO 2000).

Zerk JA, *Multinationals and Corporate Social Responsibility: Limitations and Opportunities in International Law* (CUP 2009).

Zeynalova Y, 'The Law on Recognition and Enforcement of Foreign Judgments: Is It Broken and How Do We Fix It?' (2013) 31 Berkeley J Int'l L 150.

Ziadé NB, 'Some Recent Decisions in ICSID Cases' (1991) 6 ICSID Rev—FILJ 514.

Index

For the benefit of digital users, indexed terms that span two pages (e.g., 52–53) may, on occasion, appear on only one of those pages.

Tables are indicated by *t* following the page number